# Sensory Restriction

## EFFECTS ON BEHAVIOR

# Sensory Restriction

## EFFECTS ON BEHAVIOR

*DUANE P. SCHULTZ*

*Department of Psychology*
*Mary Washington College*
*University of Virginia*
*Fredericksburg, Virginia*

1965

ACADEMIC PRESS   New York and London

ACADEMIC PRESS INC.
111 Fifth Avenue, New York, New York 10003

United Kingdom Edition published by
ACADEMIC PRESS INC. (LONDON) LTD.
Berkeley Square House, London W.1

LIBRARY OF CONGRESS CATALOG CARD NUMBER: 65-24813

PRINTED IN THE UNITED STATES OF AMERICA.

51129

# Preface

This monograph is an attempt to provide a systematic presentation of the wide variety of experimental findings emerging from the relatively recent and rapidly growing area often referred to as sensory deprivation. My purpose in gathering together this material is to provide possible empirical support for the proposition that man needs varying sensory stimulation in order to function adaptively.

I have attempted to cover the full range of effects of a reduced sensory environment and have tried to focus, wherever possible, on research utilizing objective response measures. Thus, more emphasis is placed on data obtained from objective test results or physiological measures than on strictly subjective reports with no objective referents.

This book will be of value to workers in the several disciplines from which the research has proceeded. It should also be useful as a supplementary text for undergraduate and graduate students in courses such as experimental psychology and motivation.

I am very grateful for the help of several people in the preparation of this book. Any merits it may possess is due in large part to their generous efforts in reading portions of the manuscript and supplying me with their unpublished research. They include Marvin Zuckerman of the Albert Einstein Medical Center, John Zubek of the University of Manitoba, Jack Vernon of Princeton University, William Haythorn of the Naval Medical Research Institute, Robert Lana of Alfred University, and Ralph Rosnow of Boston University. I learned much from their comments.

Permission to reproduce tables and figures has been received from many individuals and publishers. Specific acknowledgments are made in the text.

Words are inadequate to express my gratitude to my wife, Sydney Ellen, who endured five months of social isolation and numerous chapter revisions with admirable patience and tolerance. I am grateful for her always cheerful and painstaking preparation of the manuscript and her most scholarly criticisms. It is to her that this monograph is dedicated.

*Fredericksburg, Virginia*                                     D. P. SCHULTZ

*July, 1965*

# Contents

vii

# CHAPTER I

# Introduction

> A changing sensory environment seems es-
> sential for human beings. Without it, the brain
> ceases to function in an adequate way, and
> abnormalities of behavior develop. In fact, as
> Christopher Burney observed in his remarkable
> account of his stay in solitary confinement:
> "Variety is not the spice of life; it is the very
> stuff of it."
>
> WOODBURN HERON, 1957

This book will mark an attempt to provide empirical support for the proposition that man needs constantly varying forms of stimulation to function adaptively in his environment. As will be demonstrated throughout the following chapters, an absence of variety, *i.e.*, an environment offering little or no stimulus change, is an aversive state which most men seek to avoid. Too long an exposure to unchanging sensory input produces, as will be seen, physiological, cognitive, perceptual, and affective impairments.

The reader can no doubt testify to this by calling upon his own experiences. Most people find quite unpleasant the experience of being confined to bed for several days with an illness. We become lethargic, restless, irritable, and thoroughly bored. More dramatic are the effects on a person who is severely confined in a hospital with a long-term illness such as the polio victim confined to an iron lung, or orthopedic cases restricted in body casts or other complex traction. In 1958, Leiderman, Mendelson, Wexler, and Solomon collected case observations on a number of such medical and surgical patients undergoing long-term hospital confinement. They found in these patients certain psychotic-like symptoms including pathological manifest anxiety, delusions, and hallucinations. These symptoms did not respond to the usual medical or psychiatric regimen but they did respond to changes in the sensory environment of the patients such as increased social contact, keeping on a night light, and providing a radio or television set.

1

At a less severe level of confinement and restriction, the reaction of some aircraft pilots may also testify to the deleterious effects of a lack of change in stimulation. Bennett (1961) reported experiences of some RAF pilots who described feelings of being completely isolated in space and of unreality which in some cases led to apprehension while in flight. Dealing with U. S. Navy and Marine pilots, Clark and Graybiel (1957) describe what they call the "break-off" phenomenon reported by some pilots. This phenomenon included spatial disorientation in which "the pilot conceived himself to be isolated, detached, and physically separated from the earth, and no longer in contact with it" (p. 169). The experience was reported to occur most frequently when the pilots were flying alone at high altitude and with minimal task performance required. The sensory environment in this situation is rather constant and unchanging. This "break-off" effect could be abolished by increasing sensory stimulation, such as more concentration on flight tasks.

Considering a still less serious level of monotonous stimulation, most readers have no doubt driven on one of the new superhighways and have possibly experienced the effects of monotony attendant with them. The older highways provided more changing sensory stimulation in the form of stop lights, business establishments along the side of the road, curves, hills, *etc*. Most of these "diversions" are not to be found on the new roads and the driver faces the little changing sensory environment of the white line and straight road for miles ahead. Many writers have suggested that this reduction in sensory stimulation may impair the normal psychological functioning of the driver. Leiderman *et al.* suggest that the monotony of driving on the new superhighways is conducive to personal error, inattention, disorientation, excessive fantasy formation, and even falling asleep.

Working at a more homely level, one is reminded of the industrial situation where many men devote their working day to simple, routine, and highly repetitive tasks. As automation performs more and more functions, industrial workers and many military personnel have little to do but monitor a set of instruments. The monotonous vigilance task of radar operators is a case in point. The vigilance literature reports consistent deterioration in performance in as short a time as thirty minutes in an environment which offers little sensory change. Those who are forced to work at such repetitive, monotonous tasks often express complaints of boredom and job dissatisfaction. Often their job performance declines. In short, boredom seems to be a most unpleasant situation.

One of the very few laboratory demonstrations of the aversive consequences of boredom was performed by Karsten in 1928. The study involved having the subjects perform uninteresting, monotonous and repetitive tasks such as drawing vertical strokes, putting thimbles in holes, reading a short poem over and over again. They were told to work at the tasks as long as they felt like doing so, but it was implied that they should continue as long as possible. None of the tasks required the expenditure of much physical effort. As the experimental session proceeded, the quality of the performances deteriorated. Much more interesting for our discussion, however, are the often ingenious attempts of the subjects to introduce some variety into the situation. For example, the strokes were drawn with different rhythms, with the pencil held in different ways. Also evidenced by the subjects was a growing distaste for the task and everything connected with it. Feelings of aggression toward the task, the experimenter, and even toward the subjects themselves were expressed verbally and in mild violence. Finally, the subjects refused to continue.

Karsten felt that the reason for these reactions and the stopping of the tasks was not due to muscular exhaustion, for the subjects willingly used the same muscles for other responses, providing these other responses had a different meaning. Karsten accounted for these results by attributing them to the monotonous stimulation resulting from the monotonous activity.

In recent years there has been increasing interest in investigating the behavioral effects of confining a human subject under conditions of reduced sensory input. In 1951, Hebb and his colleagues at McGill University began a systematic study of the effects of prolonged exposure to a rigidly monotonous environment. In 1954 their findings were published in an article entitled, "Effects of Decreased Variation in the Sensory Environment" (Bexton, Heron, & Scott).

The twenty-two male college students who served as subjects in this study were paid twenty dollars per day to do absolutely nothing. Their task was simply to lie in a comfortable bed in a lighted cubicle for twenty-four hours a day with time out for eating and toilet activities. The cubicle is shown in Figure 1–1.

The subjects wore translucent goggles admitting diffuse light, and gloves and cardboard cuffs limiting tactual perception. Auditory stimulation was limited by a masking noise and the partial sound-proofing of the cubicle. Again, all the subjects were required to do was to rest and relax—a seemingly easy task for twenty dollars a day! It promised to be a pleasant holiday.

And yet the experimenters found that it was difficult to keep subjects for more than two or three days. Somehow they were not finding the experience to be as easy as it had appeared. After an

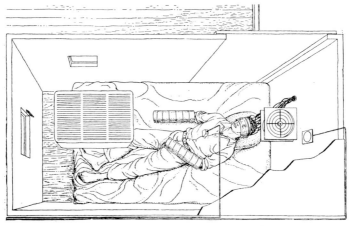

Fig. 1–1. Experimental cubicle constructed at McGill University in Montreal to study the effects of perceptual isolation. [Reprinted by permission from W. Heron, *Scientific Amer.*, 1957, **196**, 52–56.]

initial period of sleep, the subjects became very bored and extremely eager for some kind of stimulation. They seemed to find difficulty in concentrating and they reported many forms of hallucinations—visual, kinesthetic, and somasthetic. There was intellectual and perceptual deterioration. In short, the subjects found this "restful" environment to be extremely unpleasant.

Clearly, then, this limiting or restricting of stimulation was a factor deserving of further study. The importance and interest of this area is attested to by the incredible growth rate of the experimental literature. Indeed it is a rare month when perusal of the professional journals does not reveal at least one article dealing with some facet of sensory restriction.

Some of the earlier studies are reported in "Sensory Deprivation" (Solomon *et al.*, 1961) which contains the results of a symposium held at Harvard Medical School in 1958. An overview of the literature of the past eleven years reveals a clear progression in the quality of the research being undertaken. The more recent reports rely, in general, less on subjective report and more on quantitative behavioral measures. They use larger groups of subjects with an adequate control population, and are characterized by more sophisticated experimental design and data analysis. This book will review some of the studies reported in "Sensory Deprivation" but will concentrate on the more recent literature including some material which, at the time of writing, has not yet been published. At the rapid rate at which the literature is increasing, this book will enjoy a relatively short, but hopefully useful, life.

## A. SOURCES OF INTEREST IN SENSORY RESTRICTION

What are some of the practical and theoretical considerations that have led investigators from such diverse areas as neurophysiology, psychiatry, psychoanalysis, psychology, biochemistry, pharmacology, and human engineering to enter this area with such enthusiasm? Kubzansky (1961) and Zubek (1964c) suggest several different sources of influence.

One such influence was the much publicized confessions brought about by the so-called "brainwashing" techniques apparently developed to a high degree of efficiency in the Communist world. Drugs or extreme tortures were not used in these procedures; rather, the degree of prisoner-compliance was induced by solitary confinement and other means of restricting the individual's perceptual environment.

A second source of impetus has been provided by new and stressful environments in which military personnel now operate. Attention has been focused on the operating efficiency of men who are forced to function, at maximal effectiveness, in severely restricted and monotonous environments, *e.g.*, in space vehicles, submarines, and radar stations, and the monitoring of a greatly increased amount of automated equipment. Consequently, agencies of the defense establishment have initiated and supported a number of research programs concerning man's reactions to and operating efficiency in limited social and sensory environments.

A third source of interest of more theoretical concern stems from recent advances in neurophysiology concerning the role of the brain-stem reticular formation in producing a general state of arousal or alertness in the organism. This arousal or alerting function seems to be dependent on continuous exposure to varying sensory stimulation. Based partially on these findings has been the development of a neurophysiologically-based concept of motivation which may be grossly subsumed under the rubric "need for experience." This point of view refutes the notion that the human organism is a passive, automaton-like responder to stimuli, positing instead the organism as an active, aggressive seeker of stimulation. The relevance of research in sensory restriction for this "new look" in motivation is noted by Cofer and Appley (1964): "That the cortex requires activation by stimulation seems a *necessary* conclusion from the results of sensory deprivation experiments" (p. 408, italics ours).

The data from which this motivational formulation is derived come not only from the sensory deprivation literature, but also from studies on exploration, play behavior, curiosity, manipulation, and intracranial stimulation. All of these data, as a number of writers have suggested, would seem to suggest man's need for continual and varied stimulation.

## B. METHODOLOGICAL CONSIDERATIONS

In reviewing the literature on sensory restriction, one is struck by the variety of procedures which has been used to reduce environmental stimulation. There is even some ambiguity about the term "sensory deprivation" itself, *i.e.*, not all studies involve a total absence or deprivation of stimulation. The present discussion will be defined by the categorizations suggested by Kubzansky (1961) who distinguishes between sensory deprivation and perceptual deprivation.

Sensory deprivation experiments involve attempts to reduce sensory stimulation to an absolute minimum. This usually involves having the subjects lie quietly in a dark, soundproofed room with arms and hands encased in gloves and cardboard cuffs. Earplugs are worn to further reduce the level of stimulation.

A more severe procedure to attempt to bring about total deprivation has been used by Lilly (1956) and Shurley (1963) who immersed subjects in a pool of slowly circulating tepid water.

Wearing nothing but a mask covering eyes and ears (and an anxious smile), and instructed to inhibit all movement, the subjects were exposed to minimal visual, auditory, and tactile stimulation. Figure 1–2 demonstrates this water-immersion technique.

It is not possible, of course, to totally eliminate *all* external stimulation in these isolation studies. Some stimulation is invariably provided as a result of imperfect soundproofing, tactual stimuli,

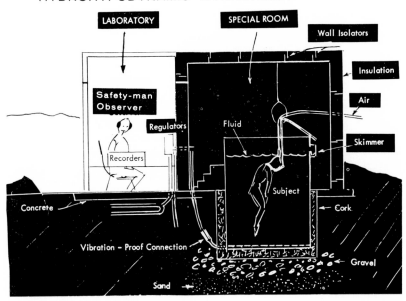

Fig. 1–2. Water-immersion technique. [Reprinted by permission from J. Shurley, *Proceedings of the Third World Congr. of Psychiat.*, Vol. 3. Toronto, Canada: Univer. Toronto Pr., 1963.]

the sound of the subjects' own voices or breathing, and so on. Zuckerman (1964) reports that in some water-immersion studies, the subjects became sensitized to bubbles, to their face masks, and to respiration and heart sounds. Thus, sensory deprivation experiments do not totally eliminate sensation but they do provide as low a level of sensory input as is possible.

Perceptual deprivation involves an attempt to reduce the patterning and meaningful organization of sensory input while maintaining a somewhat normal level of input. This was the procedure used in the study by Bexton, Heron, and Scott described above and pictured in Figure 1–1. Perceptual deprivation, then, involves a higher level of sensory input than the sensory deprivation technique but the stimulation received is totally devoid of any meaningful organization.

Figure 1–3 represents the isolation chamber used in the research at the University of Manitoba under the direction of Zubek. With

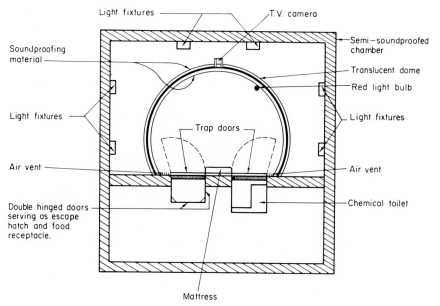

FIG. 1–3. A cross-sectional view of the University of Manitoba isolation chamber. [Reprinted (with modifications) by permission from Zubek, Sansom, & Prysiazniuk, *Canad. J. Psychol.*, 1960, **14**, 233–243.]

slight changes, the chamber is used for both sensory deprivation and perceptual deprivation techniques.

A less commonly used technique employs a monotonous sensory environment. A repetitive auditory experience is provided and the

FIG. 1–4. Experimental subject shown in tank-like respirator. The vents of the respirator were left open so that the subject breathed for himself. [Reprinted by permission of the publishers from P. Solomon, P. Kubzansky, P. Herbert Leiderman, J. Mendelson, R. Trumbull, and D. Wexler, *Sensory deprivation*, Cambridge, Mass.: Harvard Univer. Pr., Copyright, 1961, by the President and Fellows of Harvard College.]

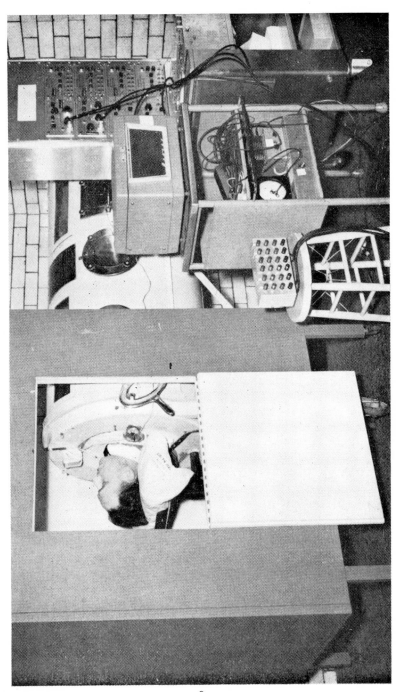

subjects are exposed to a highly restricted, though normally patterned, visual environment. This technique does not involve either sensory or perceptual deprivation, as defined above. More appropriately, it might be referred to as a state of perceptual monotony. An example of this approach is provided by the work of Mendelson, Kubzansky, Leiderman, Wexler, and Solomon (1961) who confined their subjects in polio tank respirators with arms and legs enclosed in cardboard cuffs. An auditory masking sound was provided and the visual environment was restricted to the front of the respirator and the blank walls of a screen. Figure 1–4 represents this technique.

Another technique to be discussed involves social isolation alone. All the procedures discussed above involve social isolation in that the subject has no contact with other people. However, in the social isolation technique, no attempt is made to restrict the level or patterning of stimulus input. The subjects are confined in a normal sensory environment either alone or with a small group of people. They are able to move around and to talk with the others. This represents a variation of perceptual monotony, for even with the presence of other people, the environment can soon become monotonous and repetitive.

In addition to these procedures which attempt to restrict the total organism from stimulus change, a number of studies have utilized sensory or perceptual deprivation applied to only one sense modality. Some of the research of Zubek and his associates at Manitoba, to be discussed later, involves the restriction of vision alone, or the restriction of tactile stimulation on a small area of the skin.

In discussing the research in the following chapters it is considered necessary to note in detail the experimental procedure used in each study. Comments of comparison and attempts at generalization would otherwise be rendered somewhat meaningless. Therefore, detailed information is provided on the procedure, use of controls, *etc.*, where such information is available.

## C. THE CHAPTERS TO FOLLOW

The discussion of the literature in the rest of the book focuses primarily on the effects of sensory restriction on the adult human organism. No attempt will be made to review the literature dealing with the effects of sensory restriction when imposed early in the life of the organism. However, the effects of such early sensory restriction on later adult behavior is briefly mentioned in Chapter II. This area has been the subject of rather intensive review, *e.g.*, Beach and Jaynes (1954), King (1958), Fiske and Maddi (1961).

Chapter II considers a neurophysiologically-based theoretical framework within which the author believes the various effects of sensory restriction may be reasonably accounted for. The following chapters deal with the effects of a reduced sensory input on physiology (Chapter III), cognition (Chapter IV), perception (Chapter V), and affective feeling states (Chapter VI). The discussion in Chapter VII deals with the phenomenon of individual differences in tolerance for isolation and with the various attempts that have been made to predict those subjects who can best endure conditions of sensory restriction. The effects of social isolation alone are discussed in Chapter VIII, and the final chapter attempts a summary and discussion of some of the problems involved in this rapidly growing area.

# CHAPTER II

# *Toward a Unifying Theoretical Framework*

As the title indicates, this chapter will mark an attempt at constructing a model within which the behavioral effects of sensory restriction can be discussed. The basic tenor of this attempt is that the cortex requires activation by exteroceptive stimulation. Thus, the discussion centers around man's "need" for sensory stimulation, without which adaptive behavior is not possible.

The discussion of the concepts and the literature which follows is not intended to be exhaustive or complete, as the material has already been the subject of methodical review in a number of sources, *e.g.*, Cofer and Appley (1964), Fiske and Maddi (1961). Rather, the discussion is intended to provide a perhaps crude initial theoretical structure as a basis for more advanced efforts to follow. This particular structure may or may not prove adequate to handle new data, but as Vernon (1963) has commented:

> One does not present a theory with the idea that it will be accepted; instead he offers something he knows in advance will be challenged at every quarter. The overwhelming importance of that theory, however, is not whether it is correct but whether it stimulates new ideas, new investigations, more facts, more information, and finally a revised theory so that the unending process may begin again at a higher level of understanding (p. 195).

The discussion begins with the following comment by White:

> Twenty years of research have thus pretty much destroyed the orthodox drive model. It is no longer appropriate to consider that drives originate solely in tissue deficits external to the nervous system, that consummatory acts are a universal feature and goal of motivated behavior, or that the alleviation of tissue deficits is the necessary condition for instrumental learning. Instead we have a complex picture in which humoral factors and neural centers occupy a prominent position; in

13

which, moreover, the concept of neurogenic motives without consummatory ends appears to be entirely legitimate. Do these changes remove the obstacles to placing exploration, activity, and manipulation in the category of drives? (1959, p. 305).

It is suggested that the data now available provide an affirmative answer to White's question and allow for the postulation of a neurophysiologically-based drive for stimulation.

A significant portion of these data has been concerned with the phenomena of exploration, curiosity, and a wide spectrum of related behaviors which seem to be inexplicable in terms of the traditional drive-reductionist viewpoint based on the concept of homeostasis. The drive doctrine seeks to link all activities to four or five primary drives which are considered to be the basis of all types of behavior, no matter how complex. Through the postulation of secondary or learned drives and reinforcers, there is, theoretically, no limit to the behaviors that could be acquired through the association of neutral stimuli with primary drives and reinforcers. Thus, the human organism's entire, complex, variegated patterns of behavior could be accounted for by reference to the maintenance of the internal biological equilibrium or homeostasis.

However, as noted above, the drive doctrine has been criticized on the grounds that the range of behavioral phenomena is simply too great to be based on a few primary drives. Evidence suggests that there is a great deal of behavior, both human and animal, which defies reduction to the traditional primary drives. This evidence is reviewed in Berlyne (1950, 1954, 1960), Bindra (1959), Fiske and Maddi (1961), Harlow (1953), Hebb (1949, 1955), Lana (1960), Nissen (1954), and Olds (1955). In short, there is a rapidly growing body of data which suggests that much behavior, particularly at the human level, seems to bear no relation to the reduction of hunger, thirst, or sex drives or to escape from noxious stimulation. Rather, much behavior would seem to be directed toward decreasing or increasing sensory stimulation to the end of maintaining a certain level of sensory input. White (1959) comments that:

> Human experience provides plentiful evidence of the importance of reducing excessive levels of tension. Men under wartime stress, men under pressure of pain and extreme deprivation, men with excessive work loads or too much exposure to confusing social interactions, all act as if their nervous systems craved that utterly unstimulated condition

which Freud once sketched as the epitome of neural bliss. But if these same men be granted their Nirvana they soon become miserable and begin to look around for a little excitement. Human experience testifies that boredom is a bad state of affairs about which something must be done. Hebb (1949) has been particularly insistent in reminding us that many of our activities, such as reading detective stories, skin-diving, or driving cars at high speeds, give clear evidence of a need to raise the level of stimulation and excitement. Men and animals alike seem at times bent on increasing the impact of the environment and even on creating mild degrees of frustration and fear (p. 313).

The traditional homeostatic concept of motivation, then, ignores this all-important aspect of man's existence because its primary focus is not on the vital role of the brain and central nervous system, but on the maintenance of an internal balance among vegetative functions.

## A. AROUSAL AND THE RETICULAR ACTIVATING SYSTEM

One line of evidence relating to the role of stimulus input in motivation has proceeded from a physiological basis. The reference here is to recent work on cortical arousal and the reticular activating system (RAS). This reticular formation is represented in Figure 2–1 and consists of a dense neurone network forming a central core which extends from the medulla of the lower brain stem to the thalamus in the diencephalon. Fibers descend from the formation allowing impulses from it to influence the body musculature and the autonomic nervous system. Fibers also ascend upward from the formation. Thus, the reticular formation is seen as contributing impulses upward to the cortex and downward to the musculature.

The two major sources of stimulation for the RAS are considered to be sensory stimulation and cortical impulses. Apparently, stimulation from somatic, visual, auditory, olfactory, and visceral sources can act somewhat interchangeably in activating the system. Evidence for the role of cortical impulses is provided by the work of French, Hernandez-Peon, and Livingston (1955) who found that electrical stimulation of various cortical areas led to electrical activity in the reticular formation. Also, it seems that cortical stimulation, interacting with sensory influences in the RAS, may also affect the action of the RAS upon the cortex. Duffy (1962) suggests that this interaction in moderation could lead to facilitation,

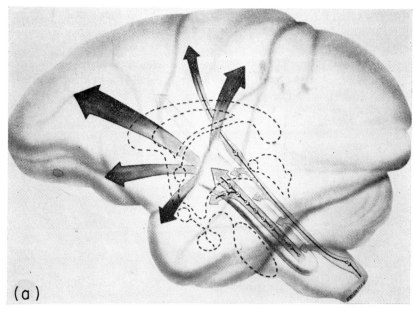

(a)

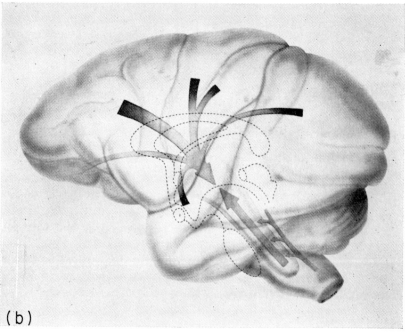

(b)

but that excessive interaction might lead to a complete blocking of the reticular activation of the cortex resulting in disturbances in awareness and attention.

Lindsley (1961) notes the existence of marked behavioral disturbances under the opposing conditions of sensory restriction and sensory overload. He believes that these similar behavioral effects can be explained in terms of the ascending reticular activating system (ARAS). Located strategically so as to sample the incoming and outgoing messages, the ARAS is able to influence alerting and attention and also serve an adjustment or adaptation function.

> The adjustment or adaptation level of the reticular formation as it monitors both incoming and outgoing messages becomes very much a part of the process of learning and habit formation, just as it does for the more elementary perceptual processes. Its changes and adjustments depend upon the ebb and flow of activity in the afferent or efferent systems and when these are restricted, compensatory adjustments are made within limits. When this fails, under more widely deviating conditions of restriction, behavior becomes disorganized (Lindsley, 1961, p. 181).

Thus, Lindsley conceives of the reticular formation as serving as a barometer regulating or adjusting input-output relations. From this he proceeds to the assumption that the reticular formation has an adaptation level and becomes attuned to certain levels of activity. This level is, then, projected on the cortex where it influences perception, learning, and emotion. The regulating system is disturbed or upset by disturbances in sensory input, *i.e.*, either sensory restriction or sensory overload.

Lindsley speaks of an activation pattern, as measured on the EEG, which is characterized by a reduction of the synchronized alpha rhythms and the induction of low amplitude fast activity. This pattern is produced by sensory stimulation and has also been demonstrated by electrical stimulation of the reticular formation.

---

FIG. 2–1. The reticular formation. (a) Pathways of ascending reticular control. (b) Pathways of cortico-reticular control. [Reprinted by permission of the publishers from P. Solomon, P. Kubzansky, P. Herbert Leiderman, J. Mendelson, R. Trumbull, and D. Wexler, *Sensory deprivation*, Cambridge, Mass.: Harvard Univer. Pr., Copyright, 1961, by the President and Fellows of Harvard College.]

Moruzzi and Magoun (1949) found that if an animal's brain showed an EEG characteristic of sleep prior to stimulation, then electrical stimulation changed the pattern at once to one of arousal or activation. It was further found that a sensory stimulus of any modality had a similar capacity for arousal, behaviorally and electrocortically. Weinberger and Lindsley (1964) have also demonstrated that stimulus offset or cessation can elicit electroencephalographic and behavioral arousal. They suggest that it is the sudden change in stimulus conditions, rather than just stimulus onset, which is responsible for cortical and behavioral arousal, and they conclude that either increase or decrease of stimulation can change the adaptation level of the reticular formation.

In addition to the arousal function of the RAS, there is evidence to indicate that it plays a role in the selectivity of attention. Hernandez-Peon, Scherrer, and Jouvet (1956) recorded responses from the cochlear nucleus in a cat during the presentation of click stimuli. When the cat was relaxed, responses of the nucleus to the click were obtained. When a mouse, fish odor, or shock were introduced, however, the response to the click stopped. Direct electrical stimulation of the RAS depresses the response of the cochlear nucleus. Hence, it was inferred that the RAS suppressed the response to the click during the presence of other strong stimuli to which the cat was attending.

Thus it appears that both interoceptive and exteroceptive stimulation affect the arousal state which, in turn, determines the organism's capacity for efficient behavior. Hebb (1955) suggests that this arousal is synonymous with a general drive state which functions as an energizer and is produced by the slower passage of sensory impulses through the ARAS, which terminate in diffuse stimulation over wide areas of the cortex. Faster traveling impulses (from the same stimulus source) provide more specific cortical stimulation and function as a cue in controlling goal responses. Hebb further suggests that intermediate levels of activation or arousal provide for efficient performance but that low or very high levels are disruptive.

An optimal level of cortical arousal is thus considered necessary for efficient adaptive behavior to occur. Both external and cortical stimulation are required but it will be demonstrated that the absence of appropriate external stimulation can reduce the arousal capacity of the cortically-produced stimulation. What little stimulation is available is repetitive, and the ARAS becomes habituated to it. This latter point is most important for the discussion which will shortly consider the role of the level of external stimulation in effecting cortical arousal.

## B. AROUSAL AND THE HYPOTHALAMUS

Though the major emphasis in this discussion focuses on the reticular formation, the role of the hypothalamus cannot be overlooked. Kubzansky and Leiderman (1961) note that stimulation of specific hypothalamic areas has been shown to influence the optic and auditory systems, possibly via the RAS and perhaps also through other central pathways. Murphy and Gellhorn (1945) indicated that peripheral motor responses produced by stimulation of the cortex occurred with greater intensity when the hypothalamus was simultaneously stimulated. Gellhorn (1964) suggests that hypothalamic stimulation may exert an excitatory influence on the cortex.

Duffy (1962) notes that stimulation of the hypothalamus in man has been shown to produce effects on blood pressure, pulse rate, respiration, and other visceral functions. Porter (1953) has demonstrated a marked increase in electrical activity of the posterior hypothalamus under the influence of stress. Stellar (1954) suggests that sensory and cortical stimulation can exert excitatory and inhibitory influences on the hypothalamus. Thus, it seems not unreasonable to suggest that in sensory restriction the altered sensory input may affect hypothalamic mechanisms with consequent effects on the behavioral functions under its control.

## C. CORTICAL AROUSAL AS A FUNCTION OF LEVEL OF STIMULUS VARIATION

A concept of a level of stimulation appropriate to the functioning organism has been considered by several writers, e.g., degree of energy mobilization (Cannon, 1929; Duffy, 1941, 1951), degree of arousal (Freeman, 1948), level of arousal (Hebb, 1955; Bindra, 1959), level of activation (Schlosberg, 1954a, 1954b). They all refer to a dimension representing the energy level or excitation level of the organism; an arousal or sensory continuum with deep sleep or anesthesia representing the lower end and epileptic seizure, extreme anger or fear, or panic behavior representing the upper end of extreme sensory stimulation.

A sleeping organism represents the lower level of activation. In sleep, the cortex and sympathetic division of the autonomic nervous system are inactive and the muscles are relaxed.

Bindra (1959) reviews the autonomic, somatic, and neural changes that take place within the organism under different levels of stimulation and notes the existence of marked individual differences in both base level and the degree of reactivity of these physiological functions.

Bindra discusses three main points of difference between high and low states of arousal. First, the involuntary bodily processes function differently in the two states. For instance, in a high arousal state, the sweat glands are more active and the blood pressure and heart rate are higher. Second, voluntary musculature activity is higher in high arousal states. Finally, the pattern of the firing of the nerve cells is different in the two states. During sleep, a preponderance of delta waves, large in amplitude and slow in speed, are noted. During periods of excitement or high arousal the pattern is characterized by rapid frequency and small amplitude.

Bindra (1959), Hebb (1955), Leuba (1955), McReynolds (1956), Berlyne (1960), among others, have suggested that between the two extremes on the sensory continuum lies an area of optimal level of stimulation and consequent arousal which results in efficient response and learning capabilities on the part of the organism. This relation is conceptually represented by Bindra (1959) in Figure 2–2. This inverted U-shaped function has been suggested by Freeman (1940), Schlosberg (1954a, 1954b), and Hebb (1955).

Figure 2–2 represents hypothetical curves for three different kinds of tasks. The arousal level required for the highest score in weight lifting is greater than that for typewriting, which is greater than that for drawing. "In each case the subject will be 'too excited' above the upper limit of the range and 'not warmed up' below the lower limit of the optimal range. The figure also shows that there are upper and lower limits of arousal level beyond which an activity cannot occur at all" (Bindra, 1959, pp. 247–248).

At too high an arousal level, the intense sensory bombardment may interfere with the delicate functions involved in the cue or guiding function (Hebb, 1955), perhaps due to the "blocking" discussed above. Thus the intense stimulation may interfere with responses already in the organism's repertoire and may further prevent the acquisition of new responses to adapt to the situation. Duffy (1962) reviews a large number of studies indicating a wide variety of performance tasks which are handicapped by a very high level of activation.

Intense pain stimulation is one way of bringing about too high an arousal level. Cofer and Appley (1964) note that intense painful stimulation can result in excited behavior and changes in skin

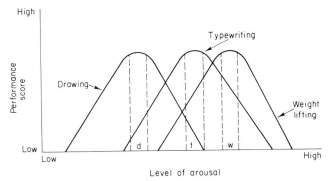

Fig. 2–2. Relation between level of arousal and performance. Curves showing hypothetical relations between level of arousal and performance. Ranges (d, t, w) of optimal levels of arousal for performance on three different tasks. [Reprinted by permission from D. Bindra, *Motivation—A Systematic Reinterpretation*. New York: Ronald Press. Copyright, 1959.]

conductance, muscle tension, blood pressure, EEG, and respiration. The person who may be "wild with pain" is less capable of dealing effectively with his environmental circumstances.

In "Panic Behavior," Schultz (1964a) postulates individual sensory thresholds for panic behavior as a contributory factor to a panic reaction. Once the stimulation has exceeded the upper end of the optimal range of stimulation for the individual, he is no longer capable of coping effectively with the situation. The individual's panic flight behavior is thus seen as a disorganized and nonadaptive attempt to reduce the level of stimulation. Thus, the organism may function less efficiently as a result of extreme levels of stimulation.

Levels of stimulation below the optimal range may be represented by studies in sensory restriction where the effect of too little stimulation can be almost as disruptive as too much stimulation. Consider first a situation with a restricted range of stimulus variability. A subject is presented with a continuing series of similar stimulus events in which his task is to detect stimulus change over relatively long periods of observation. Such would be the case with the study of human vigilance behavior. Here the subject has low intensity stimulation which is repetitive and monotonous and so offers little sensory variation. It has been suggested (Schultz, 1963, 1964b; Scott, 1957) that the decrease in efficiency found in vigilance studies is directly related to a reduction in sensory variation, and that performance occurs at a higher level of efficiency under conditions which increase the variety of the stimuli, either peripheral or task-related, e.g., higher signal rate, multiple stimulus sources.

Reducing stimulus input to an even lower level, the area of minimal stimulation represented by sensory and perceptual deprivation studies is reached. The literature reviewed in the following chapters shows a variety of stressful functions on the organism, including cognitive and emotional deterioration and a decrease in behavioral efficiency. "Most writers on the topic of restricted stimulation appear to accept the proposition that the normal and efficient functioning of the human organism depends upon external stimulation" (Fiske, 1961, p. 137). They note that not only is the intensity of stimulation minimized but also that the minimal stimulation that does exist furnishes no information of value to the subject. Because of the resulting low level of arousal, the subjects are not able to employ their own imagery to increase the level of stimulation.

Thus, when the level of stimulus input falls below the optimal range, gross disruptions of overt behavioral efficiency are reported. Disruptions in cortical activity would also be expected. In Chapter III, evidence is discussed, based on EEG tracings taken under minimal stimulus input conditions, which shows that there is a tendency toward a sleeplike pattern and toward slower frequencies in the alpha range.

Thus far the discussion has dealt with an optimal level of stimulus input. Actually, the evidence suggests that it is not the level of stimulation *per se* which is so important in cortical arousal and its resulting behavioral efficiency, but rather it is the level of stimulus or sensory variation. Thus, the concern is with the relative heterogeneity or patterning of stimulation. For example, Davis,

McCourt, and Solomon (1960) presented random visual stimulation to subjects confined in a tank respirator and reported emotional disturbances, intellectual impairment, and hallucinatory phenomena similar to those obtained under constant light and noise. They suggested that the brain needs not simply change in sensation, but a *continuous meaningful contact with the outside world.* Working with blackout and diffuse light conditions, Freedman and Greenblatt (1959) also suggested that the important factor which tends to degrade perceptual organization is the absence of order and/or meaning, rather than the specific nature of the stimulus field. Zubek, Pushkar, Sansom, and Gowing (1961) suggest that:

> What is required for normal functioning of the brain is constantly varying *meaningful* stimulation. When meaning is absent or is reduced for long periods of time, for example under darkness, silence, diffuse light, white noise, or random visual stimulation, psychological disturbances . . . will occur. Furthermore, since these sensory conditions are not equal in meaningfulness they might be expected to produce somewhat different behavioural effects (p. 98).

In summary, it might be suggested that under conditions of highly intense sensory stimulation (as in sensory overload), the intense sensory bombardment interferes with the delicate functions involved in cue function. As a result, the meaningfulness or patterning of the sensory input may no longer be perceived. Under conditions of vigilance or more extreme forms of sensory restriction, there exists not enough varied stimulation to provide meaningful patterning. Thus, a sufficient (but not too high) level of sensory variation is necessary for the occurrence of optimal cortical arousal and adaptive overt behavior. The level of stimulation must exceed the individual's lower threshold and it must be variegated in pattern and/or time. If these conditions are not met, then the arousal level is not sufficiently high to facilitate and maintain adaptive behavior.

## D. WHAT STIMULUS PROPERTIES FACILITATE AROUSAL LEVEL?

The point has been made that it is the meaningfulness or patterning of sensory input that is crucial in influencing cortical arousal and its resulting behavioral efficiency. These terms, "meaningfulness" and "patterning" are somewhat vague. In recent years, effort has been expended toward a more precise delimiting of those stimulus properties capable of affecting arousal.

Berlyne (1960) discusses the so-called "collative" properties of stimuli which depend on collation or comparison of characteristics belonging to different features of the environment. Collative properties include such characteristics as novelty, complexity, indistinctness, incongruity, and so on. Berlyne comments:

> Of these words, the most frequently used in this context is undoubtedly 'novelty', but this is a word that can mean several different things. An adult human being is hardly likely to perceive some quality quite unlike anything that he has experienced before. When he calls something 'novel' or 'new', he may mean that he is perceiving familiar features in a combination that he has never encountered before, or he may mean that he is experiencing something of a sort that he has not encountered for some time (1964, p. 7).

To Berlyne, an advantage of collative properties is that they can be discussed in the precise mathematical language of information theory. A surprising event, for example, would be one with a high information content. Along these same lines, Jones (1964) suggests the existence of at least three statistical properties of stimuli. These include: (1) information, or the unpredictability or statistical uncertainty of stimuli; (2) complexity, or the objective randomness of stimuli series which are nevertheless predictable by subjects; and (3) fluctuation, or the degree of alternation in stimulus series which are neither objectively random nor unpredictable.

If these specific collative properties can be shown to affect arousal there would be important implications for motivational theory since, as Berlyne suggested, the concept of arousal has much in common with the older notion of drive. Berlyne (1961; Berlyne, Craw, Salapatek, & Lewis, 1963) has demonstrated that the magnitude of the galvanic skin response (GSR) increases with the degree of inter-response conflict (which Berlyne claims underlies all the collative variables), with surprisingness, and with novelty. Working with complexity and incongruity, Berlyne and McDonnell (1965) found that more complex or incongruous visual patterns evoked longer EEG desynchronization than did less complex or incongruous patterns.

Thus, Berlyne and McDonnell conclude that:

We can put forward with fair confidence the view that the collative stimulus properties influence arousal processes. . . . So the findings are consonant with the conclusion, suggested by a variety of other phenomena, that such characteristics of the external environment as novelty, surprisingness and complexity can induce heightened drive independently of visceral needs and nociceptive events (1965, pp. 6–7).

## E. A POSSIBLE BASIS FOR INDIVIDUAL DIFFERENCES IN LEVEL OF AROUSAL

There is much experimental literature available which indicates the effects on adult behavior of both reduced and increased levels of stimulation imposed very early in the life of the organism (Beach & Jaynes, 1954; King, 1958; Riesen, 1961; Thompson & Schaefer, 1961). This literature will not be reviewed here but certain aspects will be briefly noted. The data suggest that both decreased and increased levels of early postnatal stimulation are capable of producing behavioral changes later in the life of the organism. For example, restriction of early environmental stimulation in animals has produced drastic and enduring effects on emotionality, learning ability, activity level, social behavior, and perception (Thompson & Schaefer, 1961). Being reared in an orphanage has produced a number of behavior changes in children, such as lack of attentiveness, impulsiveness, lowered cognitive capacity, and lessened ability to relate to others (Goldfarb, 1955).

The effects of an increased level of early stimulation in humans are suggestive of positive effects (increases in I.Q. for example) but the evidence is not conclusive. With animals, however, more reliable data indicate large gains in growth rate, intelligence, ability to withstand stress (Thompson, 1955, 1960; King, 1958), and even greater weight and thickness of cortical tissue and an increase in total acetylcholinesterase activity of the cortex (Bennett, Diamond, Krech, & Rosenzweig, 1964). Thus, a variety of response systems may be affected by abnormal levels of early stimulation.

The purpose in referring to this literature is to support the contention of Riesen (1961) and Thompson and Schaefer (1961), among others, that the growth and maintenance of neural structures are dependent upon the adequacy of functional demands placed on them by stimulation.

It is suggested that the optimal level of sensory variation of an individual is influenced by early postnatal levels of stimulation and the resulting level of cortical arousal as mediated by the reticular activating system. In other words, the level of stimulus variation to which the neonate is exposed functions to influence the optimal range of cortical arousal appropriate for adaptive behavior of the adult organism. The adaptation level of the ARAS referred to above is thus determined to some degree by the amount and variety of early stimulation.

The concern is with the dual function (arousal and cue) of stimuli. Hebb (1955) suggests that the specific cue function is responsible for the organization of behavior while the arousal function is responsible for the arousal level or (in Hebb's terms) general drive level. Thompson (1958) and Riesen (1961) suggest that this dual role of stimulation has a useful application in the problem of development. They note that the effect of stimulation on the neonate is primarily the arousal function. Thus, the level of activation or alertness produced by the amount of stimulation provided allows the opportunity for or facilitates neural organizations to be developed via the specific sensory pathways. Stimulation is provided later in life, then, mainly via the specific projection system and its consequent cue functions. How adequately the organism's neural organizations can utilize and handle the cue functions depends on the level of cortical arousal "built up" by initial levels of stimulus variability.

It is suggested that the optimal level or range of stimulus variation within which the adult organism is able to function effectively is influenced in great part by the stimulation provided at the neonate stage. Contact with a rich sensory environment would facilitate the development of differentiation of cue functions, of sensory modalities, and of events within modalities. An impoverished sensory environment would prevent such differentiation and the fuller use of cue functions later in life. Because of the low activation produced, the organism would not perform well those learning tasks which require higher levels of activation. As Maddi and Fiske note, "Thus, the restricted early environment may have a double-barreled effect: it limits or prevents the occurrence of crucial types of experiences, and it reduces the ability to learn from whatever experiences are available" (1961, p. 442). This is not to imply that the activation level remains static throughout the remainder of the organism's life. Quite possibly, the cumulative effect of sensory experience in the adult organism may serve to modify the optimal range.

Genetic factors may also operate to influence the organism's optimal level of arousal, though little evidence is available. Cooper and Zubek (1958) have studied the effects of an enriched and a restricted environment on bright and dull strains of rats. Differences between the two strains were eliminated by rearing in the restricted or the enriched environment. The dulls profited much more than the brights by the additional early stimulation. An impoverished environment, on the other hand, affected the brights much more than the dulls. Thompson and Schaefer (1961) comment that, "It seems quite clear that adding or reducing stimulation early in life will have differential effects according to the genotype of the animal involved" (p. 97).

## F. SENSORY VARIATION AS REINFORCEMENT

Thus far the following major propositions have been discussed: (1) behavioral efficiency is a function of an appropriate level of cortical activation, and (2) this level of cortical arousal is highly dependent on an optimal level of varied sensory input.

For the discussion of a "need" for stimulation as a motivational factor to proceed beyond this point, it should be demonstrated that changes in sensory variation can have reinforcing properties. Will organisms exhibit evidence of learning in situations where the only apparent reinforcement is a change in stimulation? The literature does provide much evidence indicating the existence of such behavior occurring in the absence of any reduction of the traditional, visceral, homeostatic drives. The reference here is to the many studies on exploration, alternation behavior, manipulation, curiosity, and play, and the studies showing a reinforcing effect of intracranial stimulation. These studies, which have been the subject of intensive review (Berlyne, 1960; Bindra, 1959; Cofer & Appley, 1964; Dember, 1960; Fiske & Maddi, 1961), do demonstrate the reinforcing effects of a change in stimulation.

Utilizing relatively simple behavior with less complex stimulation, a number of studies have demonstrated the reinforcing properties of light onset and light increment in rats (Girdner, 1953; Marx, Henderson, & Roberts, 1955; Berlyne and Koenig, 1964) and in mice (Barnes, Kish, & Wood, 1959; Kish, 1955). Using rats, Barnes and Kish (1961) have demonstrated the reinforcing properties of the onset of auditory stimulation.

Additional evidence has demonstrated the reinforcing effects of stimulation following periods of sensory restriction. Butler (1953) confined a rhesus monkey in a cage covered with an opaque box and found that it learned a color discrimination response where the only reinforcement was a thirty-second peek through a window into the laboratory. Furthermore, the response showed no satiation tendencies over ten four-hour testing sessions.

Butler and Alexander (1955) found that monkeys spent 40 per cent of their time (in a ten-hour test period) in visual exploration activity. The rate of this activity increased as a function of the amount of deprivation of visual exploration (Butler, 1957).

Fox (1962) confined monkeys in a dark box where they learned to bar-press for a reward of 0.5 second of light. The rate of response correlated positively with the length of preceding visual deprivation. The response was decreased monotonically by adding various amounts of ambient light. When the reward light and the ambient light were of equal intensity, the response rate was markedly reduced.

Using human subjects, Jones, Wilkinson, and Braden (1961; Jones, 1961) demonstrated the existence of instrumental responses that produced visual stimuli after varying periods of isolation in lightproof chambers. Additional evidence with human subjects is discussed in Chapter VII.

It has also been suggested that subjects under conditions of minimal stimulation may exhibit approach tendencies to stimuli usually perceived as noxious, stimuli which would be avoided under a more normal stimulus environment. Dember (1960) comments that "there may be occasions on which a small dose of a primary drive may be welcome. If there is no other source of variety, a little bit of hunger, or a mild electric shock, may be enjoyable" (p. 366). Leuba (1955) suggests that stimulation of pain sense organs may be pleasant and irresistible if it increases stimulation from a minimal to an optimal level.

Thus, it seems not unreasonable to postulate that a change in sensory variation can have reinforcing properties leading to the learning of instrumental behaviors. The discussion of an optimal level of stimulus variation suggests the occurrence of instrumental behavior to bring about a decrease in stimulation also, when preceding levels are too intense. For example, Barnes and Kish (1957) have demonstrated the reinforcing properties of the termination of intense auditory stimulation. Berlyne and Koenig (1964) found light decrement to be reinforcing with rats. As Fiske and Maddi (1961) note:

> When there is a large discrepancy between current level of activation and the optimal level or range for the given situation, the organism will typically engage in behavior designed to increase or decrease impact and thus to shift activation to reduce the discrepancy, thereby making effective instrumental responses more possible (p. 15).

Speaking in traditional drive-reductionist terms, it might be said that some behavior is tension-reducing while other behavior is tension-increasing.

## G. A DRIVE FOR SENSORY VARIATION: *SENSORISTASIS*

Berlyne (1960) notes three logically distinct characteristics of the concept of drive: (1) drive is an energizing condition that affects the level of activity, (2) drive has a selective function making certain overt responses more likely than others, and (3) drive is a condition the alleviation of which is rewarding. In amending the third concept, Berlyne noted that increases in arousal as well as decreases can be rewarding.

One may reasonably ask why it is proposed to add another drive to the perhaps already overcrowded list of non-visceral drives. Behavior theory has at times postulated drives which serve to bring the individual into greater diversified contact with his environment, *e.g.*, exploration, curiosity, manipulation, and the like. Research has demonstrated that opportunity to explore or to manipulate, without any primary drive reduction, can serve as a reinforcer. There is much evidence suggesting that an exploratory drive, primary in the sense that it is not derived from any of the traditional internal drives, can be elicited in higher organisms. Although Montgomery (1952) and Berlyne (1960) described the exploratory drive as non-homeostatic in nature, Lana (1960) suggests that satiation of this drive may produce some kind of equilibrium in the organism.

This exploratory drive "is of an external nature in the sense that both deprivation and satisfaction associated with the drive depend totally on the presence or absence of the relevant stimulus, *i.e.,* novelty" (Lana, 1960, p. 13). The exploratory drive, then, motivates the organism to increase stimulation.

All of these postulated drives possess the three characteristics of drives noted above. However, it appears that the behavioral ends or goals of manipulation, exploration, *etc.,* are exactly the same, *i.e., the bringing about of an optimal level of sensory variation.* One suspects that the specific behaviors elicited (exploration, for example) are situationally determined. The monkeys in Harlow's manipulatory behavior experiments manipulated the puzzle so diligently over a twelve-day period because there was nothing else they could do to change their sensory environment. Butler's chimps worked so hard to look out the window for brief periods because they had no puzzles to manipulate. It is submitted that the animal subjects in these experiments were making the best of a bad situation (so to speak) and attempting to find sensory variation with whatever means the experimenter had provided for them. Anyone who has observed monkeys in the relatively free environment of a zoo has noted that they exhibit visual exploration, curiosity, manipulation, play activity, and a host of other seemingly endless activities. Thus it is suggested that the specific overt behavioral phenomena reported as exploration, curiosity, *etc.,* are simply specific behavioral mechanisms by which the organism is best able to maintain an optimal level of sensory variation/cortical arousal. If this proposition, that the end goals of these behaviors are the same, can be accepted, then in the interest of parsimony it would seem much more practicable to discuss these behaviors in terms of one drive state which the author chooses to call *sensoristasis.*

Sensoristasis can be defined as a drive state of cortical arousal which impels the organism (in a waking state) to strive to maintain an optimal level of sensory variation. There is, in other words, a drive to maintain a constant range of varied sensory input in order to maintain cortical arousal at an optimal level. Conceptually, this sensory variation-based formulation is akin to homeostasis in that the organism strives to maintain an internal balance, but it is a balance in stimulus variation to the cortex as mediated by the ARAS. The word, *sensoristasis,* is used in the same manner in which Cannon (1932) spoke of homeostasis. "The word does not imply something set and immobile, a stagnation. It means a condition—a condition which may vary, but which is relatively constant" (p. 24). Thus, sensoristasis is concerned with a fluctuating constant —an optimal range which is capable of shifting as a function of task and subject variables. The monitor serving to maintain the sensoristatic balance is the reticular formation which (as discussed above) Lindsley conceives of as serving as a regulator adjusting input-output relations. The sensoristatic balance is disturbed or upset by conditions of sensory restriction and sensory overload.

The essential corollaries of the sensoristatic model are seen as the following:

(1) The drive mechanism invoked in the concept of sensoristasis is synonymous with arousal as facilitated or mediated by the RAS.

(2) An optimal range or level of external stimulation exists which functions to influence the level of cortical arousal. The organism is able to function adaptively in his environment only when this optimal range is maintained. Too much or too little stimulation disrupts learned responses and prevents new learning.

(3) The organism will behave so as to maintain this optimal arousal level. Those behaviors which increase or decrease sensory variation to the optimal level will be reinforced while those which increase stimulation above the optimal level will not be reinforced. Thus, the organism is sometimes motivated to increase stimulation and sometimes to reduce it.

(4) The optimal range of sensory variation is capable of shifting as a function of several variables such as the task to be performed, present state of the organism, and level of preceding stimulation. More important, the range is subject to both inter- and intra-organism differences. Thus, one may speak of individual differences in need for sensory variation as well as differences over time within the same subject. This point will be considered in greater detail in Chapter VII.

Of theoretical importance in the development of the sensoristatic model is the question of what predictions can be made from it. The following seven predictions are offered. It is noted that they apply specifically to conditions of reduced or minimal stimulus variation. With slight modification in wording they would also apply to conditions of too intense stimulation. The remaining chapters, however, will deal only with evidence concerning sensory restriction.

(1) Conditions of reduced sensory input will result in measurable changes in activation level.

(2) The sensoristatic drive state is induced by conditions of restricted sensory variation input and becomes increasingly intense as a function of time and amount of deprivation or restriction.

(3) When conditions of sensory restriction disturb the sensoristatic balance, the organism will exhibit gross disturbances of functioning; e.g., perception, cognition, learning.

(4) When stimulus variation is restricted, central regulation of threshold sensitivities will function to lower sensory thresholds. Thus, the organism becomes increasingly sensitized to stimulation in an attempt to restore the balance.

(5) Organisms will exhibit evidence of learning in situations where the only apparent reinforcement is a change in sensory variation. Thus, under conditions of sensory restriction, increases in stimulus variability will have reinforcing properties.

(6) There exist individual differences in the need for sensory variation. These individual differences may be partially due to the early postnatal levels of stimulation as discussed above.

(7) Reduction of the patterning of stimulus input will result in greater behavioral effects than simply reduction of the level of stimulation. Deprivation of variation in stimulation rather than level of stimulation *per se*, induces a more intense sensoristatic drive state. Hence, behavioral disturbances should be greater under perceptual deprivation conditions than under sensory deprivation conditions, as these were defined in Chapter I.

The validity of these predictions is considered in the following chapters.

## H. IMPLICATIONS OF *SENSORISTASIS* FOR DRIVE REDUCTION AND HOMEOSTASIS

The sensoristatic notion involves the shifting of the drive reduction notion upward, so to speak, "out of the gut and into the brain," as Rosnow (1964)* so succinctly commented. The mechanisms of drive in this system thus remain the same as in the traditional homeostasis-based drive reduction system.

Lana (1960) argues that the existence of an exploratory drive,

---

* Personal communication.

whether internal or external in nature, does not invalidate the drive-reduction hypothesis, although some revision may be necessary. He notes:

> Yet it appears that the fundamental idea contained in the drive-reduction hypothesis of the necessity of drive-reduction for the occurrence of learning has not been badly disturbed. The fact that satiation occurs at all in manipulation-exploration experiments, and it almost invariably does, suggests that an exploratory or manipulatory drive is being reduced and that the instrumental act involved is being reinforced (p. 23).

It is suggested that this holds equally true for the sensoristatic drive state.

The proposed sensoristatic drive does not follow the "rules" of the traditional primary drives. White (1959), in discussing the addition of an exploratory drive to the list of primary drives, noted that:

> If we admit exploration to the category of drive we are thus committing ourselves to believe that drives need have no extraneural sources in tissue deficits or visceral tensions, that they are not necessarily activated by strong or persistent stimuli, that they do not require consummatory responses, and that drive increase can sometimes be a mechanism of reinforcement (p. 302).

These four characteristics are applicable to the concept of sensoristasis. In our own culture, where primary drive deprivation is known by very few, the homeostatic drive concept falls short of accounting for complex human behavior. Postulating the sensoristatic drive does not in any way eliminate the viscerogenic drive states. It does suggest, however, the possible operation of a dual-drive motivational system with the sensoristatic drive occupying the more central position of importance in explaining the behavior of man.

Lana suggests (1964)* that sensoristasis might be postulated as a theoretical process independent of the concept of drive because of the many and varied criticisms inherent in the drive concept. This can be easily accomplished—the supporting data and predictions remain the same; only the tie with drive states changes. The relative utility or futility of positing sensoristasis as a drive state, or as some other independent process, is beyond the scope of this

* Personal communication.

work. Whatever label or theoretical process is ultimately invoked, it is demonstrated in the remaining chapters that sensory restriction is indeed an unpleasant experience which seems to result in a "need" or striving for contact with an increased level of stimulus variation.

# CHAPTER III

# *Physiological Effects of Sensory Restriction*

The research to be discussed in this chapter will bear directly on two items of central importance discussed in Chapter II: activation level and threshold sensitivities under conditions of reduced sensory input.

The discussion in Chapter II led to the prediction of a decline in activation level when stimulus input is curtailed. Once external stimuli are reduced, the only other sources of impact become interoceptive and cerebral stimuli. As a consequence, then, of sensory restriction, "the major potential source of impact is the nervous system itself, especially cortical states. Unless the subject's thoughts and imagery have considerable impact, his activation level necessarily declines" (Fiske, 1961, p. 140).

The sensoristatic model also predicts a shift in receptor sensitivities as the ARAS performs its regulative function in adjusting input-output relations. Thus, one would expect the organism to become increasingly sensitive to stimulation as the level and variety of input decreases.

## A. ELECTROENCEPHALOGRAPHIC CHANGES

The prototype work at McGill, reported by Heron (1961), contains a report of EEG tracings on eight subjects who underwent isolation for ninety-six hours under the following conditions. The subjects lay on a bed in a lighted cubicle with auditory and tactual perception severely limited. The translucent goggles worn by the subjects admitted diffuse light but prevented any pattern vision.

Electroencephalographic records were taken immediately upon entrance into isolation and twice daily thereafter. In addition, some readings were taken during hallucinations and a final recording was taken after the subject completed a battery of perceptual tests upon

35

termination of the isolation period. It is important to note that records were taken only when the subject was awake, *i.e.*, when he was able to carry on a conversation.

The bipolar parieto-occipital tracings indicated slower frequencies at the end of the isolation period than at the beginning. Heron also noted that the tracings at the end of isolation "appear somewhat less tidy, as if whatever mechanisms are involved in the synchronization of alpha rhythms are affected" (1961, p. 24).

A quantitative analysis of wave frequencies within a given time interval revealed progressively slower activity as time in isolation increased. For instance, there was more slow activity after ninety-six hours than after forty-eight hours. The regular progression was still evident even when the records were analyzed in twenty-four-hour periods. Moreover, these changes persisted for three and one-half hours after termination of the isolation experience.

EEG records taken during reported hallucinations were similar to those usually obtained from persons in an alerted state.

Mendelson, Kubzansky, Leiderman, Wexler, and Solomon (1961) reported EEG tracings of two subjects who endured a state of perceptual isolation for six hours in a tank-type respirator (see Figure 1–4). Tactual stimulation was reduced by encasing arms and legs in rigid cylinders. A dull, repetitive auditory masking sound was provided. The subjects wore no goggles and could see the white walls and ceiling and the front of the tank. Artificial light was minimal and constant. Two-minute EEG tracings were taken every fifteen minutes. No post-isolation recordings were made, nor were any control subjects used.

The results indicated a great deal of fluctuation from states of drowsiness to those of alertness. It is noted that the subjects were allowed to talk and, in general, the periods of no verbal activity were accompanied by slower frequencies which increased during periods of verbalization. The authors reported a consistency between behavioral and physiological responses. "Where there is a behavioral index of anxiety there is a generally parallel physiological response. Where there is no behavioral activity, parallel physiological activity is also relatively absent" (Mendelson, *et al.*, 1961, p. 110).

A report by Cohen (1958b) discussed the "white-out" phenomena and its correlated EEG measures. The "white-out" phenomena often result after prolonged exposure to a uniform visual field. The subjective experience seems to be that of cessation of vision, as though the subject has stopped seeing. Different apparatus was necessary to produce binocular and monocular situations. These are described by Cohen (p. 3):

> Two Ulbricht type spheres, with a diameter of 1 m., were joined, and appropriate illumination produced either a completely uniform field or one containing a small differentiated area. The subject, using his right eye alone, looked through a specially designed mask into one of the spheres and was presented with either the uniform field or one containing an 8 cm. circular figure at a distance of 1 m.

For binocular stimulation, the following was used (Cohen, p. 4):

> The new apparatus consisted of a dome with a diameter of 35 cm. at the base and was made of milk glass 4 mm. thick. The dome was placed over the head of the subject who was seated in a tent-like structure made of white cloth. A battery of 30 small 12 volt D.C. bulbs were distributed so as to provide uniform stimulation from all directions of the visual field. In addition, translucent plastic material was hung between the subject and the light source. The diffusion of light through both the translucent plastic and the milk glass dome resulted in a relatively uniform visual field.

Eleven subjects participated for three to eight hours each, with each experimental session lasting about one hour. Periods of continuous stimulation lasted from three to ten minutes with a five-minute rest period between exposures. The subject sat alone in a room and was instructed to signal the duration of a "white-out" by depressing a key.

In the occipital records taken, strong alpha activity usually followed the onset of a "white-out" with the latency of about one second.

> The amount of alpha activity was dependent upon the conditions of stimulation. Uniform stimulation resulted in a much higher percentage of alpha than stimulation with a spot in the field. Monocular uniform stimulation produced more alpha activity than binocular uniform stimulation. Low levels of illumination resulted in more alpha than high levels of illumination. Under those conditions favoring alpha, the reappearance of bursts of alpha usually occurred within 10 sec. On the other hand, stimulation with a spot often suppressed alpha for over 60 sec. (Cohen, 1958b, p. 8).

There was a considerable range of individual differences in EEG tracings.

In general, the onset of alpha activity occurred when visual experience spontaneously became less differentiated, *i.e.*, when the spot in the visual field disappeared with the field appearing as a uniform fog, when the fog disappeared and the subject reported the experience of "light," and when everything disappeared with the subject seeing nothing.

Zubek and his associates have performed several well-controlled studies yielding EEG measures. Zubek's method of measuring occipital frequencies in the studies to be discussed below involved the selection of two hundred one-second samples of artifact-free occipital lobe tracings. Using a special calibrated ruler, the frequency of each one-second sample was determined and the average for the two hundred samples was then computed.

Zubek, Pushkar, Sansom, and Gowing (1961) exposed sixteen subjects to sensory deprivation. Fourteen subjects remained for seven days, one for eight and one-half days, and one for ten days. The purpose of the study was to investigate perceptual changes and is therefore discussed in more detail in Chapter V. Its relevance for the present chapter is that EEG records were taken from eight subjects who remained for a week and one subject who endured ten days of sensory deprivation. Records were taken before isolation and within three hours after confinement.

The post-isolation record of the ten-day subject consisted mainly of fast activity at 12 to 20 c.p.s. and an excess of theta activity particularly in runs involving the temporal lobes. In attempting to relate hallucinatory activity to EEG variations, it was found that alpha activity diminished during some of the hallucinations. An EEG taken two weeks later indicated a quite normal pattern although some temporal lobe slow activity was still evident.

Dealing with the eight one-week subjects, it was found that two of them showed normal post-isolation records, three showed a slowing of the alpha, and three showed a slowing of the alpha together with an above average amount of slow or theta activity. The authors suggest the presence of fast activity in the ten-day subject and its absence in the seven-day subjects may be a function of individual differences.

Zubek, Welch, and Saunders (1963) isolated three subjects under conditions of perceptual deprivation for a period of fourteen days under the following conditions. The subject lay on a mattress wearing translucent goggles and gloves to reduce tactual stimulation. White noise, slightly above the threshold of hearing, was constantly presented through earphones. Subjects were instructed not to engage in any vocal activities and were allowed to move but not to exercise. EEG readings were taken at the following times: before isolation, at seven, ten, twelve, and fourteen days during isolation, and after isolation at three hours, and at one, two, and seven days.

Zubek, Welch, and Saunders reported a highly consistent progressive decrease in mean occipital frequencies as indicated in Table 3–1. This decrease was more than twice as great during the second

TABLE 3–1

MEAN FREQUENCIES (WAVES PER SECOND) FOR THE OCCIPITAL LOBE FOR
THREE SUBJECTS AT VARIOUS TIMES DURING AND AFTER 14 DAYS
OF PERCEPTUAL DEPRIVATION[a]

| Subject | During deprivation | | | | | After deprivation | | | |
|---|---|---|---|---|---|---|---|---|---|
| | Day 0 | Day 7 | Day 10 | Day 12 | Day 14 | Hour 3 | Day 1 | Day 2 | Day 7 |
| A | 10.10 | 9.16 | 8.60 | 7.48 | 7.15 | 7.50 | 7.89 | 8.62 | 9.57 |
| B | 13.03 | 12.65 | 11.40 | 10.94 | 10.44 | 10.80 | 11.04 | 11.34 | 12.50 |
| C[b] | 11.56 | | 10.14 | 8.84 | 8.00 | 9.00 | 10.21 | | 11.01 |

[a] Reprinted by permission from Zubek, Welch, and Saunders, Science, 1963, 139, 490–492.
[b] No encephalographic records were taken for this subject during day 7 of deprivation or on day 2 after deprivation.

week as compared with the first. The post-isolation records showed a consistent progressive increase in mean frequencies.

Zubek (1964a) isolated fifteen subjects for fourteen days of perceptual deprivation. EEG's were taken before isolation, at seven, ten, and fourteen days during isolation, and at one, two, seven, and ten days after isolation. The data available from seven of the subjects revealed a progressive decrease in mean occipital lobe frequency with time in isolation. The mean decrease during the second week was approximately twice as great as that occurring during the first week; this difference borders on significance. The data also revealed a progressive increase in mean frequency following release from isolation. However, indications of EEG abnormality were still present even ten days after release from confinement.

An important finding was the large individual differences noted among the subjects. The mean decrease in frequency ranged from 3.56 to only 0.26 c.p.s. This indication that some individuals are more tolerant of sensory restriction than others will be discussed in Chapter VII.

Next, Zubek and Welch (1963) proceeded to determine the difference in brain wave activity between sensory deprivation and perceptual deprivation, as these two conditions were defined in Chapter I. Ten subjects were utilized in each of four conditions, each lasting for one week. EEG readings were taken before isolation and some two and one-half hours after isolation. The perceptual deprivation conditions were the same as described above (Zubek, Welch, & Saunders, 1963). The sensory deprivation condition was similar except that constant darkness and silence (70 db. attenuation) were maintained. The last two groups were control conditions. One was a control for the supine position assumed by the experimental groups most of the time. In this condition, small groups of three to four subjects lay quietly on mattresses in a large room. Aside from minimizing gross body movements, their environment was quite normal with radio, TV, talking and reading permitted. The final control group simply came to the laboratory twice (with a one-week interval) for the EEG recordings.

The results indicated that all twenty subjects in the two experimental groups showed a post-isolation decrease in mean occipital lobe frequency. This decrease was significantly greater in the perceptual deprivation condition than under sensory deprivation. The two control groups exhibited no consistent trend whatsoever. In addition to these changes in occipital lobe frequencies, the experimental subjects also showed an excess of slow or theta activity, particularly in tracings from the temporal lobes. Moreover, the incidence of theta waves was similar for both sensory deprivation and perceptual deprivation conditions.

The next step in Zubek's research program (Zubek & Wilgosh, 1963) was to determine if the same effects could be produced by tactile-kinesthetic immobilization alone. Twenty-two subjects were "laid to rest" for one week in a box 7 ft. long, 28 in. wide, and 18 in. high and lined with foam rubber. The subject's head rested on adjustable padded devices above which were frames to which pictures could be attached. The feet were immobilized by two V-shaped restraining devices and the arms were placed in rigid cylinders which were fastened down. They were unstrapped for fifteen minutes at mealtimes and one hour in the afternoon. Otherwise their environment was as normal as possible, with no auditory or visual restrictions imposed.

EEG's were recorded from ten subjects before and after their immobilization. Data from ten control subjects were also obtained. The resulting difference in occipital lobe frequencies between the two groups was significant at the .001 level, with the experimental group exhibiting a greater mean decrease. Comparing these results with his earlier research, Zubek concluded that a decrease in frequency is less after immobilization than after a week of sensory

TABLE 3–2

MEAN "PRE-POST" DIFFERENCES IN OCCIPITAL LOBE FREQUENCIES BEFORE
AND AFTER TWO EXPERIMENTAL AND ONE CONTROL CONDITION
(30 SUBJECTS, TEN IN EACH GROUP)[a]

| | Perceptual deprivation subjects | | |
|---|---|---|---|
| | No-exercises | Exercises | Controls |
| | −1.74 | −1.28 | −0.26 |
| | −1.64 | −0.78 | −0.25 |
| | −1.47 | −0.61 | −0.06 |
| | −1.26 | −0.56 | −0.03 |
| | −1.23 | −0.50 | +0.01 |
| | −1.16 | −0.33 | +0.03 |
| | −1.10 | −0.31 | +0.10 |
| | −1.07 | −0.27 | +0.12 |
| | −1.06 | −0.15 | +0.13 |
| | −0.41 | −0.01 | +0.28 |
| Mean | −1.21 | −0.48 | +0.01 |

[a] Reprinted by permission from J. Zubek, *Science*, 1963, **142**, 504–506.

deprivation. But this point of interest remains: tactile-kinesthetic deprivation alone, with no reduction in auditory or visual stimulation, did significantly influence cortical activity. In line with this finding is a study by Hodes (1962) who reported a slowing down of EEG activity in cats when injected with flaxedil, a neuromuscular blocking agent.[*] This has important implications for sensory restriction research and will be discussed in Chapter IX.

[*] The author is grateful to Dr. Zubek for noting the relevance of this important study.

Zubek (1963a) studied the effects of physical exercise during a week of perceptual deprivation. The conditions of isolation were similar to those in the other perceptual deprivation studies conducted at Manitoba with one important difference. Subjects were permitted to engage in six five-minute exercise periods each day. The exercises had been rehearsed prior to confinement and were begun at the sound of a signal. They could also be performed at any other time if a subject so desired.

Occipital lobe frequencies were reported for ten subjects before and after a week of perceptual deprivation. These mean frequencies were compared with those of ten "no exercise" and ten control subjects used earlier (Zubek & Welch, 1963), under the same conditions of deprivation and testing. The results are shown in Table 3–2 (see p. 41). Both experimental groups differed significantly from the controls and the mean decrease of the exercise group was significantly less than that of the "no exercise" group.

## B. GALVANIC SKIN RESPONSE

One of the variables studied by Vernon, McGill, Gulick, and Candland (1961) was galvanic skin response (GSR). The conditions of the study were those of sensory deprivation as defined in Chapter I. Eighteen subjects were confined in a dark, lightproof and soundproof cubicle measuring $4 \times 9$ ft., for periods of twenty-four, forty-eight, or seventy-two hours. Wearing gauntlet-type gloves, subjects were instructed to lie quietly and make as little noise as possible. Measures were taken before confinement (Test A), at the end of the confinement period (Test B), and twenty-four hours after release from confinement (Test C).

The authors predicted that skin resistance would increase from Test A to Test B since an increase occurs in sleeping subjects. As Table 3–3 indicates, all confinement groups showed a decrease from Test A to Test B, while a control group registered an increase. The forty-eight- and seventy-two-hour confinement groups showed a statistically significant loss from Test A to Test B. The gain for the twenty-four-hour control group was also significant.

The GSR drop was only 400 ohms after twenty-four hours, 3300 ohms after forty-eight hours, and 4100 ohms after seventy-two hours. The authors suggested that longer confinements would lead to greater alertness.

A study by Cohen, Silverman, Bressler, and Shmavonian (1961) tested four subjects undergoing four hours of isolation in a sound-proof chamber where they were instructed not to move and to stay awake. Sensory restriction was apparently minimal: the above being the only reported conditions. Two of the subjects had previously been diagnosed as schizoid personalities, the other two as well

TABLE 3–3
GALVANIC SKIN RESISTANCE (OHMS × 1000)[a]

| Group | Tests of confined subjects | | | Tests of control subjects | | |
|-------|------|------|------|------|------|------|
|       | A    | B    | C    | A    | B    | C    |
| 24-hr. | 12.0 | 11.6 | 11.6 | 16.0 | 22.6 | 24.3 |
| 48-hr. | 10.0 | 6.7  | 12.0 | 11.0 | 13.0 | 15.0 |
| 72-hr. | 15.7 | 11.6 | 11.0 | 11.3 | 13.0 | 11.7 |

[a] Reprinted by permission of the publishers from P. Solomon, P. Kubzansky, P. Herbert Leiderman, J. Mendelson, R. Trumbull, and D. Wexler, *Sensory Deprivation*, Cambridge, Mass.: Harvard University Press, Copyright, 1961, by the President and Fellows of Harvard College.

integrated. These latter two subjects showed higher levels of nervous system arousal as indicated by their skin resistance records, than did the two schizoid personalities. No mention of the amount of the differences was made by the authors. They did note that the two schizoid subjects appeared to be more comfortable and less upset by confinement.

Cohen, Silverman, and Shmavonian (1962) dealt with only two hours of perceptual deprivation and reported that most of their subjects showed increases in skin resistance and decreases in number of nonspecific GSR reactions. This was indicative of decreased arousal.

Leiderman (1962) studied galvanic skin potentials in six subjects using four counter-balanced conditions: (1) vision absent, sound present, (2) vision and sound present, (3) vision present, sound absent, and (4) both vision and sound absent. The readings were taken at fifteen-minute intervals during the two-hour sessions and revealed no relationship to the stimulus conditions.

Zuckerman, Levine, and Biase (1964) took GSR measures under conditions which they called total perceptual isolation (darkness and silence) and partial isolation (darkness with sound or silence with light). Thirty-six female college undergraduates were confined for three hours of isolation, twelve under each of the following conditions: (1) no sound–no light, subjects lay on a bed in a dark soundproof cubicle and were instructed not to sleep or talk; (2) light–no sound, the conditions were the same as above except the cubicle was illuminated; (3) sound–no light, conditions were similar to (1) except recorded "Muzak-type" music was played into a speaker.

A five-minute base line GSR recording was obtained on entrance into the cubicle. Thereafter, readings were taken every two minutes or before and after any marked changes in resistance. The nonspecific GSR index indicated that total isolation was more stressful than either condition of partial isolation and that light deprivation was more stressful than sound deprivation. These stress effects did not appear until after one and one-half hours of isolation. There were significant decreases in skin resistance in all groups but the differences between groups were not significant while the groups by periods interaction was significant. The authors also reported a significant correlation between GSR fluctuations and anxiety ratings, based on post-experimental interviews, during the last one and one-half hours of confinement.

Biase and Zuckerman (1965)* reported on a replication of the above study using three groups of male subjects run under the same conditions as the female subjects utilized above. Again, significant decreases in skin resistance were found in all groups and the number of nonspecific GSR's was significantly higher in the total isolation group. For the confined male and female groups, there was a significant difference in nonspecific GSR. The males tended to show a greater rise in conductance (or drop in resistance) than the females.

## C. BIOCHEMICAL CHANGES

Murphy *et al.* (1955) investigated eleven oxycorticoids using urine from nine subjects in the Bexton, Heron, and Scott (1954) study. The results indicated no consistent increase in excretion of

---

* Personal communication.

corticoids during the one- to six-day period of isolation. The authors concluded that the adrenal cortex was not affected by perceptual deprivation to a greater degree than it would have been affected by the minor exigencies of everyday life. However, Zuckerman (1964) noted that the subjects were resting much more than people exposed to the exigencies of everyday life and suggested that a recumbent control group confined with some perceptual distractions might show a drop in corticoids.

Mendelson, Kubzansky, Leiderman, Wexler, DuToit, and Solomon (1960) determined catechol amine levels using urine collected from ten male subjects isolated for periods of 3.5 to 30.8 hours. The subjects were confined in a tank-type respirator, with arms and legs placed in rigid cylinders to inhibit movement and tactile contact. A dull auditory stimulus was provided and the subject's visual field was limited to the blank white walls and ceiling of the room with minimal, constant illumination. Urine samples were collected prior to, during, and after isolation.

The investigators were concerned with the adrenal medullary hormones, epinephrine and norepinephrine, the former secreted only by the adrenal medulla and the latter secreted primarily by the endings of the peripheral sympathetic nerves and secondarily by the adrenal medulla. The authors cited a number of studies showing that a variety of stress situations had produced adrenal medullary hormonal response.

The results indicated that both epinephrine and norepinephrine rose from the pre-confinement to the confinement period, and then fell from the confinement to the post-confinement period. Thus, there was a rise of both hormones during confinement and a fall toward control values after the experience was over. There was a wide individual variation in the response measure but, in general, those subjects who had the greatest rise in either epinephrine or norepinephrine during confinement had the greatest fall after confinement.

Finally, brief mention is made of the study by Cohen, Silverman, and Shmavonian (1962) who reported no consistent direction of change in epinephrine or norepinephrine during a two-hour period of perceptual deprivation. However, as Zuckerman (1964) suggested, the period of confinement may have been too short to induce the stress response.

## D. OTHER PHYSIOLOGICAL FINDINGS

Davis (1959) recorded three indices of somatic activity as a function of two conditions of sensory restriction. Measures were taken of muscular tension and certain circulatory and respiratory variables. One group of twenty-two subjects lay on cots in a dark and soundproof room for forty minutes ("reduced stimulus" group), while the other group of twenty-eight subjects received unpatterned auditory and visual stimulation ("stimulus" group). The results indicated significantly greater increased muscular and circulatory activity and a decreased respiration in the "reduced stimulus" group.

Davis discusses this and other physiological findings of sensory restriction studies in terms of increased sensitization, commenting that:

> The visual receptor, of course, gains sensitivity in the absence of stimuli and loses in their presence, and there is reason to think the process occurs elsewhere as well. 'Central' regulation of sensitivity now seems to play an important role (Bruner, 1957). Such operations resemble the automatic volume control of a radio receiver. That device is intended to maintain a constant output in the face of signal variations. But, if the intended signal is weak or absent, the device seeks ever weaker input levels and causes the system to respond to the noise level. So the sensitized organism may be brought into contact with an underlying field of weak tactual, kinesthetic, even auditory and visual stimuli or system noise, a field which one may easily suppose is more densely populated than are the higher energy levels (Davis, 1959, pp. 313–314).

## E. THRESHOLD CHANGES

### 1. VISION

A study designed to determine the effects of sensory restriction on visual recognition thresholds was performed by Rosenbaum, Dobie, and Cohen (1959). The conditions of sensory deprivation and perceptual deprivation were compared by utilizing one group under total visual deprivation and another group under unpatterned visual stimulation. The subjects, sixteen in each group, each sat in a chair in a room, wearing earplugs and padded earphones. In addition, a constant masking sound was provided by an electric fan. Subjects in the sensory deprivation group wore blacked-out rubber goggles while those in the perceptual deprivation group wore frosted goggles admitting diffuse formless light. After the period of deprivation, subjects were allowed several minutes for peripheral adaptation to normal light. The deprivation periods were zero, five, fifteen, and thirty minutes on four different days.

Subjects' recognitive thresholds were determined tachistoscopically for a list of thirteen five-digit numbers. The results showed no appreciable decrement in threshold for either of the deprivation conditions. An interesting finding was that visual efficiency increased under both conditions after five minutes of deprivation but then returned to normal. On their failure to verify visual impairments reported in other studies, the authors comment that, "It seems more likely that such visual disturbances are a complex derivative of a prolonged isolation-experience in which the reduced variation of all exteroceptive stimulation and the stress-effects of social isolation interact to produce the phenomena observed" (Rosenbaum et al., 1959, p. 433).

The research of Doane, Mahatoo, Heron, and Scott (1959) suggests an increase in visual acuity. Thirteen subjects underwent four days of perceptual deprivation in the McGill cubicle and took a test of visual acuity before and after confinement. Thirteen control subjects also took the test at the same time intervals and showed no change in visual acuity. The confined subjects improved from pre- to post-confinement, although the results do not reach significance.

## 2. CUTANEOUS SENSITIVITY

Several different methods of restricting sensory input have been utilized in the research dealing with cutaneous sensitivity. The discussion will consider first two studies involving isolation in a chamber under perceptual deprivation, then studies dealing with restriction of vision alone, and finally studies dealing with restriction of the cutaneous system itself.

The study by Doane, Mahatoo, Heron, and Scott (1959) discussed above also measured the two-point limen in five subjects undergoing four days of perceptual deprivation. The tests were given prior to isolation, after forty-eight hours of isolation, and again after seventy-two hours. Measurements were taken with a standard aesthesiometer on the tip of the left index finger, volar surface of the left forearm, the inner surface of the right upper arm, and the forehead one inch above the nasion. The results, as shown in Table 3–4, showed a decrease in the two-point limen in three of the four loci, two of which reached significance.

One subjective phenomenon of interest was noted while the subjects were being tested. They were sometimes uncertain as to whether or not they were being touched, and frequently responded when no stimulus was being applied.

TABLE 3–4

MEAN VALUES FOR TWO-POINT LIMEN FOR 5 EXPERIMENTAL SUBJECTS (4 IN THE 72-HOUR TEST) AND 20 NORMAL CONTROL SUBJECTS[a]

| Locus | Group | Test periods | | | p-values (U test)[b] | |
|-------|-------|--------------|--------|--------|------|------|
| | | Pre-isolation | 48 hr. | 72 hr. | 1–2 | 1–3 |
| Finger | Experimental | 1.70 | 1.70 | 1.75 | NS | |
| | Control | 1.75 | 1.50 | 1.60 | | |
| Forearm | Experimental | 29.6 | 26.7 | 24.0 | .15 | .15 |
| | Control | 23.4 | 23.3 | 23.7 | | |
| Upper arm | Experimental | 29.1 | 21.9 | 23.8 | .002 | .05 |
| | Control | 32.8 | 32.8 | 32.4 | | |
| Forehead | Experimental | 19.8 | 16.9 | 19.2 | .02 | .02 |
| | Control | 9.2 | 9.2 | 9.2 | | |

[a] Reprinted by permission from B. Doane, W. Mahatoo, W. Heron, and T. Scott, Canad. J. Psychol., 1959, 13, 210–219.

[b] p-values are based on each subject's change in score as between his first and second, and first and third test.

Zubek (1964b) confined twelve subjects for one week under conditions of perceptual deprivation in the Manitoba dome. The tactual acuity of the index finger and forearm were measured by the "flicker" technique as described by Shewchuck and Zubek (1960). This technique utilizes an interrupted jet of air, the frequency of which can be increased until the subject reports a constant sensation of pressure. Measurements were taken before and after isolation under a constant level of illumination. A group of thirty control subjects were tested at the same interval.

The results indicated that the tactual acuity of both the index finger and the forearm was significantly increased. This increase was quite uniform; all twelve subjects showed increased forearm acuity and eleven of the twelve showed an increased finger acuity.

The control data revealed a chance distribution of increases and decreases.

A study by Zubek, Flye, and Aftanas (1964) was designed to determine the influence of visual deprivation alone on cutaneous sensitivity. Sixteen subjects were placed two at a time in a room for one week. Aside from constant darkness the sensory environment was quite normal with no restrictions on movement or conversation.

Measures of tactual acuity were taken before and immediately after the week of confinement and thereafter at one, two, five, and seven days, with measurements taken from the palm, index finger, and forearm. The sensitivity of the palm was measured by the two-point threshold technique while that of the index finger and forearm was measured by the "flicker" technique described above.

All three measures revealed an increase in tactual acuity which persisted for several days: one day for palm, two days for the finger, and seven days for the forearm. Examination of the individual data for all sixteen subjects revealed a very uniform effect. The increase in sensitivity appeared over all subjects and on all skin areas.

> The subjects verbal reports are also of interest: Several individuals reported that during darkness the soles of their feet or their arms were very sensitive. One subject also stated that he was ticklish for the first time in his life. There were also indications of auditory hyperacuity. Several subjects reported, on their return home, that the radio was unusually loud. It is possible, therefore, that a general enhancement of sensory functioning may occur as a result of visual deprivation (Zubek, Flye, & Aftanas, 1964, p. 1593).

The next logical step from Zubek's methodical Manitoba laboratory was to study the effects of visual perceptual deprivation on cutaneous sensitivity (Zubek, Flye, & Willows, 1964). Having ascertained the effects of visual deprivation, this study was undertaken to determine if similar effects could be produced by exposure to diffuse homogeneous illumination.

Eighteen subjects were placed in groups of two or three in a constantly illuminated room for a period of one week. Wearing translucent goggles admitting diffuse light, the subjects were free to move about in the room and suffered no other restrictions. The techniques, locations, and times of measurements were identical to those reported above.

The results indicated an increase in tactual acuity for the finger, which persisted for one day, and for the forearm with no persistence. A slight, though not statistically significant, increase was demonstrated on the palm, which the authors explained in terms of the lesser sensitivity of the two-point threshold. The individual subject data revealed uniformity though not as striking as under the visual deprivation condition.

Hence, Zubek and his associates demonstrated an increased cutaneous sensitivity under conditions of both darkness and homogeneous illumination. In an effort to account for the less dramatic effects under the unpatterned light condition, the authors suggested the existence of random fluctuations in illumination as a function of head movement (away from the light source) and opening and closing of the eyes. During darkness this could not be a factor, but during exposure to unpatterned illumination these random variations in illumination might alert the neurovisual system intermittently hence diminishing the magnitude of the cutaneous effects.

The discussion now turns to studies involving interference with the cutaneous system itself. Heron (1961) noted some preliminary studies conducted at McGill on cutaneous sensitivity. Sensory restriction was brought about by covering an area on the volar surface of the forearm with a plastic cup 3 × 6 cm. Sensitivity was tested by means of von Frey hairs before and after isolation. The two subjects exhibited a trend toward a post-isolation lower threshold which, however, was not significant. Heron also noted the subjects' reports of changes in sensory functioning, e.g., feelings of pain, warmth, or itching when touched with the hairs on the isolated area.

Aftanas and Zubek (1963a, 1963b) investigated tactual acuity under three conditions: (1) no stimulation, (2) constant stimulation, and (3) a control condition. In all three conditions the area involved was on the volar surface of the forearm 8 cm. below the elbow. The no stimulation condition involved attaching a perforated plastic cup to the skin. The constant stimulation was provided by attaching a slightly curved perforated disc. In the control condition, an open ring was attached to the forearm. Each condition lasted one week with eleven subjects in each group. Measurements were taken before and immediately after each condition and then daily for six days thereafter.

Tactual acuity was measured by the "flicker" technique described above. The results are shown in Figure 3–1. Both experiments yielded the same results: a significant increase in tactual acuity for the no stimulation group and a decrease for the constant stimulation group. The pre-post differences for all three conditions were significant as were the differences between the two experimental groups and the control group. The results also suggested

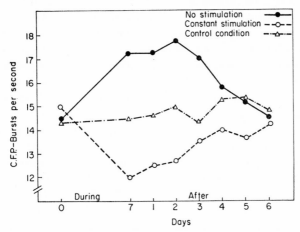

Fig. 3–1. Tactual acuity of the control and two experimental groups before and after a week, and 1, 2, 3, 4, 5, and 6 days later. [Reprinted by permission from M. Aftanas & J. Zubek, *Percept. mot. Skills*, 1963, **17**, 867–870.]

aftereffects which persisted for five days for no stimulation and up to six days or longer for constant stimulation. The authors discussed the results in terms of central rather than peripheral mechanisms arguing that the peripheral factors (impaired circulation and skin distortion) could not likely account for such persisting aftereffects.

Another study by Aftanas and Zubek (1964) was designed to determine if similar changes in acuity could be demonstrated with a two-point threshold technique and if these changes would transfer to the contralateral limb. The conditions were identical to those described above with ten subjects in each condition. Measures were taken before and immediately after the seven-day period and one and two days later.

The results, using the tactual flicker technique, verify Aftanas and Zubek's earlier findings though the aftereffects persisted only one day. Identical results were obtained using the two-point threshold technique though no aftereffects were evident. The most dramatic results relate to the effects on the contralateral arm. Significant changes in tactual acuity, similar to those produced on the experimental arm though less pronounced, were found on a homologous skin area of the contralateral arm. This transfer effect was quite specific: there was no effect on a more distally located skin area. This finding provides rather clear support for Aftanas and Zubek's earlier contention that these changes in acuity are a function of central neural mechanisms.

The authors present additional evidence to support their results:

> Heron and Morrison, in an unpublished paper, also reported an increase in tactile sensitivity, as measured by a modified von Frey hair technique, after four days of isolation of an area on the forearm. Furthermore, a similar change, although not as pronounced, occurred on a homologous but not on a non-homologous skin area of the contralateral arm. Unfortunately, no observations were made on the duration of the phenomenon or on the effects of constant stimulation. Our results on the "no stimulation" condition are also in agreement with a series of studies on unilateral amputees, Ss who may be viewed as possessing a limited degree of tactual deprivation. These studies have all demonstrated an increased sensitivity to touch at the stump as compared with the homologous area of the intact limb or with either limb of control Ss (Haber, 1955; Katz, 1920; Teuber, Krieger, & Bender, 1949; Wilson, Wilson, & Swinyard, 1962). Furthermore, Wilson et al. (1962) have shown that a unilateral congenital amputation increases the sensitivity of the contralateral limb. This sensitivity, however, is not as great as that of the stump but it is greater than that of either limb of matched controls (Aftanas & Zubek, 1964, p. 441).

## 3. PAIN SENSITIVITY

Vernon and McGill (1961) utilized eighteen adult male subjects under conditions of sensory deprivation. The subjects first spent several practice periods in the deprivation chamber to allow their pain thresholds to become relatively stable. Pain thresholds were determined by a modified method of limits (the 50 per cent value being calculated) and pain was delivered by electrical current of 1000 c.p.s.

After the pain thresholds had been determined, nine of the subjects underwent four days of sensory deprivation in a small lightproof and soundproof cubicle. The other nine subjects served as a control group. The pain thresholds were measured again at the end of the four-day period while the subject was still in the deprivation chamber. Results are contained in Table 3–5.

The thresholds for the confined group dropped 0.108 m.a. which was a significant difference as compared to the control group. The thresholds for the experimental group were still lower four days later.

Working with perceptual deprivation of one week duration, Zubek, Aftanas, Hasek, Sansom, Schludermann, Wilgosh, and Winocur (1962) found that confined subjects were significantly more

TABLE 3–5
MEAN PAIN THRESHOLDS (IN MILLIAMPERES)[a]

| Test No. | Sensory deprivation group | Control group |
|----------|---------------------------|---------------|
| 1        | 0.290                     | 0.240         |
| 2        | 0.182                     | 0.221         |
| Difference | 0.108                   | 0.019         |

[a] Reprinted by permission from J. Vernon and T. McGill, *Science*, 1961, 133, 330–331.

insensitive to pain than a control group. The authors explained this discrepancy with the previous findings as being due to the action of the analgesic properties of the white noise utilized in the study.

The previously reported study by Zubek, Flye, and Aftanas (1964) also investigated pain and heat sensitivity under visual deprivation alone. Measurements were taken on the forearm before and after the week of darkness by the Hardy-Wolff-Goodell dolorimeter. A group of matched control subjects were also utilized. As Figure 3–2 indicates, there was a significant increase in sensitivity to heat and pain which persisted two days for pain and one day for heat.

The study by Zubek, Flye, and Willows (1964) reported above using exposure to unpatterned light, also demonstrated a significant increase in pain sensitivity which persisted for one day after confinement.

The following two studies were designed primarily to study intellectual and perceptual impairments under sensory restriction and will therefore be discussed in more detail in Chapters IV and

V. Brief mention of them is made here in reference to their findings on pain sensitivity.

Zubek, Aftanas, Kovach, Wilgosh, and Winocur (1963) utilized body immobilization for periods of three to twenty-four hours and

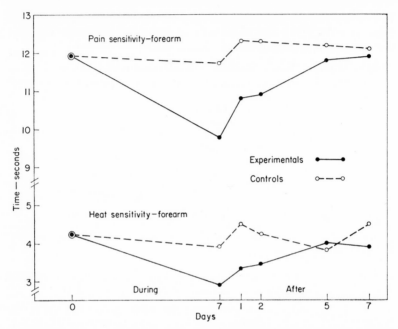

Fig. 3–2. Heat and pain sensitivity of the forearm before and after a week of darkness, and 1, 2, 5, and 7 days later. [Reprinted by permission from J. P. Zubek, J. Flye, & M. Aftanas, *Science,* 1964, **144**, 1591–1593.]

found no significant difference between confined and control subjects in pain sensitivity.

Working with a longer period of body immobilization (one week), Zubek and Wilgosh (1963) again found no differences in pain sensitivity.

## 4. AUDITORY SENSITIVITY

A very common post-isolation report of many of the sensory and perceptual deprivation studies involving long-term isolation was that sounds in the external environment seemed to be louder to many of the subjects. This raises the interesting possibility that sensory restriction may increase auditory sensitivity. Duda and Zubek (1965)* performed a study in which visual deprivation alone resulted in an increase in auditory sensitivity. Twelve subjects were confined in darkness for one week and given two auditory tests prior to and at the end of the isolation period, and then at intervals of one, two, five, and seven days. A control group of seven subjects were given the same tests at the same intervals. The first test measured auditory flutter fusion using an interrupted white

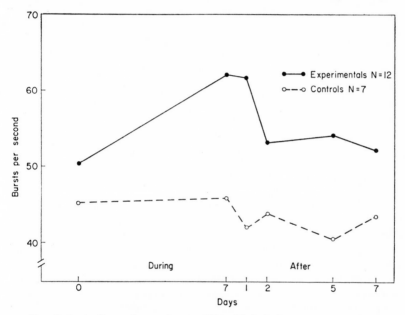

Fig. 3–3. Auditory flutter fusion. [Unpublished data. Reprinted by permission from P. Duda and J. Zubek, 1965.]

noise at an on-off ratio of 90:10. The second test measured the threshold of hearing for the following frequencies: 100, 300, 1000, 5000, and 9000 c.p.s.

The results indicated a significant increase in auditory flutter fusion for eleven of the twelve subjects. This significant increase was still present one day after return to a normal sensory environment. The control group showed a chance distribution of increases and decreases. The results of the auditory flutter fusion tests are shown in Figure 3–3. Zubek notes that these results are almost

* Personal communication.

identical to those for tactual fusion. The results of the other test revealed a slight but non-significant lowering of absolute thresholds for the various frequencies.

Zubek (1965)* also reported that subjects often commented that their sense of smell was better and that food seemed tastier after visual deprivation. Thus, it may be that olfactory and gustatory sensitivity are also increased.

## F. DISCUSSION

Impressive evidence does exist to support the proposition that level of activation, as reflected in EEG tracings, is influenced by sensory restriction. A clear shift to the lower frequencies in the alpha band has been consistently demonstrated. Furthermore, this decrease seems to persist for some time after return to a normal sensory environment.

Heron (1961) suggested that these effects could be defined in terms of the ARAS, as discussed in Chapter II, and noted that the activity of this mechanism is closely related to overt behavior and is intimately connected with sensory systems. Zubek and Wilgosh (1963) also attributed the EEG changes to a disturbance of the activity of the ARAS as a result of the decrease in the level of varied sensory input. Their study on tactile-kinesthetic deprivation indicated that, "Interference with these sense modalities alone may be sufficient to produce certain behavioral changes, especially in the light of several reports pointing to the 'powerful excitatory influence of somatic sensory excitation' upon the reticular activating system†" (p. 308).

That the critical factor is variation in sensory input rather than level of input *per se* is demonstrated by Zubek and Welch (1963) who found a greater disturbance of electrical activity of the brain under perceptual rather than sensory deprivation. The authors also noted a close correspondence between behavioral performance under deprivation and the state of electrical activity of the brain. There were greater behavioral impairments under perceptual than under sensory deprivation.

---

* Personal communication.

† J. D. French, in *Handbook of Physiology*, section 1, *Neurophysiology*, vol. 2, J. Field, Ed. (Williams & Wilkins, Baltimore, 1960), p. 1281; H. Bernhaut *et al.*, *J. Neurophysiol.*, 1953, **16**, 21.

Of great interest is the suggestion of possible fluctuation in brain wave activity as a function of behavioral activity. The observation of Heron (1961) that EEG records obtained during hallucinations were similar to those usually obtained in a waking state suggests the operation of interoceptive stimulation in increasing level of activation. The changing EEG activity as a function of presence or absence of verbal activity as noted by Mendelson *et al.* (1961) also indicates the importance of self-generated stimulation in maintaining activation. Continuous EEG tracings taken during isolation and correlated with overt and covert activity would most likely provide stronger evidence for the effects of interoceptive and exteroceptive stimulation on cortical arousal.

Along these lines, Cohen (1958b) presented some interesting conjectures derived from his study of the "white-out" phenomenon. He suggested that a low alpha index would tend to reflect an activation pattern which might be correlated with excessive blinking, which would disrupt continuous stimulation and thereby prevent "white-out." He also suggested that the temporal correspondence of alpha pattern with "white-out" might indicate that little, if any, neural activity initiated by visual stimulation was reaching the visual cortex during "white-out." The presence of slow brain waves usually associated with sleep, as well as the drowsiness reported by the subjects, might serve to indicate that areas of the brain, other than those associated with vision, are of importance for the "white-out" effect. It is suggested that this is a function of a too low arousal level due to the low level of sensory variation.

Finally, physical exercise was shown by Zubek (1963a) to produce less of a decrease in mean frequencies. As he suggested, exercising may provide varied kinesthetic and proprioceptive stimuli to counteract to some degree the restriction of varied visual and auditory inputs. Thus, somatic sensory stimulation may exert an excitatory influence on the reticular formation.

Thus, the data reveal reduced electrical activity of the brain which is more severe under perceptual as compared to sensory deprivation and which can be counteracted, to some extent, by kinesthetic and proprioceptive sensory input. It is important to note that large individual differences are reported, with some subjects showing considerable disturbance of brain wave activity while others reveal an almost normal record. This point will be discussed further in Chapter VII.

The studies by Zuckerman, Levine, and Biase (1964), Cohen, Silverman, Bressler, and Shmavonian (1961), and Vernon, McGill, Gulick, and Candland (1961) revealed a decrease in skin resistance (or increase in skin conductance) as a function of time in isolation. The implications of these findings for our sensoristatic model are suggested by Vernon *et al.* (1961):

> The change in the electrical resistance of the skin may possibly be related to general alertness. Skin resistance increases during sleep and decreases when the subject awakens. It might be concluded that as the subject becomes less alert, resistance goes up and as he becomes less drowsy, resistance goes down. Under the conditions of sensory deprivation the skin resistance goes down, which may mean that the confined individual has become a more alert individual. It is reasonable to assume that the subject is constantly tuned to receive any and all stimuli during confinement. In a sense he has become more sensitive to changes of any sort since he has so few. He may be a more awake and more alert individual. Thus, it would be predicted that the longer the confinement, the greater the change in skin resistance, a prediction which is verified by the data (p. 55).

This suggestion that the stimulus-deprived subject will become more sensitive to stimulation has considerable support from the data reported.

The work of Mendelson *et al.* (1960) on catechol amine excretion suggests that some forms and durations of sensory restriction may be classed with other stresses which have measurable physiological effects. Their finding that subjects with the lowest control norepinephrine values had the greatest rise in excretion during confinement is consistent with the law of initial values of other physiological variables. That epinephrine excretion does not follow this pattern is of interest. The authors noted that, "these data converge to suggest that epinephrine excretion is more dependent upon and sensitive to situational determinants which may induce psychological stress, whereas norepinephrine excretion is more closely related to basal physiological processes" (Mendelson *et al.*, 1960, p. 154).

The research reviewed has revealed consistent increases in cutaneous sensitivity with some suggestion of an increased visual sensitivity. Pain sensitivity showed an increase only under conditions of sensory deprivation, visual deprivation alone, and diffuse light alone. The most systematically studied threshold change has been cutaneous sensitivity by Zubek and his associates. They have shown tactual acuity to increase under conditions of no tactual stimulation, visual deprivation alone, and perceptual visual deprivation. Most striking has been their demonstration of an increased acuity on a homologous area of the contralateral arm, strongly suggesting the operation of central factors serving to regulate threshold sensitivity.

Thus the evidence reviewed in this chapter lends support to several of the predictions set forth in Chapter II. Reduced sensory input results in measurable changes in activation level (Prediction 1), the organism becomes increasingly sensitized to stimulation (Prediction 4), and disturbances are more pronounced under perceptual as compared to sensory deprivation (Prediction 7).

# CHAPTER IV

# Cognitive and Learning Effects

This chapter will focus on sensory restriction research which has investigated intellectual efficiency, rate of learning, and attitude change.

## A. INTELLECTUAL EFFICIENCY

A number of studies in sensory restriction have indicated subjective reports of difficulties in concentration, attention, and problem solving following isolation. Upon release from confinement, subjects have given fairly consistent reports indicating the existence of cognitive decrements. As will be seen, however, somewhat less consistent results have emerged from studies using objective tests of cognitive functioning.

The prototype study of Bexton, Heron, and Scott (1954) investigated the effects of perceptual deprivation on cognitive processes. The study has been described in Chapter I. Subjective reports indicated that the subjects were unable to concentrate on any topic for long and found it difficult to solve intellectual problems. Most of the subjects abandoned attempts at organized thinking and there existed blank periods during which they were unable to think of anything at all.

The following tests were administered to twelve of the confined subjects and twelve controls: multiplying two- and three-digit numbers, arithmetical problems, completion of number series, making a word from jumbled letters, and making as many words as possible from the letters of a given word (word-making). These tests were given prior to isolation, after twelve, twenty-four, and forty-eight hours in isolation, and three days after isolation. The authors reported that the experimental subjects performed worse than the controls on all the tests, but the differences reached significance only for the error scores on the second anagram test, as shown in Figure 4–1.

Scott, Bexton, Heron, and Doane (1959) also investigated cognitive effects of perceptual deprivation under the same conditions as in the Bexton, Heron, and Scott study described above. The same tests were also used. The statistical analysis was based on a comparison of the mean difference score (between the pre-isolation

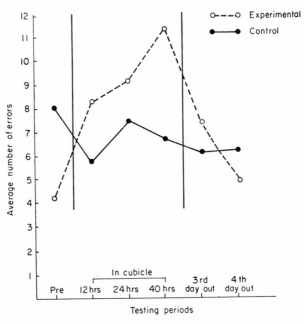

Fig. 4–1. Errors in word-making (wrong words, misspellings, repeats). Mean error scores for experimental and control subjects, before, during, and after the isolation period. [Reprinted by permission from W. H. Bexton, W. Heron, & T. H. Scott, *Canad. J. Psychol.*, 1954, 8, 70–76.]

and subsequent tests) of the confined and control groups. The confined group performed significantly worse than the controls on the word-making test and the number series. On the other tests, the experimental group also performed poorer although the results were not significant.

Subjective reports during isolation revealed that nearly all subjects reported inability to concentrate, lack of clarity in thinking, and difficulty in thought organization. Also, the thought disorganization became more pronounced as time in isolation increased.

Post-isolation comments revealed that these subjectively reported impairments persisted for two days after the experiment, with reports of lack of interest in study, loss of motivation, and absent-mindedness.

Freedman, Grunebaum, and Greenblatt (1961) placed eight subjects under conditions of perceptual deprivation in a small room, wearing translucent goggles, and with a constant white noise, for a period of eight hours. The study was concerned primarily with perceptual changes, but the authors did report subjective changes in cognitive functioning. All subjects commented on the difficulty in thinking coherently and concentrating. Those who tried were often unable to count consecutively for more than twenty or thirty digits.

Goldberger and Holt (1958) confined fourteen male subjects in a cubicle for eight hours under perceptual deprivation similar to the McGill experiments except that the subjects were encouraged to talk. Tests of arithmetic reasoning, logical deduction, digit span, and story recall were given before and after confinement. Pre- and post-test comparisons yielded significant impairment on the test of logical deduction only. No control group was utilized.

Davis, McCourt, and Solomon (1958) confined ten male subjects for ten hours in a respirator under perceptual deprivation. The subjects were confined in pairs and though they could not see one another, they were able to converse. The authors found no pre-post test differences on a block design task.

Cohen, Silverman, Bressler, and Shmavonian (1961) confined four subjects in a soundproof chamber for four hours. Subjects were instructed to stay awake and were seated in a chair. Before isolation, subjects were given the vocabulary, digit span, similarities, arithmetic, and comprehension sub-tests of the Wechsler Adult Intelligence Scale (WAIS). After isolation, the remaining six sub-tests of the WAIS were given. There were no control subjects. Though no statistical data were provided, the authors reported that short-time retentive ability (digit span) was increased while arithmetical reasoning, ability to abstract and generalize, and reasoning ability showed a decrease.

Smith and Lewty (1959) confined twenty subjects in a cubicle under perceptual deprivation for as long as they could stand it. The average periods of confinement were 29.24 hours for men and 48.70 hours for women. No objective tests of intellectual functioning were used but the subjects reported that thinking became disordered and concentration was lost.

Myers, Murphy, Smith, and Windle (1962), in the HumRRO* research program, have conducted a number of studies in which military personnel serving as subjects were confined to lightproof and soundproof cubicles for ninety-six hours. A battery of five tests was administered prior to confinement, after about seventy-five hours of isolation, and again after release from confinement. The tests were taken over the intercom system and included immediate memory, numerical facility, verbal fluency, successive subtraction, and inductive reasoning.

In comparison with the performance of a control group, the authors reported that the isolated subjects tended to perform at a poorer level during isolation, though only two of the tests (successive subtraction and inductive reasoning) reached significance. The results are shown in Table 4-1. The post-confinement results yielded

TABLE 4-1
RELATIVE PERFORMANCE OF CUBICLE AND CONTROL GROUPS ON THE
DURING-ISOLATION INTELLECTUAL EFFICIENCY TEST BATTERY[a]

| Subtest | Superior group (Cubicle or control)[b] | $x^2$ | $p$ |
|---|---|---|---|
| Immediate memory | Cubicle | 0.53 | NS |
| Numerical facility | Cubicle | 0.24 | NS |
| Verbal fluency | Control | 3.76 | NS |
| Successive subtraction | Control | 4.76 | $<.05$ |
| Inductive reasoning | Control | 4.76 | $<.05$ |

[a] Reprinted by permission from T. I. Myers, D. B. Murphy, S. Smith, and C. Windle, HumRRO res. memo., February 1962.
[b] Cubicle group $N = 34$; control group $N = 34$.

no decrement in intellectual efficiency. A post-confinement questionnaire revealed that the isolated subjects rated themselves as being considerably less efficient in thought processes.

The authors concluded that the two tests on which significant impairments were shown probably involved more complex operations than the other tests used. They suggested, therefore, that sensory deprivation impaired involved or complicated intellectual tasks but not necessarily fairly easy and routine activities.

* Human Resources Research Office operating under contract with the Department of the Army.

Zuckerman, Albright, Marks, and Miller (1962) isolated twenty-five female subjects in an iron lung for seven hours in total darkness with white noise presented through earphones. A battery of tests was administered to confined and control subjects. The study is discussed in greater detail in Chapter VI, but two of the tests are of interest in the present context. A Mental Arithmetic Test and the Digit Span Test from the Wechsler Memory Scale were given to the subjects after entering confinement and again after six hours of confinement. No significant differences were reported on either test, however, an interesting difference between two control conditions was revealed on the Mental Arithmetic Test. One control group (C1) remained in the iron lung for seven hours but suffered no visual or auditory restrictions. The other control condition (C2) endured neither confinement nor sensory restriction but were simply tested at appropriate times. The C1 group had an increase in the number of problems right which was significantly greater than the decrease in the C2 group. The authors suggested that confinement without sensory restriction may have exerted a facilitating effect on this test. The experimental subjects reported difficulty in thought and concentration.

Zubek, Sansom, and Prysiazniuk (1960) confined subjects in the Manitoba dome isolation chamber under conditions of darkness and silence. The subject group consisted of fourteen who remained for seven days, one for eight and one-half days, and one for ten days. Six other subjects terminated within the first three days. A battery of tests was administered inside the chamber at the beginning of the isolation period, at intervals of approximately twenty-four hours, and again one day after isolation had ended. Total testing time was forty-five minutes. The testing procedure was as follows:

A 15-watt red light bulb located in the ceiling of the dome was put on; S removed the test battery and clipboard which were placed inside the food receptacle by E through a door in the bottom of the receptacle; S sat down on the "step-down" toilet seat located below the red light bulb; E gave S instructions for taking the tests over the two-way speaker system; the completed test battery was replaced in the food receptacle; S was asked to report any experiences he might have had since the last test session; the red light was extinguished (Zubek, Sansom, & Prysiazniuk, 1960, pp. 235–236).

A group of control subjects were tested at the same time intervals under the red light inside the chamber.

The tests included the following: verbal reasoning, rote learning, abstract reasoning, space relations, verbal fluency, number facility, numerical reasoning, recall, and recognition. Significant impairments were reported for the confined subjects only on the tests of recall and recognition. The confined subjects performed better (though not significantly) on verbal reasoning and rote learning. The control group performed better (though not significantly) on verbal fluency and numerical reasoning.

Subjective reports revealed that four subjects consistently reported intellectual impairments, while five reported impairments from the fifth day of confinement on. Seven subjects reported no intellectual impairments whatsoever.

Also, on the recall and recognition tests, several subjects reported a feeling of great frustration and a blankness when they tried to recall or recognize words they had seen several minutes before. The memory lapses and absentmindedness persisted in several subjects a day or so after isolation.

The authors concluded that purely intellectual abilities (excluding recall and recognition) did not seem to suffer any impairment. They suggested that some of these abilities, e.g., rote learning, verbal and abstract reasoning, and space relations, might even improve, at least during the first few days of isolation.

Zubek next proceeded to determine the effects of perceptual deprivation on various intellectual functions (Zubek, Aftanas, Hasek, Sansom, Schludermann, Wilgosh, & Winocur, 1962). Forty subjects were confined in the Manitoba isolation chamber under diffuse illumination and white noise. Twenty-nine of these subjects successfully endured the seven days of isolation. Two control groups of forty subjects each were also utilized. The "ambulatory" control group came to the laboratory for testing on nine occasions. The "recumbent" controls remained in a room, in groups of five or six, for a week. Aside from lying down for the period of confinement, their sensory environment was quite normal.

The tests were administered before isolation, at various intervals during isolation, and one day after the release from confinement. The testing required about one hour per session and was conducted inside the chamber with instructions given over the intercom. The two control groups were given the same tests at the same time intervals.

The results for those subjects completing the week of isolation and those terminating early are shown in Table 4–2.

Following the analysis of variance, the differences between the various groups were evaluated by 2-tailed $t$ tests. This revealed that the experimentals performed significantly worse than the controls on the following tests: cancellation, dexterity, number facility, abstract reasoning, space relations, and verbal fluency. With the

TABLE 4–2

VALUES OF $F$ AND $x^{2a}$ FOR 12 INTELLECTUAL TESTS DURING A WEEK OR LESS THAN A WEEK OF PERCEPTUAL DEPRIVATION[b]

| Week of isolation | | | Less than week of isolation | | |
|---|---|---|---|---|---|
| Tests | $F$ | $p$ | Tests | $x^2$ | $p$ |
| Cancellation | 8.90 | <.001 | Cancellation | 6.30 | <.05 |
| Dexterity | 7.51 | <.01 | Dexterity | 8.75 | <.02 |
| Number facility | 3.26 | <.05 | Number facility | 7.40 | <.05 |
| Abstract reasoning | 7.40 | <.01 | Abstract reasoning | 7.40 | <.05 |
| Recall | 2.88 | NS | Recall | 5.00 | NS |
| Recognition | 1.06 | NS | Recognition | 6.20 | <.05 |
| Verbal reasoning | 1.17 | NS | Verbal reasoning | 3.20 | NS |
| Numerical reasoning | 8.80 | <.001 | Numerical reasoning | 1.55 | NS |
| Space relations | 14.51 | <.001 | Space relations | 6.20 | <.05 |
| Verbal fluency | 3.18 | <.05 | Verbal fluency | 7.80 | <.02 |
| Rote learning | 0.76 | NS | Rote learning | 3.15 | NS |
| Digit span | 2.00 | NS | Digit span | 1.30 | NS |

[a] Friedman two-way analysis of variance by ranks.
[b] Reprinted by permission from J. P. Zubek et al., Percept. mot. Skills, 1962, 15, 171–198.

test of numerical reasoning, the performance of the experimental group was significantly worse than that of the ambulatory controls, and the recumbent controls were also significantly worse than the ambulatory controls. This, together with suggested, though not significant, evidence on space relations and verbal fluency suggested that the postural condition may have influenced these abilities. None of the post-isolation tests revealed any differences in performance. Also, the authors suggested that the impairment observed during the first few days of isolation was about the same as that at the end of isolation.

The data for those subjects terminating within the first three days of isolation is contained in the right half of Table 4–2. The results were quite similar to those who endured the week success-fully. There were significant impairments in cancellation, dexterity, number facility, abstract reasoning, space relations, and verbal fluency. Numerical reasoning was not impaired significantly as it was with longer confinement subjects, and recognition was impaired in this group while it was not in the main group.

Finally, the authors examined the performance of four of the twenty-nine successful subjects who had served a year earlier in a sensory deprivation experiment lasting one week. Three of these subjects noted that the second condition was much easier to en-dure, while the fourth found it more difficult. Comparing the per-formance of these four with a matched group of four of the "non-repeaters" it was found that the "repeaters" obtained higher mean scores on nine of the twelve tests, though the differences were not significant.

Thus, these two studies of Zubek and his associates have demon-strated greater intellectual impairment under conditions of per-ceptual deprivation as compared to sensory deprivation.

Zubek (1963a) then investigated the effect of exercise on twenty-seven subjects confined in the Manitoba chamber for one week under conditions of perceptual deprivation. The study has been described in Chapter III. The subjects were given the twelve intellectual tests noted above (Zubek *et al.*, 1962) before isolation and at six intervals during the week of confinement. The exercise group did not differ significantly from a no-exercise group on any of the tests except cancellation. The no-exercise group did perform significantly worse than matched controls on seven of the tests (cancellation, numerical reasoning, space visualization, arithmetic problems, abstract reasoning, dexterity, recall). Thus, the perform-ance of exercise can eliminate many of the impairments produced by perceptual deprivation.

Pushing methodically onward, Zubek, Aftanas, Kovach, Wilgosh, and Winocur (1963) investigated the effects of severe immobiliza-tion of the body on intellectual processes. The forty experimental subjects were immobilized in the coffin-like box described in Chapter III, with no visual or auditory restrictions. Eight subjects were able to endure the isolation for the prescribed twenty-four-hour period. A group of "recumbent" controls were individually placed in the same box for the same time period but suffered no restrictions on their motility except for assuming the supine position. The "ambulatory" control group simply came to the laboratory for the testing sessions.

The tests were administered prior to and immediately after immobilization and consisted of the following: space relations, numerical reasoning, verbal reasoning, verbal fluency, digit span, recall, and recognition. The results indicated no significant differences on any of the tests and the existence of no particular trends. Also, no trends were reported when the data were analyzed in terms of the duration of immobilization.

A questionnaire given after immobilization indicated that a significantly greater percentage of the experimental subjects reported that their ability to concentrate was impaired, thoughts were jumbled, thought and reflection were a great effort, and ideas tended to perseverate.

Next, Zubek and Wilgosh (1963) immobilized twenty-two subjects for a period of one week under the same conditions as noted in the above study (Zubek *et al.*, 1963). Twelve tests were given before confinement and at various intervals during the week of confinement and included the following: simple arithmetic problems, mathematical reasoning, abstract reasoning, verbal fluency, verbal reasoning, space visualization, digit span, rote learning, recall, recognition, cancellation, dexterity. The authors reported that the mean performance of the experimental subjects was worse than that of the matched controls on all twelve tests, though only cancellation, recall, and verbal fluency were impaired significantly. Thus, immobilization for a longer period of time did result in greater intellectual impairment than immobilization for only twenty-four hours.

A different approach to the cognitive effects of sensory deprivation is reported by Suedfeld, Vernon, Stubbs, and Karlins (1964). The authors believed the discrepancy between subjective reports of cognitive impairment and actual objective test results was due to the use of clear and structured objective problems in previous research. The subjective reports, on the other hand, dealt with unstructured tasks. An earlier study (Suedfeld, Grissom, & Vernon, 1964), using an oral TAT technique and requesting long and detailed responses, found that after twenty-four hours of sensory deprivation subjects told much shorter stories than before isolation. This, they concluded, demonstrated a lessened ability to concentrate as a result of sensory deprivation.

The Suedfeld, Vernon, Stubbs, and Karlins study was designed to replicate the earlier study and to determine if repeated confinement would reduce the cognitive impairment. The subjects were fifty-eight males who were isolated on a bed in a dark silent chamber for two twenty-four-hour periods one week apart. The findings after the first confinement session verified the earlier study, *i.e.*, shorter stories were told after confinement. Thus, the authors concluded that subjective reports of cognitive impairment can be experimentally verified with the use of appropriate tests. The difference was not found in the second confinement session suggesting that cognitive impairments produced by sensory deprivation might be negated through adaptation.

## B. RATE OF LEARNING

Vernon and Hoffman (1956) confined four male subjects to the Princeton floating room cubicle for forty-eight hours under conditions of sensory deprivation. Their purpose was to test the effects of sensory deprivation on rate of learning. The learning tasks were twelve item adjective lists presented aurally. The subject's ability to learn by the anticipation method was determined prior to confinement, after twenty-four and forty-eight hours of confinement, and twenty-four and forty-eight hours after release from confinement. Tests were administered in an antechamber by the light of a fifteen watt red bulb. The results of the confined subjects compared with those of a control group are shown in Figure 4–2. They indicate that the ability to learn adjective lists improved with continuing sensory deprivation. Subjective reports obtained after confinement did not reveal any difficulties in thought, concentration, *etc.*

A second study by the Princeton group (Vernon & McGill, 1957) confined twelve subjects for a period of seventy-two hours under the same conditions as noted above. Nine subjects successfully completed the period of confinement. Lists of fourteen adjectives were presented prior to confinement, after twenty-four hours, then every twelve hours. After release from isolation, the lists were again presented after twenty-four, thirty-six, and forty-eight hours. The tests in this study were administered while the subjects were inside the confinement chamber and seated on the edge of the bed. The results showed no significant difference between experimental and control groups. Performance of the learning task was neither facilitated nor inhibited.

A more recent study by Arnhoff, Leon, and Brownfield (1962) confined twelve subjects for forty-eight hours under conditions of perceptual deprivation with low level diffuse illumination and masking noise. The subjects wore gloves and cardboard cuffs. Six word lists of fifteen adjectives each were presented aurally prior to

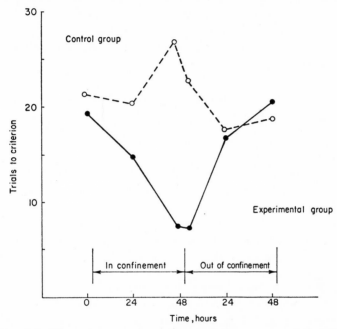

FIG. 4–2. Effect of sensory deprivation on learning rate in human beings. Each point is the mean value of four subjects. [Reprinted by permission from J. Vernon & J. Hoffman, *Science*, 1956, **123**, 1074–1075.]

confinement, four times during confinement, and twenty-four hours after confinement. All tests were given in the cubicle. Analyses made for the total confinement period, and for each twelve-hour period revealed no significant differences between the confined subjects and a control group. Thus, learning was neither facilitated nor impaired by perceptual deprivation.

Using retention of verbal material as a response variable, Grissom, Suedfeld, and Vernon (1962) confined twenty subjects individually for twenty-four hours in a soundproof and dark room where they were instructed to lie quietly on a bed. After one minute of confinement, subjects were aurally presented with a 182-word passage from "War and Peace." They were told they would be asked to repeat the passage after it was presented. After subjects completed their attempt at repeating the passage, control subjects were released from confinement and told to return twenty-four hours later while experimental subjects remained in the chamber for twenty-four hours. Both groups were then asked to repeat the passage verbatim. The authors reported that only one subject anticipated a retest. The results indicated that the memory retention did not change significantly for the confined group. A significant decrease in performance was noted with the members of the control group who went about their normal everyday activities during the twenty-four-hour test-retest period. Thus, sensory restriction did facilitate retention of the verbal material.

## C. ATTITUDE CHANGE AND CONFORMITY

Before discussing attempts to change attitude through sensory restriction techniques, it is relevant to mention the study of Bexton (1953) who showed that subjects in isolation elected to listen to material they would ordinarily find tedious. Under conditions of perceptual deprivation, subjects were given the opportunity to hear five-minute recordings of eight repetitions of the sixteen-bar chorus of "Home on the Range," two talks for children from a religious primer, soap commercials, and a portion of a stock market report. One group of four subjects heard the records prior to isolation while the other four knew nothing about them until they had been in isolation for several hours. Subjects were told they could hear any of the records as often as they wished.

The subjects who had previously heard the records asked for them a total of only nine times, while the other group asked for them fifty-three times and reported that they helped relieve the boredom. It was also found that the rate of requests increased greatly during the second half of the isolation period. Voluntary exposure to communicative material seems to be of great importance in subsequent acceptance of its contents and in changing attitudes in the direction advocated.

Scott, Bexton, Heron, and Doane (1959) investigated opinion change under conditions of perceptual deprivation. Twenty-four subjects still remaining in isolation after eighteen hours were exposed to recorded propaganda material which consisted of a ninety-minute talk on a series of records read in a boring monotone. The talk argued for belief in various types of psychical phenomena (telepathy, clairvoyance, ghosts, poltergeists, and psychical research). The attitude questionnaire consisted of a series of Bogardus-type scales measuring attitude toward the above topics, the amount of interest in the topic, and how important the subject felt the topic was.

After a subject had been in isolation for about eighteen hours he was told that he might listen to a series of records if he wished. There were nine records in all and they were played one at a time as the subject requested them. A control group was treated in the same way, being told about the records at the same time in the testing schedule. The questionnaire was given prior to confinement and again when the subjects stated definitely that they did not want to hear the records again.

The results indicated that both groups showed a significant change in attitude but the change was significantly greater in the confined subjects. Also, while both groups showed more interest in the topic and felt it was more important after hearing the records, the confined subjects were affected to a greater degree than the controls. Although no systematic followups were obtained, anecdotal evidence suggests that the effects persisted in some subjects for three to four days.

Vernon (1963) reported on a study conducted by Suedfeld which measured the effect of sensory deprivation upon susceptibility to propaganda. On the basis of a pretest questionnaire, subjects with neutral views toward Turkey were chosen for the experimental and control groups. A group was confined in the Princeton floating room under what was described as the most severe conditions of sensory deprivation. At the end of the twenty-four-hour period, each subject heard a tape containing propaganda favorable to Turkey. A control group also heard the tape in the confinement chamber. Immediately after hearing the tape, the posttest questionnaire was given.

A significant change in attitude was reported for the confined group with no significant change for the control group. The average change of the confined group was over eight times as great as the controls.

Personality differences were also investigated in this study. Subjects were identified by personality tests as either concrete, abstract, or intermediate individuals. A concrete individual is one who accepts information at face value, needs extended information, and feels stressed when such is lacking. The abstract individual seeks to evaluate information received and is more self-reliant ( Harvey, Hunt, & Schroder, 1961). As had been predicted, the concrete subjects showed greater attitude change in the direction advocated, as is shown in Table 4–3.

TABLE 4–3
AVERAGE ATTITUDE CHANGE[a]

|  | SD (%) | Non-confined (%) | System average (%) |
|---|---|---|---|
| Concrete | 32 | 10 | 21 |
| Intermediate | 18 | 3 | 11 |
| Abstract | 8 | −6[b] | 1 |
| Treatment average: | 20 | 3 | |

[a] Reprinted by permission from J. Vernon, *Inside the black room*. New York: Potter, 1963.
[b] A negative score means that these subjects change their attitudes opposite to that of the propaganda, *i.e.*, became less favorable toward Turkey.

A study from the HumRRO program ( Myers, Murphy, & Smith, 1963) utilized 109 enlisted Army volunteers of above average intelligence. The experimental group consisted of forty-five subjects who were confined for forty-eight hours of sensory deprivation. The remaining sixty-four control subjects were not confined and simply reported to the laboratory for testing. Pretest questionnaires were given to determine the subject's initial attitudes toward Turkey.

After forty-eight hours of confinement ( and while still in isolation), the experimental subjects were permitted to hear a three-minute recording about Turkey as often as they wished during a seventy-five-minute test period. The control group was also allowed to hear the propaganda after forty-eight hours of normal sensory experience. Each subject received information which was contrary to his initial attitude. Both groups were then immediately given the posttest questionnaire in the form of an auditory version of the Semantic Differential.

The results indicated that the confined subjects requested the propaganda recordings significantly more often than did the control subjects, even though the information was contrary to each subject's belief. However, in spite of this greater exposure of the confined group to the propaganda material there was no significant difference in attitude change between the two groups. It was found that those subjects who held more extreme initial views did shift significantly more than those with less extreme initial attitudes.

Finally, two studies on the effects on ninety-six hours of sensory deprivation on conformity to group influence will be mentioned. Myers, Murphy, and Smith (1961) used techniques similar to those of Asch and Crutchfield to determine if isolated and control subjects would be differentially influenced by the judgments of others. Subjects were required to make judgments on a series of multiple-choice problems involving the ability to count various series of brief tones presented in rapid succession. Subjects were exposed to the "judgments" of other subjects.

The results indicated that both confined and control subjects were greatly influenced by the group influence situation. There was, however, no substantial difference between experimentals and controls in amount of influence.

Smith, Murphy, and Myers (1963) utilized thirty-nine experimental subjects and forty controls in another study on conformity. Again, techniques similar to Asch and Crutchfield were used with the subjects hearing the alleged judgments of "other subjects." An overall comparison of the data revealed no significant difference between the control and confined subjects.

The interaction between level of intelligence and confined versus control group assignment was significant, however. Experimental subjects of lower intelligence yielded greater conformity while in isolation than did lower intelligence subjects in the control group. For those subjects of higher intelligence, there was no significant difference between the two conditions.

It is noted that those subjects designated as lower intelligence were in the top forty per cent of the Army population, hence they were a fairly bright sample. The authors suggested that using subjects of even lower intelligence would result in greater conformity.

## D. DISCUSSION

In attempting to provide a general overview of the research reported in this chapter, the results of some tests of cognitive functioning are provided in Table 4–4. It is noted that only those tests which have been investigated under two or more conditions of isolation are reported. Significant impairments were also produced by ninety-six hours of sensory deprivation on successive subtraction and inductive reasoning (Myers, Murphy, Smith, & Windle, 1962) and by eight hours of perceptual deprivation on logical deduction (Goldberger & Holt, 1958). These tasks, however, were not tested under other conditions of sensory restriction. Of the tests in Table 4–4, verbal reasoning, arithmetic problems, and digit span showed no impairment under any form of sensory restriction.

The extent of changes in intellectual efficiency seems to be related to some degree to the type of deprivation employed. There are indications that impairments are greater after perceptual deprivation than after sensory deprivation, lending further support to Prediction 7. Zubek (1964b) noted that post-sensory deprivation testing seemed to give no evidence of any cognitive deficits whereas with tests given during sensory deprivation some indications of intellectual inefficiency have been found. Zubek ascribed these effects to differences in the subjects' motivational states during and after isolation. It seems fairly safe to conclude that intellectual impairments produced by sensory deprivation are not particularly severe.

A degree of agreement exists among those studies using perceptual deprivation. For example, the study of Zubek, Aftanas, Hasek, Sansom, Schludermann, Wilgosh, and Winocur (1962) essentially confirmed the original McGill experiments observing significant deficits in arithmetic problems, numerical reasoning, verbal fluency, visualization in two- and three-dimensional space, and abstract reasoning. Other functions, e.g., digit span, rote learning, recall, and recognition suffered no impairment. There was also agreement in that no relationship was found between degree of impairment and duration of isolation.

It has been suggested (Goldberger & Holt, 1958) that simple tasks involving a highly overlearned set of operations were perhaps less impaired by perceptual deprivation while tasks involving reflection and manipulation of ideas were the most impaired. The more recent data reported here do not bear out this suggestion. For example, it has been noted that the complex ability of verbal reasoning was not impaired under any condition whereas the simple task of verbal fluency was impaired by perceptual deprivation and by a long period of body immobilization. The recent data also suggest that the duration of the task and the interest value of the test may not be important.

Zubek *et al.* (1962) also suggested that the intellectual impairments that do occur do not get any worse with time. Furthermore, in some cases, the degree of impairment decreases toward the end of confinement. This suggests that the subjects possibly adapt to the reduced sensory environment, which is discussed in Chapter IX.

One provocative finding which appeared in some of the studies is that some abilities might actually improve as a function of sensory restriction; though the evidence is suggestive only and contradictions have been reported. Zubek (1964b) noted that digit span seemed not to be affected by sensory restriction and that rote learning may be somewhat improved. The proposition that some mental processes might show facilitation as a function of sensory restriction is also lent support by the significant improvements in sensory thresholds as discussed in Chapter III.

The findings under conditions of body immobilization are of interest. Short-term immobilization of up to twenty-four hours (Zubek, Aftanas, Kovach, Wilgosh, & Winocur, 1963) produced not even the suggestion of any intellectual impairment while immobilization for seven days produced impairments similar to prolonged sensory deprivation. However, the longer immobilization did not affect as wide a range of functions as sensory or perceptual deprivation.

Finally, the role of exercise in eliminating many impairments produced by perceptual deprivation (Zubek, 1963a) indicated that the degree of motor activity permitted during isolation may be one of the most important variables in sensory restriction research. Zubek noted that some of the contradictory results in this area may be related to differences in motor activity of the subjects. The influence of somatic sensory excitation on the RAS has been discussed in Chapter III.

TABLE 4-4

REVIEW OF FINDINGS ON COGNITIVE FUNCTIONING

| Task | Impairment | Conditions of deprivation | Duration of deprivation | Author(s) |
|---|---|---|---|---|
| Multiplication of 2 and 3 digit numbers | NS | Perceptual | 48 hr. | Bexton et al., 1954 |
| | NS | Perceptual | 3-4 days | Scott et al., 1959 |
| Arithmetic problems | NS | Sensory (iron lung) | 7 hr. | Zuckerman et al., 1962 |
| | NS | Perceptual | 48 hr. | Bexton et al., 1954 |
| | NS | Perceptual | 3-4 days | Scott et al., 1959 |
| | NS | Perceptual | 8 hr. | Goldberger & Holt, 1958 |
| | NS | Body immob. | 7 days | Zubek & Wilgosh, 1963 |
| Completion of number series | NS | Perceptual | 48 hr. | Bexton et al., 1954 |
| | Significant | Perceptual | 3-4 days | Scott et al., 1959 |
| Making a word from jumbled letters | NS | Perceptual | 48 hr. | Bexton et al., 1954 |
| | NS | Perceptual | 3-4 days | Scott et al., 1959 |
| Making as many words as possible from a single word | Significant | Perceptual | 48 hr. | Bexton et al., 1954 |
| | Significant | Perceptual | 3-4 days | Scott et al., 1959 |
| Digit span | NS | Sensory (iron lung) | 7 hr. | Zuckerman et al., 1962 |
| | NS | Perceptual | 8 hr. | Goldberger & Holt, 1958 |
| | NS | Body immob. | 7 days | Zubek & Wilgosh, 1963 |
| | NS | Body immob. | 24 hr. | Zubek et al., 1963 |
| Numerical facility | NS | Sensory | 96 hr. | Myers et al., 1962 |
| | NS | Sensory | 7-10 days | Zubek et al., 1960 |
| | Significant | Perceptual | 7 days | Zubek et al., 1962 |
| | Significant | Perceptual | 1-3 days | Zubek et al., 1962 |
| Cancellation | Significant | Perceptual | 7 days | Zubek et al., 1962 |
| | Significant | Perceptual | 1-3 days | Zubek et al., 1962 |
| | Significant | Body immob. | 7 days | Zubek & Wilgosh, 1963 |

| Test | Significance | Type | Duration | Reference |
|---|---|---|---|---|
| Verbal fluency | NS | Sensory | 96 hr. | Myers et al., 1962 |
|  | NS | Sensory | 7–10 days | Zubek et al., 1960 |
|  | Significant | Perceptual | 7 days | Zubek et al., 1962 |
|  | Significant | Perceptual | 1–3 days | Zubek et al., 1962 |
|  | NS | Body immob. | 24 hr. | Zubek et al., 1963 |
|  | Significant | Body immob. | 7 days | Zubek & Wilgosh, 1963 |
| Verbal reasoning | NS | Sensory | 7–10 days | Zubek et al., 1960 |
|  | NS | Perceptual | 7 days | Zubek et al., 1962 |
|  | NS | Perceptual | 1–3 days | Zubek et al., 1962 |
|  | NS | Body immob. | 24 hr. | Zubek et al., 1963 |
|  | NS | Body immob. | 7 days | Zubek & Wilgosh, 1963 |
| Abstract reasoning | NS | Sensory | 7–10 days | Zubek et al., 1960 |
|  | Significant | Perceptual | 7 days | Zubek et al., 1962 |
|  | Significant | Perceptual | 1–3 days | Zubek et al., 1962 |
|  | NS | Body immob. | 7 days | Zubek & Wilgosh, 1963 |
| Recall | Significant | Sensory | 7–10 days | Zubek et al., 1960 |
|  | NS | Perceptual | 7 days | Zubek et al., 1962 |
|  | NS | Perceptual | 1–3 days | Zubek et al., 1962 |
|  | NS | Body immob. | 24 hr. | Zubek et al., 1963 |
|  | Significant | Body immob. | 7 days | Zubek & Wilgosh, 1963 |
| Recognition | Significant | Sensory | 7–10 days | Zubek et al., 1960 |
|  | NS | Perceptual | 7 days | Zubek et al., 1962 |
|  | Significant | Perceptual | 1–3 days | Zubek et al., 1962 |
|  | NS | Body immob. | 24 hr. | Zubek et al., 1963 |
|  | NS | Body immob. | 7 days | Zubek & Wilgosh, 1963 |
| Numerical reasoning | Significant | Perceptual | 7 days | Zubek et al., 1962 |
|  | NS | Perceptual | 1–3 days | Zubek et al., 1962 |
|  | NS | Body immob. | 24 hr. | Zubek et al., 1963 |
|  | NS | Body immob. | 7 days | Zubek & Wilgosh, 1963 |

The studies dealing with attitude change under conditions of both sensory and perceptual deprivation revealed contradictory findings.

The studies of Scott, Bexton, Heron, and Doane (1959) and Suedfeld (reported by Vernon, 1963) revealed a significant attitude change as a function of sensory restriction while the research of Myers, Murphy, and Smith (1963) revealed no such change. Myers *et al.* suggested that complex set factors were responsible for this inconsistency. They further contended that the HumRRO procedure was more likely to have induced subject resistance to showing any effects of the influence attempt. The fact that the confined subjects had a higher degree of self-exposure to the propaganda may have increased the transparency of the manipulation attempt.

In his book, "Inside the Black Room" (1963), Vernon described a fascinating procedure based on sensory restriction for developing a superior brainwashing system. His subject is a hypothetical prisoner who is a strong Protestant with, however, little understanding of his belief. To "convert" him to Islam, Vernon described the following procedure:

> First, place him in S.D. for four days in order to get him receptive to novelty—any novelty. At the end of four days introduce two switches without any instruction into the cubicle. If he operated Switch A, he would hear a thirty-second speech favoring his brand of Protestantism. If he operated Switch B, he would hear a thirty-second speech favoring Islam. The main difference between the two switches is that Switch A always produces the *same* speech, whereas Switch B always produces a *different* one and always by a different voice. In this manner the monotony of S.D. would become associated with the monotony of the repetitive speech on Protestantism, and the desire for novelty would lead to the selection of Switch B. Now arrange the switches so that he can operate them less often, and our battle is practically won. We have caused this individual, by *his own choice,* to listen to our propaganda. If we can get him to listen, we can get him to believe by making our propaganda clever enough (pp. 28–29).

Once the subject is listening (by choice) to the propaganda, any evidence of conversion would be rewarded. For example, questions about Islam might be presented to him aurally. Correct answers might be reinforced first by a little light, then by a novel food, and later by social contact. These responses are not forced out of him by torture and pain but only through the positive reinforcement of sensory variation.

Vernon noted the similarity between this approach and that of the Red Chinese and commented that, "our hypothetical case would not convert everyone, but very likely it could be a much more effective system than has been used to date" (1963, p. 31).

Evidence discussed in this chapter, then, lends support to Predictions 3 and 7.

# CHAPTER V

# *Perceptual and Motor Effects*

One of the findings of the McGill research on sensory restriction was the reporting of gross disturbances in perception. After several days of isolation, subjects reported movement of the visual field, changes in size, shape, and brightness of objects, after-images, and other perceptual distortions. For the most part, these disturbances disappeared within thirty minutes after isolation, though some subjects did continue to experience them a day later. As will be seen, the research which followed this initial study has not found perceptual changes of so gross a nature. The disturbances which have subsequently been demonstrated are, in general, minimal and somewhat transitory in nature.

## A. RELATED FINDINGS

Some relevant data have appeared from studies not involving sensory or perceptual deprivation *per se*, but rather a reduction in the level of stimulus variation. The literature on vigilance behavior, for example, which has been reviewed by Holland (1958) and Fiske and Maddi (1961), is of interest. This situation provides a homogeneous level of variation in stimulation—a series of repetitions of the same or similar stimuli. It has been suggested (Fiske & Maddi, 1961; Schultz, 1963, 1964b) that adaptation to such a monotonous and repetitive situation readily develops. As a consequence, alertness and attention are decreased. Continued exposure to the stimuli results in the loss of their nonspecific effects which has been called "sensory habituation" (Scott, 1957). Hence, performance, *i.e.*, overt response to the continuing stimuli, would be expected to deteriorate, as the vigilance literature testifies.

Detection in this situation seems to be improved by introducing a novel stimulus. This serves to increase alertness and the vigor of ongoing behavior, with its concomitant focusing of attention and arousal of interest. There exists in the vigilance situation, then, a demonstration of the influence of the level of stimulus variation upon the performance of a perceptual task. When the stimulus environment contains minimal sensory variation, then production of perceptual deficits seems to follow.

Evidence is also available on the disturbing effects of a completely homogeneous visual field—a Ganzfeld. Hochberg, Triebel, and Seaman (1951) created a Ganzfeld by placing half a ping-pong ball over one eye of the subject which resulted, in most cases, in the complete disappearance of color.

Also working with a colored Ganzfeld, Cohen (1957, 1958a) utilized two intersecting spheres both illuminated by a highly saturated red light. On first looking into the apparatus the subject sees a poorly saturated red fog. Shortly this color begins to fade and appears achromatic in about three minutes. This disappearance of color in a Ganzfeld demonstrates the vital role played by spatial inhomogeneity and temporal change in perception.

In another study restricting stimulus input to homogeneous visual stimulation, Cohen (1958b) demonstrated the "white-out" phenomenon (cessation of vision) under both monocular and binocular conditions. The apparatus and conditions of the study were described in Chapter III. The "white-out" phenomenon tended to be suppressed by factors which introduced sensory change such as blinking and eye movement and the presence of an object in the visual field.

## B. SENSORY RESTRICTION RESEARCH

Bexton, Heron, and Scott (1954) reported that when their subjects were released from perceptual deprivation they experienced disturbances in visual perception lasting for one or two minutes. Specifically these disturbances included difficulty in focusing, objects appearing fuzzy and not clearly distinct from their backgrounds, the environment appearing two-dimensional, and colors seeming unusually saturated.

In order to further investigate these reported changes in visual perception, Heron, Doane, and Scott (1956) served as subjects themselves for six days under perceptual deprivation. The author-subjects reported a high degree of similarity among their subjective experiences which they summarized in five categories. These observations were made immediately after isolation and included: (1) apparent movement independent of movement by the subject, (2) apparent movement associated with head or eye movement, (3) distortions of shape, (4) accentuation of after-images and perceptual lag, and (5) colors appeared bright and highly saturated and color and brightness contrast was exaggerated.

Scott, Bexton, Heron, and Doane (1959) in their investigation of cognitive effects of three to four days of perceptual deprivation, discussed in the preceding chapter, administered a mirror drawing task before and after isolation. There was no significant difference between the performance of the confined and control groups.

Doane, Mahatoo, Heron, and Scott (1959) investigated changes in perceptual functioning in thirteen subjects after four days of perceptual deprivation. Visual tests were given prior to and after confinement and compared with a control group given the tests at the same time intervals. The authors noted that the test battery took over an hour to administer and suggested that some of the later tests may have shown smaller differences than had they been given more immediately after termination of confinement. The test results are briefly mentioned in the order in which they were given. No effect was found on critical flicker frequency. A significant increase of figural aftereffect was reported. Size constancy was significantly decreased while no differences were found in the phi-phenomenon or in brightness contrast effects. The autokinetic effect was significantly increased as was color adaptation. No differences were reported in shape constancy, brightness constancy, or Necker cube reversals.

Qualitative reports obtained as soon as the translucent mask was removed revealed gross visual disturbances similar to those reported by Heron, Doane, and Scott (1956) and lasting for about one-half hour. Specific distortions reported by most of the subjects included spontaneous movements, induced movements (produced by head and eye movements), surface distortions, and linear distortions. There were also reports of increased contrast and saturation, luminosity of colors, and pronounced positive and negative after-images.

Freedman, Grunebaum, and Greenblatt (1961) isolated one group of eight subjects under conditions of perceptual deprivation in a small room where they lay on a bed, wearing translucent goggles, gloves and cuffs, and earphones. Subjects were tested before and after the eight-hour session for their perception of simple figures. They were asked to describe in detail the appearance of the figures and to draw the figures if the descriptions were distorted. Altered perception was reported for only one control subject, but all of the confined group reported changes. "Subjects reported that triangles seemed to change shape, straight lines appeared to move, halos developed and arrowheads became larger or smaller. . . . Perceptual aberrations in one case persisted for over one hour" (Freedman, Grunebaum, & Greenblatt, 1961, p. 65).

Differences between experimentals and controls on a series of perceptual tests are shown in Table 5–1. On the size constancy test,

TABLE 5–1

DIFFERENCES BETWEEN EIGHT EXPERIMENTAL AND SIX CONTROL SUBJECTS
FOLLOWING SENSORY DEPRIVATION[a]

| | $p$ |
|---|---|
| Perceptual distortions | |
| Experimentals > Controls | .03 |
| Figure-ground stability | |
| Experimentals < Controls | .05 |
| Change in amount of Müller-Lyer effect | |
| Experimentals > Controls | .05[b] |
| Deterioration of form-quality on Bender Motor Gestalt Test | |
| Experimentals > Controls | .05 |
| Improvement in pursuit-rotor performance | |
| Experimentals < Controls | NS |
| Size constancy | NS |

[a] Reprinted by permission of the publishers from P. Solomon, P. Kubzansky, P. Herbert Leiderman, J. Mendelson, R. Trumbull, and D. Wexler, *Sensory deprivation*, Cambridge, Mass.: Harvard Univer. Pr., Copyright, 1961, by the President and Fellows of Harvard College.
[b] Based on Moses Test of Extreme Reactions. All other probabilities based on Mann-Whitney U Test.

confined subjects showed hyper-constancy or hypo-constancy with changes of greater magnitude than controls. Similar results were found with the Müller-Lyer Illusion. On a pursuit-rotor task, confined subjects improved an average of 13.9 per cent while controls improved 33.2 per cent. Much greater instability was shown on ambiguous or reversible figures by confined subjects who also showed deteriorations on the form-quality of Bender-Gestalt reproductions.

The authors concluded that, "thus, experimental subjects do not have veridical perception after an 8-hour exposure to 'non-patterned' stimulation, and their visual-motor coordination is impaired" (Freedman, Grunebaum, & Greenblatt, 1961, p. 66).

Vernon, McGill, Gulick, and Candland (1959) isolated subjects under conditions of sensory deprivation for three different periods of confinement: twenty-four, forty-eight, and seventy-two hours. Three subjects served under each condition and were not told how long they would be confined. Testing was conducted prior to confinement (A), upon release from confinement (B), and twenty-four hours after confinement (C). Comparisons were made between the performances of the confined group and a control group matched on the basis of Test A performance. The tests used were color perception, depth perception, pursuit rotor, mirror drawing, and rail walking.

The results indicated that color perception was adversely affected, particularly for the forty-eight- and seventy-two-hour confinement groups, though significance was reached only for the forty-eight-hour group. With depth perception, the greatest loss occurred for the twenty-four-hour period of confinement but this was not significant due to the large individual variation. Rotary pursuit ability was significantly adversely affected only for the forty-eight-hour confinement group. Similar results were obtained from the mirror tracing task, but errors were fewer after forty-eight hours and significantly increased after twenty-four and seventy-two hours of isolation. Finally, gross motor behavior, as measured in the rail walking task, was adversely affected particularly for the seventy-two-hour group.

The authors suggested caution in interpreting these results due to the small N and the wide range of individual differences for some tasks. The tests given twenty-four hours after confinement revealed a tendency toward elimination of the effects.

Vernon and Hoffman (1956), in the study of human learning rate discussed in the preceding chapter, isolated four subjects for forty-eight hours under conditions of sensory deprivation. Though no objective perceptual tests were used, post-isolation reports of the subjects in which they were questioned about focusing difficulty, saturation of hues, and a three-dimensional perception, revealed negative findings. This is in disagreement with the work cited by Heron, Doane, and Scott (1956) above.

Freedman and Greenblatt (1959) utilized an eight-hour period of perceptual deprivation in which the thirteen subjects lay on a bed, wearing translucent goggles and being exposed to white noise. The purpose of the study was to measure perceptual lag, *i.e.*, the perceived distortion in the shape of a line which is rotated slowly against a dimly illuminated screen. The authors noted the earlier work of Heron, Doane, and Scott (1956) who reported that their subjects perceived the line as S-shaped because the ends "lagged" behind the center part. Held and White (1959) found no distortion in the shape of the line but did report a change in apparent speed of rotation.

In the Freedman and Greenblatt (1959) study, the subjects viewed the line after eight hours of perceptual deprivation viewing a homogeneous diffuse field. The subjects perceived the sweep of the apparatus as moving more slowly than before isolation. Control subjects showed no such change in performance.

Further work on this phenomenon was undertaken by Freedman and Held (1960) who used three exposure conditions with a three-hour period of perceptual deprivation under the same conditions as in the Freedman and Greenblatt (1959) study. The perceptual lag test was given prior to confinement and thereafter at thirty-minute intervals. All three conditions involved isolation on a bed, with white noise to mask ambient sounds, and gloves and cuffs to reduce tactile perception. One condition (Diffuse) involved perceptual deprivation with a homogeneous diffuse visual field (30 ft. candles). A second group (Random Flash) involved viewing, through translucent goggles, three incandescent lamps set in a row six inches apart and twenty-four inches above the eyes. The lamps flashed at different rates, durations, and interflash intervals. The final condition involved sensory deprivation, *i.e.*, complete darkness (Blackout). The results are shown in Figure 5–1.

As had been predicted, the Random Flash condition produced a greater effect at each measurement. The differences between Blackout and Diffuse conditions were not significant while the Random Flash effects were significantly greater than the other two except at 150 minutes. The authors explained the lack of difference between Blackout and Diffuse effects in terms of spontaneous random activity in the homogeneously stimulated eye. The subjects tended to return slowly to normal speed perception after the confinement was ended.

Ormiston (1958) investigated change in perception of the phi phenomenon under three different conditions: perceptual deprivation, sensory bombardment, and a control condition. Thirty subjects served in each group, with each condition lasting thirty minutes. The perceptual deprivation group sat in a bare room, wearing

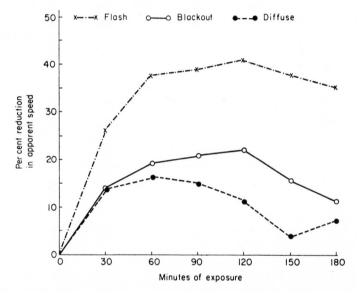

Fig. 5–1. Perceptual lag in sensory deprivation. [Reprinted by permission from S. J. Freedman & R. Held, *Percept. mot. Skills*, 1960, 11, 277–280.]

translucent goggles, earplugs, and earmuffs. In the sensory bombardment condition subjects were exposed to motor tasks, varied sound effects, taste and smell stimuli, and a variety of colored goggles. The perceptually-deprived group showed a significant increase in perception of phi while the bombardment group showed a trend toward a decrease in phi perception. There was no change with the control group.

Part of the HumRRO research program (Myers, Murphy, Smith, & Windle, 1962) dealt with auditory vigilance under sensory deprivation. The conditions of the ninety-six-hour confinement have been described in the preceding chapter. Each time a subject heard the short tone signal (500 c.p.s. presented for $\frac{1}{10}$ second) he was required to release a lever which he had been holding.

A pre-confinement test was given to establish baseline speeds of response. The vigilance task was performed on the third day of isolation with the session consisting of twelve signals given over a forty-eight-minute period. Two control conditions were utilized, one group taking the test in a lighted room and the other in darkness. The results of the three groups are contained in Figure 5–2.

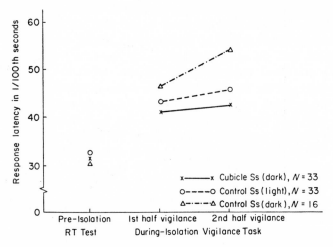

FIG. 5–2. Average response latency on the first and second halves of an auditory vigilance task for cubicle subjects tested after three days of prior isolation, and for two control groups, one tested in darkness and the other in the light. [Reprinted by permission from T. I. Myers, D. B. Murphy, S. Smith, & C. Windle, HumRRO res. memo., February, 1962.]

The results showed the classic performance decrement previously referred to in vigilance research. The performance of the lighted room control group was significantly better than that of the darkness control group. The average response latencies of the confined group were faster than those of both control groups, but only the confined-darkness control difference was significant. Thus, vigilance performance of the confined subjects was not significantly better than that of the subjects tested in light, but they did significantly outperform those subjects tested in darkness.

A number of carefully controlled studies are available from the

Manitoba laboratories. Zubek, Pushkar, Sansom, and Gowing (1961) investigated perceptual changes after seven to ten days of sensory deprivation under conditions of darkness and silence. A battery of perceptual-motor tests was administered prior to and immediately after isolation. (It is noted that these same subjects were also given tests of intellectual abilities described in Chapter IV, which tests were given during isolation.)

The test battery consisted of the following: visual vigilance, auditory discrimination, depth perception, size constancy, reversible figures, perception of lines, and perception of colors. In addition to these tests, subjects were required to estimate various intervals of time before isolation and at various times during isolation. A control group took the same tests and made the time estimates.

The statistical analysis based on the difference between the mean scores of the two groups after a week of isolation, relative to their pre-isolation scores produced the following results. On depth perception, the confined subjects did less well than the controls, though this was not significant. Similarly, on the size constancy test, there was a non-significant decrease in constancy for the experimental group. The authors noted that these results bordered on significance and suggested that with a larger $N$ they might have reached significance. The confined group showed fewer figure reversals per minute than the controls but the difference again was not significant. On the auditory discrimination task, there was no significant difference between the two groups. On the visual vigilance task, the overall performance of the confined subjects after a week was significantly poorer than that of the controls. Both groups overestimated the short intervals of time (one, three, five, fifteen, and thirty minutes) but the differences between the groups was not significant. On the longer time intervals (60 and 120 minutes), both groups underestimated, with the confined subjects showing significantly more underestimation on the 120-minute estimate.

Post-isolation interviews revealed that none of the confined subjects reported gross perceptual changes of the type reported earlier (Heron, Doane, & Scott, 1956). However, some of the subjects did report that colored objects were brighter and more vivid.

Zubek, Aftanas, Hasek, Sansom, Schludermann, Wilgosh, and Winocur (1962) investigated perceptual functioning under conditions of perceptual deprivation in the Manitoba dome under diffuse illumination and white noise. The perceptual test battery was administered prior to and after seven days of isolation. Ambulatory and recumbent control groups took the tests at the same time intervals.

The battery of tests included the following: color discrimination, reversible figures, depth perception, size constancy, visual vigilance, auditory vigilance. The experimentals performed significantly worse than both control groups on color discrimination, reversible figures, and visual and auditory vigilance. As with the above-mentioned study utilizing sensory deprivation, post-confinement interviews produced no mention of gross perceptual changes. However, 48 per cent of the subjects reported objects to be brighter and more vivid on leaving isolation. Interestingly enough, similar experiences were mentioned by roughly the same percentage of recumbent controls who suffered no restriction of vision expect that their visual field was restricted to a room for the one-week period.

Next, Zubek, Aftanas, Kovach, Wilgosh, and Winocur (1963) investigated perceptual processes under conditions of twenty-four-hour body immobilization as described in Chapter III. No visual or auditory restrictions were imposed. The tests were administered before and after confinement and included the following: cancellation test, dexterity, reversible figures, perception of patterns, color discrimination, and kinesthetic acuity. Immobilization produced significant impairments on dexterity, kinesthetic acuity, color discrimination, and reversible figures. Perception of simple patterns was also affected to some degree. There were also reports of increased brightness and vividness of objects and colors by both confined and control subjects.

Using a seven-day period of body immobilization, Zubek and Wilgosh (1963) investigated perceptual-motor phenomena under the same conditions as in the twenty-four-hour immobilization study. The tests were given before and after the week of confinement and included depth perception, size constancy, reversible figures, and color discrimination. Of these tests, only color discrimination and reversible figures were impaired significantly.

Finally, as discussed in Chapter III, Zubek (1963a) determined the counteracting effects of physical exercise during one week of perceptual deprivation. Color discrimination and reversible figure tests were given before and after isolation. The exercise group showed no impairment on either test.

## C. PERCEPTION WITHOUT OBJECT: HALLUCINATIONS

A most dramatic aspect of the original McGill research was the report of a variety of hallucinatory phenomena. After several days of perceptual deprivation, the majority of the subjects reported such experiences which were largely visual in nature and ranged from simple geometric forms to complex picture-like scenes. Some hallucinations invoking other senses were also reported. Most of the earlier research reported similar findings, but as Zubek (1964c) notes, since 1959 the picture has changed considerably and fewer hallucinations are being reported.

A most thorough review of the sources of reports of hallucinatory phenomena in sensory restriction research was recently published by Zuckerman and Cohen (1964a). In their discussion, Zuckerman and Cohen chose to substitute for "hallucinations" or "images" the more operational terminology of Murphy, Myers, and Smith (1962) who invoked the terms "reported visual sensations" (RVS) and "reported auditory sensations" (RAS).

These reported visual sensations showed a rather wide range in degree of structuredness or meaningfulness, from simple flashes of light to complex integrated scenes. The same variation existed with reported auditory sensations. Accordingly, Zuckerman and Cohen suggested the grouping of these reported sensations into two categories based on degree of meaningfulness. The first category (A) includes meaningless sensations such as flashes of light, spots, and simple noise. The second category (B) includes meaningful sensations such as people, objects, or complex scenes, and the sound of human voices or music. Zuckerman and Cohen suggested that the term "hallucination" should be applied only to the B type of reported sensations since the "A phenomena may include simple idioretinal responses or illusions while the B phenomena seem to signify a greater cortical involvement" (1964a, p. 2).

Zuckerman and Cohen found little in the way of any consistent relationship between incidence of reported sensations and the wide variety of confinement, subject, and response variables.

Since the impetus for this book is the attempt to provide a meaningful review and interpretation of literature which has not yet been brought together, a review of Zuckerman and Cohen's article will not be provided. Instead, attention is directed toward the suggestion that hallucinatory phenomena may be of less significance than earlier research had implied.

Of primary interest is the notion that fewer hallucinatory phenomena are being reported in more recent research. Zubek (1964c) notes that the reports in recent studies (1959–1963) indicated that hallucinatory phenomena occurred in only a small percentage of their subjects (0–20 per cent). Those hallucinations that have been reported are rarely of the complex picture-like variety (type B) but rather are usually simple and brief in the form of light flashes, spots, and geometric forms (type A).

Zubek (1964c) offered four explanations for this discrepancy between the early and the more recent research. First, the criteria for differentiating among hallucinatory phenomena have become much more precise in recent years. He suggested that if these criteria had been applied to the earlier studies, fewer hallucinatory phenomena would have been reported. Second, he noted that much more care is now being paid to the factors of suggestibility and expectancy and their role in influencing both the frequency and the complexity of hallucinatory reactions. His third point relates to the widespread publicity accorded this kind of research which may have influenced the subjects' reactions (or more properly, lack of reactions). For example, in the fall of 1964, this author heard a lengthy discussion of "sensory deprivation research" on a popular late-evening television show with numerous references to the "wild hallucinations" experienced by the subjects. It may become increasingly difficult to find naive subjects who enter the situation without any expectations as to what is "supposed" to happen. Finally, Zubek suggests that "the original dramatic results may have been produced by some unique interaction of procedural, personal, and motivational variables" (1964c, p. 39).

One final important point is to be noted. Various hallucinatory reactions described in the early literature have been found to be quite common under relatively normal sensory conditions. Subjects exposed to ten to thirty minutes of darkness (Myers, Murphy, & Smith, 1961; Ziskind & Augsburg, 1962), or just lying quietly in a room with no restriction of sensory input (Zubek et al., 1962), have frequently reported hallucinatory experiences of varying degrees of complexity. Thus, a baseline of hallucinatory reactions occurring under more normal sensory conditions must be established against which those occurring under deprivation conditions can be evaluated.

## D. DISCUSSION

An overview of the more frequently used tests given under conditions of sensory restriction is provided in Table 5–2.

The table does not include every perceptual test used in the studies discussed but only those tests investigated under more than one condition of isolation. Also, it is noted that impairments are reported only where they have reached statistical significance. In several of the studies non-significant trends are discussed. When these are considered, of course, the frequency and variety of impairment are greater than that shown in Table 5–2. With this in mind, it is noted that depth perception and size constancy were not impaired under sensory or perceptual deprivation or body immobilization. Color perception was affected under perceptual deprivation and body immobilization, and sensory deprivation of forty-eight hours but not twenty-four or seventy-two hours (Vernon, McGill, Gulick, & Candland, 1959). A longer period of sensory deprivation, seven days (Zubek, Pushkar, Sansom, & Gowing, 1961), produced no impairment.

The results on the reversible figures indicate that sensory deprivation of seven to ten days duration produced no effect whereas seven days of perceptual deprivation and twenty-four hours and seven days of body immobilization did produce significant impairments. Visual vigilance was impaired by both sensory and perceptual deprivation while auditory vigilance suffered only under perceptual deprivation and may have improved under sensory deprivation.

Expanding the scope a bit to include non-significant trends and a wider range of perceptual tests, it becomes exceedingly difficult to discuss the results due to the vast range of differences in duration of isolation, degree of restriction, capacities measured, types of subjects, control data, etc. Because of these factors, a study-by-study comparison is somewhat meaningless.

It is possible to conclude generally that the effects of perceptual deprivation seem, again, to be greater than those of sensory deprivation, though this does not hold true in every case. Kubzansky

TABLE 5–2

REVIEW OF PERCEPTUAL-MOTOR TEST PERFORMANCES UNDER SENSORY RESTRICTION

| Test | Results | Conditions of deprivation | Duration of deprivation | Authors |
|---|---|---|---|---|
| Size constancy | NS | Sensory | 7–10 days | Zubek et al., 1961 |
| | Consistent overestimation by confined Ss. | Perceptual | 6 days | Heron et al., 1956 |
| | NS | Perceptual | 8 hr. | Freedman et al., 1961 |
| | NS | Perceptual | 7 days | Zubek et al., 1962 |
| | NS | Body immob. | 7 days | Zubek & Wilgosh, 1963 |
| Color perception | NS | Sensory | 7–10 days | Zubek et al., 1961 |
| | Signif. impairment at 48 hours | Sensory | 24, 48, and 72 hr. | Vernon et al., 1959 |
| | Signif. impairment | Perceptual | 7 days | Zubek et al., 1962 |
| | Signif. impairment | Body immob. | 24 hr. | Zubek et al., 1963 |
| | Signif. impairment | Body immob. | 7 days | Zubek & Wilgosh, 1963 |
| Depth perception | NS | Sensory | 24, 48, and 72 hr. | Vernon et al., 1959 |
| | NS | Sensory | 7–10 days | Zubek et al., 1961 |
| | NS | Perceptual | 7 days | Zubek et al., 1962 |
| | NS | Body immob. | 7 days | Zubek & Wilgosh, 1963 |
| Reversible figures | NS | Sensory | 7–10 days | Zubek et al., 1961 |
| | Signif. impairment | Perceptual | 7 days | Zubek et al., 1962 |
| | Signif. impairment | Body immob. | 24 hr. | Zubek et al., 1963 |
| | Signif. impairment | Body immob. | 7 days | Zubek & Wilgosh, 1963 |
| Visual vigilance | Signif. impairment | Sensory | 7–10 days | Zubek et al., 1961 |
| | Signif. impairment | Perceptual | 7 days | Zubek et al., 1962 |
| Auditory vigilance | Confined Ss signif. better than Ss tested in darkness, but no difference when compared to Ss tested in light. | Sensory | 96 hr. | Myers et al., 1962 |
| | Signif. impairment | Perceptual | 7 days | Zubek et al., 1962 |

(1961) suggested that most of the impairments are confined to the visual modality and include, in addition to visual-motor coordination, changes in apparent movement phenomena, persistence of autokinetic effect, larger figural aftereffects, difficulty in focusing, fluctuating curvature of lines and surfaces, and a general decrease in the efficiency of perception of stimuli.

Body immobilization alone with no auditory or visual restrictions produced some of the perceptual impairments brought about by more traditional confinement techniques. Impairments were noted in color perception and reversible figures. However, immobilization did not affect as wide a range of performance tasks. The fact that any functions were impaired is of interest, however, for it demonstrates the importance of variability of input from the tactile-kinesthetic senses as well as from visual and auditory senses.

It is of interest that the gross perceptual changes reported by the subjects in the Heron, Doane, and Scott (1956) study do not seem to be confirmed as discussed in the research from Manitoba. Zubek et al. (1962) suggested that this difference may be due to the intrusions of the testing sessions in the later research, which perhaps functioned to increase the level of arousal.

The post-confinement reporting of increased brightness and vividness of colors is probably not due to sensory restriction. As Zubek et al. (1962) noted, the recumbent controls also reported the same experiences. This phenomenon can probably be attributed to simple forgetting of certain features of the "real world" as a result of prolonged removal from it.

Thus, a variety of perceptual and motor functions are susceptible to impairment as a function of sensory restriction but the range of effects does not seem to be as great as was first believed. Kubzansky (1961) suggested that, "these effects may be best characterized as a general loosening of subjects' ability to perceive reality and the weakening of stable internal norms against which to evaluate perceptual (visual) experience" (p. 63). What perceptual impairment does occur, moreover, seems to be temporary in nature with little persistence beyond the immediate post-confinement period.

Evidence discussed in this chapter, thus provides support for Predictions 3 and 7.

# CHAPTER VI

# *Affective Changes*

This chapter deals with three related aspects of sensory restriction: changes in subjective feeling states in normal subjects, effects of sensory restriction on emotionally disturbed subjects, and the possible therapeutic value of a reduced level of sensory variation.

## A. AFFECTIVE CHANGES IN NORMAL SUBJECTS

As discussed in the preceding chapters, there seems to be little doubt that exposure to conditions of sensory or perceptual deprivation is a stressful experience for many, though not all, subjects. As will be shown below, confined subjects often report extreme boredom, restlessness, irritability, anger, unrealistic fears and anxieties, depression, and physical complaints, rarely reported by subjects in control conditions. Most of the early research utilized subjective, introspective reporting but some of the more recent research to be discussed in this chapter attempts to deal with these affective changes in more objective and quantitative fashion. Some of the representative early studies will be discussed first.

Bexton, Heron, and Scott (1954) in their perceptual deprivation study reported that their subjects showed boredom, a very unpleasant degree of restlessness, and a marked increase in irritability as a function of time in isolation. Later work in the McGill laboratory by Scott, Bexton, Heron, and Doane (1959) involved perceptual deprivation of three to four days for eighteen subjects. Reports obtained during isolation indicated boredom, development of a childish sense of humor, exaggerated emotional reactions, excessive irritation by small things, and annoyance with the experimenters. A few subjects reported that they spent a great deal of time brooding about things and dwelling on imagined injustices. Post-isolation interviews revealed the subjects' frequent surprise about the way they had felt during isolation, saying that they had been irritated out of proportion to the situation.

Leiderman, Mendelson, Wexler, and Solomon (1958) discussed certain clinical aspects of sensory restriction based on their observations in two hospitals during the course of their regular psychiatric duties. It is noted that these observations did not involve sensory or perceptual deprivation in the traditional sense but rather exposure to a somewhat constant, unvarying sensory environment. Cases were presented which illustrated the possible effects of sensory restriction in different clinical situations. Brief case histories were presented of a few selected patients such as those confined in tank-type respirators, body casts or traction, or simply monotonous immobilization. The authors reported the appearance of transient psychotic-like symptoms which they found in old and young, male and female, and in a wide range of acute and chronic clinical conditions. These symptoms were said to be unrelated to the specific disease but rather to the adequacy of the sensory environment. The specific symptoms included pathological manifest anxiety, delusions, and visual, auditory, and somesthetic hallucinations. The psychotic-like state did not respond to the usual medical or psychiatric regimen but, the authors noted, it did respond promptly to appropriate manipulation of the sensory environment, e.g., keeping on a night light, providing a radio or television set, or the presence of another person.

Freedman, Grunebaum, and Greenblatt (1961) confined their eight subjects for eight hours of perceptual deprivation and found that some subjects slipped into hypnagogic states and that one became overtly paranoid, accusing the experimenter of trying to drive him insane (which, apparently, was not the case). Other subjects were able to relax, found the situation pleasant, and evidenced a willingness to return for another session. Those who found it unpleasant terminated before the end of the rather short period of isolation. Four of the subjects experienced changes in body image, e.g., arms seemed to be dissociated from the body; while others described fears of an unreal or paranoid nature such as imagining that the building were burning down.

A number of studies were reported by Ruff, Levy, and Thaler (1961) involving a wide range of both sensory and perceptual deprivation conditions. One study involved a number of four-hour isolation periods under perceptual deprivation with each subject serving twice. A rather boring vigilance task was introduced which resulted in many complaints centering around boredom. In another experiment, the subjects were not told exactly how long they would be confined (as they had been in previous experiments). This produced an increased restlessness and a vigorous use of mechanisms to reduce anxiety. In a similar experiment, subjects were encouraged to verbalize their thoughts and feelings during confinement which resulted in fewer manifestations of anxieties.

A study reported by Cohen, Silverman, Bressler, and Shmavonian (1961) involved isolating ten male and female subjects individually in a small cubicle where they sat in conditions of sensory deprivation. They were not told how long they would be so confined. After two hours, the lights were turned on and each subject interviewed. Following this, the subject left the chamber, filled out a questionnaire, and was interviewed again. Finally, a day after the experience, the subject was interviewed a third time. During the first twenty minutes of the initial interview, the authors reported a slurring of the subject's speech and poor sentence structure which indicated (to the authors) a disorganized and perplexed state. "Their facial expressions were bizarre, and reflected a marked feeling of confusion. It also appeared that the interviewer became involved, in a vague, abstract way, with the fantasies or fears the subject was experiencing" (p. 119). A number of specific and varied fears were expressed. For example, several subjects reported that they were afraid of losing control of their thoughts to the point of insanity. Another subject feared that he could no longer speak which led to a fear of being unable to move. Only two of the ten subjects appeared to be comfortable in the chamber. Generally speaking, these reported reactions were quite severe when one considers the very short period of isolation (two hours).

Goldberger and Holt (1961a) working within a psychoanalytic conceptual framework, which will be discussed in Chapter IX, confined fourteen male subjects for eight hours under perceptual deprivation. The subjects were encouraged to verbalize their thoughts and feelings during confinement. The subjects' behavior was evaluated by the Rorschach (which all subjects took a few weeks prior to confinement), by recorded "in-isolation" verbalizations, by observations through a one-way mirror, and by a post-isolation interview. Affective disturbances were reported which, in three cases, were so severe that these subjects terminated within three and one-half hours. Other disturbances included fantasy, depersonalization, and changes in body image. The results of the Rorschach will be discussed in Chapter VII.

Cohen (1958b), in the study involving short-term exposure to a uniform visual field discussed in Chapter III, found that most subjects reported feelings of drowsiness and yawned excessively. In addition, their voices took on a hesitant, drawling quality and they often seemed disoriented and reported feeling confused.

Smith and Lewty (1959) confined twenty male and female subjects in sensory deprivation for as long as each subject could stand it. The average length of deprivation was 29.24 hours for men and 48.70 hours for women. The subjects were visited and questioned four times a day. The authors reported that all subjects experienced anxiety and frequent "panic" attacks either early in the session or, more usually, at the end of confinement. One subject experienced a severe depressive reaction with crying. Those who terminated early (five–six hours) gave unbearable anxiety, tension, and "panic" attacks as their reasons for leaving. Eighteen subjects became agitated and restless while seven experienced body-image disturbances. Nightmares involving suffocation, drowning, and killing people were reported by five subjects.

The authors reported a fairly clearcut chain of events during confinement:

> At first most volunteers show a tendency to sleep, some for an unduly long time. Then follows a period of growing agitation, tension, and restlessness. Disturbed thinking, particularly obsessional, occurs about this stage; and most subjects experience panic which makes them leave the room. But some of our volunteers, even when perspiring profusely, with trembling limbs, dry mouth, and tachycardia, still clung to the conventional dislike of "anything psychological" and maintained that their reason for giving up had been backache, headache, or some other "socially approved" symptom (Smith & Lewty, 1959, p. 344).

The research of Mendelson, Kubzansky, Leiderman, Wexler, DuToit, and Solomon (1960), discussed in Chapter III, is also of interest in the present context. The ten subjects were confined in a tank-type respirator for up to thirty-six hours under conditions of constant noise, minimal and constant light, and a visual field restricted to blank white walls and ceiling. Recordings were made of the subjects' verbalizations during confinement and a post-confinement interview was conducted. Only one subject was able to stay for as long as thirty hours with the others terminating between 3.5 and 10.2 hours. The reasons for termination were classified as: "1. Anxiety: Verbalized feelings of fear, tension, nervousness, or panic, followed by a request to end the experiment. 2. Somatic: Verbalized complaints of pain, discomfort, or bodily distress, followed by a request to end the experiment" (p. 151).

The total amount of verbalization by each subject was actually quite low. Two other points of interest are noted. The longer the subject remained in confinement, the fewer somatic references he made. Also, the more verbalizations the subject offered, the greater were the somatic references. Daydreams and fantasies were also reported by a number of subjects.

Several of the studies by Zubek and his associates, reported in previous chapters, present reports of changes in affective feeling states. Zubek, Pushkar, Sansom, and Gowing (1961) confined subjects in the Manitoba chamber under sensory deprivation. Fourteen subjects remained for seven days, one for eight and one-half days, and one for ten days. The authors reported that certain emotional changes were evident in many of the subjects. Irritability, as characterized by annoyance with trivial matters and the experimenters, was the most commonly reported. This irritability was most noticeable during the second and third days and was followed by depression, brooding, and dwelling on imaginary injustices in many subjects. After the fifth day of confinement, four of the subjects reported feelings of contentment and well-being, and two reported feelings of euphoria. The authors suggested that this state of well-being, which is not usually reported in confinement studies, may either have been the result of the very long isolation or been brought on by the realization that the experience was nearing an end and that a sizeable monetary reward awaited.

Reports of dreams were quite numerous, particularly during the first three to four days. Their primary content was of an anxiety nature with the main theme concerning death, e.g., standing on an erupting volcano, being surrounded by ferocious Indians, or being in a knife fight with a giant. Another dream theme concerned restricted space. About half the subjects reported a loss of motivation after confinement but this persisted little more than a day.

Zubek, Welch, and Saunders (1963), in the study described

in Chapter III, confined three subjects for fourteen days under perceptual deprivation in the Manitoba dome. The primary purpose of the study was to record EEG changes but a post-isolation interview was also conducted to note subjective reactions. Two of the subjects reported severe motivational losses which lasted for eight days in one case and six days in the other. The third subject reported similar motivational losses lasting only three days after isolation.

The study by Zubek, Aftanas, Kovach, Wilgosh, and Winocur (1963) involving body immobilization for twenty-four hours was described in Chapters IV and V. In addition to the intellectual and perceptual functions studied, emotional changes were observed. The authors reported that significantly more confined subjects were anxious and worried about their well-being; these subjects also feared that they might lose control over their emotions and feelings. In addition they were restless, irritable, and angry. Eighty-five per cent of the subjects reported immobilization to be a stressful experience while only twenty-five per cent of the recumbent controls found the experience stressful. Significantly more confined subjects reported changes in body image, depersonalization, and unusual body sensations. Some of these same phenomena were also reported by the recumbent controls but the incidence was not nearly as high. Many more immobilized subjects made complaints dealing with discomfort and physical symptoms. Specifically, these included periodic aches and pains, numbness, dizziness, physical discomfort, chills, perspiration, weakness, strong desire to scratch, and trouble sleeping.

The sensory deprivation research program of HumRRO, discussed in earlier chapters, contains some work of relevance on the objective measurement of the stress effects of isolation. Myers, Murphy, and Smith (1961), Myers, Murphy, Smith, and Windle (1962), and Myers (1964a) reported on the use of the Subjective Stress Scale. This scale, developed by Kerle and Bialek (1958) for another HumRRO program, is a series of descriptive words or phrases semantically graded as to degree of affect on a well being-stressfulness dimension.

The Subjective Stress Scale was given to both confined and control subjects about one hour after the termination of the ninety-six-hour session. Two judgments were obtained from each subject who circled the word or phrase best describing his feelings with respect to three points in time: (1) how he felt under the normal stress of Army life before becoming a part of the experiment, (2) how he felt while in confinement (or in normal activities, for the control group), and (3) how he felt at the time of testing.

There were clearcut differences between confined and control groups. The base line ratings were quite similar for both groups but the confined subjects rated themselves as being under greater stress both during isolation and one hour later at the time of testing, than did the control subjects at both points in time. Myers (1964a) reported on the administration of the scale immediately after subjects were told of their assignment to control or confined condition just prior to beginning isolation. Subjects were asked for "How do you feel now?" and "How do you feel normally?" ratings. The "now" stress ratings were significantly higher for those slated to begin deprivation as compared to those in the control group. The "normally" ratings did not differentiate between the two groups.

Zuckerman, Albright, Marks, and Miller (1962) reported on research which attempted to measure more objectively the stress effects of isolation by tests, verbal reports, and association and performance measures. Twenty-five student nurse subjects were confined in an iron lung for seven hours under total darkness with white noise delivered through earphones. Two control groups were utilized. One group consisted of thirteen subjects who were confined in the iron lung for seven hours but with the lights remaining on and the experimenter in full view. The other control group consisted of eleven subjects who reported for testing and endured no confinement. A number of measures were administered at various times throughout the experimental session. Before and after confinement the subjects were given the Affect Adjective Check List (AACL) and the Somatic Check List (SCL). The AACL, developed by Zuckerman (1960), consists of sixty-one affectively toned adjectives with an anxiety key of twenty-one scored adjectives. The SCL consists of twenty-one somatic complaints frequently associated with anxiety. Tests of Free Association, Word Naming, and Word Association were given prior to confinement and after three and six hours of confinement. (Two tests of intellectual functioning were also given as discussed in Chapter IV.) The following personality tests were given prior to or several months after confinement: Taylor Manifest Anxiety Scale, MMPI, Edwards Personal Preference Schedule, Rohde Sentence Completion

Test. Also, peer ratings and self-ratings were obtained on three scales designed to measure dependency traits.

Some of the more pertinent results of this formidable testing program will be discussed. The pre- and post-confinement mean scores on the AACL showed a significantly greater increase in the experimental group as compared to the two control conditions. The difference in increase between the two control groups was not significant. The authors thus concluded that the anxiety feelings were produced by the sensory restriction and not by confinement alone. An item analysis revealed that the experimental group exhibited a significantly greater checking of the following words: afraid, desperate, fearful, gloomy, lonely, nervous, and panicky. A significantly smaller number of these subjects checked the following after confinement: contented, friendly, joyful.

The increase in the number of somatic complaints checked by the experimental subjects on the SCL was significantly greater than for both control groups. However, the increase with the confined control subjects was also significantly greater than that of the unconfined control group. Apparently, just confinement itself produced a significant amount of somatic discomfort, although the more severe sensory restriction did produce even greater discomfort. Item analysis revealed three specific complaints which showed significantly greater change in the experimental subjects: dry mouth, difficulty in breathing, change in heartbeat. Flushing and nausea also approached significance.

In discussing the results of the various tests, the authors noted that the isolation experience was stressful to some degree for most subjects. There was a greater manifest anxiety for the experimental group. It is interesting that verbalizations of manifest anxiety and claustrophobia, which showed an increase as a function of time in isolation, were decreased in the fourth hour after the sensory variation introduced by a testing session.

The authors discussed the isolation experience as occurring in two phases, the first of which was characterized by hyper-alertness. The second stage was characterized by a loss of interest in the very sterile environment and an increased focus on internal processes. "Loss of orientation, difficulties in directed thinking, anxiety from personal thoughts, and increasing somatic discomfort during the latter period leads to a mounting stress reaction in most subjects" (Zuckerman, Albright, Marks, & Miller, 1962, p. 14).

Thus far, evidence has been presented indicating anxiety and stress under sensory restriction when these have been measured by verbal techniques such as self-reporting, check-lists, and questionnaires. The next study to be discussed attempted to find evidence of stress using physiological as well as verbal measures. The study by Zuckerman, Levine, and Biase (1964) has been discussed in Chapter III. To reiterate briefly, the thirty-six female subjects were isolated, twelve in each of three conditions: Group I (no sound, no light), Group II (light, no sound), and Group III (sound, no light). All subjects were confined to a bed in a small room for three hours. GSR data were obtained and subjects were given the AACL and SCL described above. While in isolation, a subject could signal periods of subjective anxiety by depressing a button held in the right hand. The subjects were prevented from sleeping by means of a buzzer which sounded when their hand slipped off a switch. All subjects were interviewed after confinement.

A five-minute base line GSR recording was obtained immediately upon entrance into the cubicle. Thereafter, readings were taken every two minutes or before and after any marked change in resistance. The nonspecific GSR index revealed that the total isolation situation was more stressful than either of the partial isolation conditions. These data also revealed that light deprivation was more stressful than sound deprivation. The three groups showed no differences on the base line recordings and those obtained during the first one and one-half hours of isolation. It was during the last one and one-half hours of confinement that significant differences were obtained between groups with the total isolation group evidencing the greatest stress reaction.

The results of the verbal testing revealed that all groups taken together showed a significant pre- to post-confinement rise on the AACL anxiety score with the total isolation group showing somewhat less of an increase as compared to the two partial isolation groups. The pre- and post-isolation scores on the SCL were significantly different for all groups taken together with no significant difference in amount of change between groups.

The anxiety signal button was used by approximately one-third of the subjects in each group but was used considerably fewer times in the sound deprivation group than in the other two conditions. The sleep control buzzer was allowed to sound by many subjects when they were not sleeping. In fact, the authors commented that the number of buzzer soundings may have been a better index of restlessness than of sleep. There were no significant differences between the groups for the anxiety button or the sleep buzzer.

The subjects in the total isolation group were divided into six high and six low responders on the basis of their nonspecific GSR measures in the last one and one-half hours of isolation. These high and low responders were compared on ratings obtained from the post-isolation interviewing. High responders were rated significantly higher on need for activity and complaints of sensory deprivation, and somewhat higher on time disorientation and loneliness.

## B. THERAPEUTIC EFFECTS OF SENSORY RESTRICTION

A number of investigators have claimed therapeutic benefits among psychiatric patients as a result of exposing them to sensory or perceptual deprivation. Among these reported effects have been reduction in hallucination intensity, increased ego strength, a less rigid utilization of defenses, and an increased desire for social contacts.

The first report to be considered is that of Azima and Cramer in 1956 who investigated the disorganization effects of sensory restriction in mentally disturbed patient-subjects. The subjects consisted of two hebephrenics, five depressives, two obsessive neurotics, and five neurotic anxiety states who were isolated for an average period of four days. Confinement took place in an ordinary hospital room which was darkened by heavy curtains over the windows. The subjects lay or sat on the bed, wore translucent eyegoggles, and had their hands and arms encased in cardboard cylinders. They were put on demand feeding and evacuation schedules. The procedure was explained to each patient as a method of treatment and they were told that they could terminate any time they wished. The subjects were checked every hour but were interviewed only once or twice a day for a period of from fifteen to thirty minutes.

The authors reported that eight of the patients showed a de-personalization state and that beneficial therapeutic effects were observed in the five depressed cases; in two of these the effect was considered permanent. The two obsessive neurotics displayed acute psychotic episodes which were then treated with electric shock resulting in improvement in obsessional and paranoid features. The remaining patients were reported to show moderate increases in motivation, socialization, and self-assertiveness.

The authors noted that their "data" demonstrated that, "perceptual isolation provokes a disorganization of psychic structure which, according to the kind and quality of defenses, may lead to a psychotic state. This disorganization in most cases leads either to a temporary or to a relatively permanent reorganization of some aspects of a previously unsteady psychic state" (p. 120). Their results are presented in case history form which, while providing fascinating reading, renders evaluation difficult for the non-clinically-oriented.

Azima and Cramer-Azima (1957) reported on another study in which four obsessive-compulsives were placed in isolation for a period of three to six days. The conditions of confinement were the same as in the previously discussed study. Psychodynamic changes were investigated by the following procedures: analysis of dreams, fantasies, free association, Rorschach, and Figure Drawings. Each subject was his own control with the longitudinal picture of his history being used as a base line against which to evaluate changes.

As in the previous study, lengthy case histories were provided which will not be reproduced here. As for results, the authors noted that three of the four subjects developed a depersonalization syndrome which led in one case to a paranoid state. They further noted that the state of depersonalization seemed to be concomitant with the suppression of aggressive behavior. In three patients, there were no changes in the original clinical symptomatology. However, after confinement they showed an increased communicativeness and desire to socialize which lasted for four to five days. The one patient who developed a paranoid psychotic episode was subjected to electric shock treatment which resulted in a moderate improvement in his paranoid and obsessive states.

Harris (1959) isolated twelve schizophrenic patients under sensory deprivation in a soundproof cubicle, wearing opaque goggles, gloves, and cardboard cuffs over the arms. The patients were confined on two separate occasions. The first experience was only a half-hour while the second, which took place "on another day," was for a period of up to two hours. It is unfortunate that longer isolation periods were not used. The author concluded that the schizophrenic patients were, "more tolerant than normal subjects of these conditions, which seemed to reduce the intensity of hallucinations" (p. 237). The hebephrenic patients seemed particularly to "enjoy" the experience and were reluctant to leave.

Cohen, Rosenbaum, Dobie, and Gottlieb (1959) confined ten subjects for a period of only one hour. The subject group included four normals, one neurotic, two sociopaths, and three schizophrenics. Subjects were confined in a room, wearing earplugs and elbow-length mittens. Some subjects wore blacked-out goggles while others wore frosted goggles permitting diffuse light. The subjects were seated in chairs and were told how long they would be confined. Hallucinatory effects were strongly suggested to them prior to confinement.

The results are in agreement with those of Harris (1959) reported above. The normal and neurotic subjects were reported to be generally more anxious and restless during isolation than the sociopaths and schizophrenics. These conclusions were based on continuous observation of the subjects through a one-way screen. The authors also noted that those subjects who were in poorest contact with reality showed the least discomfort and the most positive reactions. As an example, a chronic schizophrenic found the isolation experience restful and peaceful, describing it in somewhat "hip" fashion as comfortable and "cool."

Gibby, Adams, and Carrera (1960) investigated therapeutic changes in a group of psychiatric patients who underwent up to six hours of sensory restriction. The subjects consisted of thirty male patients under the following diagnostic classifications: schizophrenic reactions, psychoneurotic disorders, psychophysiologic visceral and autonomic disorders, personality trait and pattern disturbances. Subjects were isolated in a quiet air-conditioned room where they lay on a bed, wearing earplugs and blindfolds. The authors described this condition as partial sensory deprivation. An observer stayed in the room with the subject but there was no communication until the confinement session ended. Subjects were told they might leave the confinement situation when they wished but were not told of any time limit.

Each subject was constantly observed and his verbalizations were recorded. The observer made a rating every fifteen minutes of the degree of anxiety overtly manifested in the subject's behavior and movement. Prior to confinement, each subject was interviewed by a psychologist and given a battery of psychological tests. On the second day of confinement, the interviews and tests were repeated. On the day after confinement the subject was interviewed a third time. An overall rating was then made on a Symptom Rating Scale by four interviewers.

The results indicated that positive changes in the direction of less severe symptoms greatly outnumbered the negative changes, and also that the positive effects were more long-lasting. The group as a whole demonstrated amelioration of pathological symptoms following isolation. However, a wide range of individual differences were noted. Some subjects showed no change on any of the twenty symptom items rated while others changed for the better on thirteen out of the twenty items.

The authors noted that the subjects demonstrated, in general, an increased desire for social contact, particularly for therapeutic relationships. Subjects also manifested an increased awareness of inner conflicts and anxieties and a heightened perception that their difficulties stemmed from inner rather than outer factors. The experience of sensory restriction appeared to have brought about a social "stimulus hunger" manifested behaviorally by generalized efforts to relate and communicate with others. Thus, the subjects displayed a greatly increased need for contact with other people.

Another post-isolation change noted by the authors was a less rigid utilization of inhibitory and repressive defenses:

> The reduction of incoming stimulation led to recall and verbalization of previously forgotten experiences in many instances. For some subjects this recall was anxiety-inducing, . . . In others sensory deprivation brought about a decrease of inhibitory defenses, resulting in open expressions of hostility, which then subsided. . . . The blocking off of accustomed stimulation for a few hours may have facilitated a process of reassessment and reorganization of stimulus-response patterns carried over from earlier life experiences (Gibby, Adams, & Carrera, 1960, p. 39).

Cooper, Adams, and Gibby (1962) investigated ego strength changes following sensory restriction using these same thirty subjects. At a later time (not specified) these same subjects were again exposed to isolation under the same conditions as in the earlier study (Gibby, Adams, & Carrera, 1960). They were interviewed and given the Rorschach on the day before and the day after isolation. Three aspects of ego strength were noted on the

Rorschach: (1) the ability to respond emotionally to the outer world with adequate control; (2) the ability to have good reality contact; and (3) the ability to deal with real human relations in an empathic manner. (The reader interested in the specific aspects of the scoring is referred to the original article.) The highest two of these scores were added together to yield a total Strength Score, an overall measure of ego strength.

The results revealed that the mean changes (pre-post) were positive on all Rorschach scores indicating, according to the authors, improved ego functioning. The increase in Strength Score was significant as was the increase in scale (2) above. The latter result suggests a more adequate reality contact following isolation. A positive though not significant trend in scale (1) suggested an improved ability to make well-controlled and appropriate emotional responses to others.

A second major finding related to differential effects in individual subjects. Those subjects with the lowest scores on each measure prior to isolation tended to show the greatest improvement after isolation. Thus, it appeared that those patients who had functioned least effectively were the ones deriving the greatest benefit from the isolation experience.

Behavioral observations of the patients by the authors indicated that those patients with the most severe overt symptoms prior to confinement generally evidenced the greatest reduction in overt symptoms after confinement. Also, the authors noted that the behavioral changes in the subjects after their confinement in the pilot study discussed above (Gibby, Adams, & Carrera, 1960) were consistent with the Rorschach changes found after the later isolation period. They noted that the patients demonstrated an increased desire for social contact and, in particular, a desire for therapeutic relationships.

The other major behavioral change observed was a less rigid utilization of repressive and inhibitory defenses. The authors suggested that, due to the lower level of external stimulation, the reassessment and reorganization of older maladaptive behavior patterns may have been facilitated.

These two studies (Gibby, Adams, & Carrera, 1960; Cooper, Adams, & Gibby, 1962) both suggested an increased need for social contact in psychiatric patients who had undergone short periods of sensory isolation. This raises the interesting possibility that patients might be rendered more receptive and susceptible to therapeutic communications as a function of confinement under conditions of reduced sensory input. To test this hypothesis, Gibby and Adams (1961) confined forty-two male psychiatric patients for four hours of sensory deprivation under the same conditions as in the above two studies. Before and somewhat after confinement, each subject was given the Self-Rating Inventory developed by Brownfain (1952). There were four conditions of the study: Group I (pre-recorded verbal message plus isolation); Group II (isolation but no message); Group III (message but no isolation); and Group IV (no message and no isolation).

The subjects in Group I remained in isolation for four hours, after which a fourteen-minute tape recording was played to them through a bone conductivity speaker buried in the blindfold bandages. The message was such that it might have been applicable to almost any hospitalized patient and stressed the following points: (1) the patient did not consider himself as a worthwhile person; (2) there was a discrepancy between the way he saw himself and the way others saw him; and (3) he was more likeable and more acceptable to others than he realized. Fifteen minutes after hearing the tape, the subject was removed from isolation, fed, and immediately given the Self-Rating Inventory a second time. The other three conditions are self-evident.

The results indicated that the mean pretest scores for the four groups did not differ significantly. The mean pre-post ratings were significantly greater in Group I than in the other three conditions. The mean differences for the other three groups were not significant. Thus, the authors concluded that isolation under conditions of reduced sensory input resulted in an increased acceptance of a message designed to enhance the subject's self-concept. Particularly important was that Group III, which received the identical message but was not isolated, showed essentially no change in self-concept whereas there was a marked increase in Group I.

Adams, Robertson, and Cooper (1963) reported on a study utilizing sensory deprivation and an individually prepared message for each subject. They reasoned that since the standardized message had produced such beneficial effects in the study reported above, a message specifically prepared for each subject should facilitate the therapeutic processes of understanding, insight, and self-awareness.

The subjects were forty-three male patients who were either in psychiatric wards or referred from medical wards for psychiatric evaluation. Every patient had a functional psychiatric diagnosis at the time of his selection as a subject. Before and after isolation all subjects were given the MMPI and the Interpersonal Check List (ICL). On the ICL, subjects were first asked to check those items which they felt described themselves, and then to check those which they felt best described the ideal person.

Subjects were divided into three groups: Group I (taped personal message plus sensory deprivation), Group II (sensory deprivation only, no tape), and Group III (control condition, pre- and posttesting only). The taped messages were prepared after the pretesting and were based on the test results for each subject. The messages included such points as the subject's own self-description, his conception of the ideal person, and his patterns of overt interpersonal behavior. After coverage of these points, each message then explained how psychotherapy might help the patient to resolve his personal conflicts and modify his maladaptive behavior patterns.

Subjects in Groups I and II were confined in sensory deprivation for a period of not more than three hours. The conditions of isolation were the same as noted above (Gibby, Adams, & Carrera, 1960). After two hours of isolation, the taped messages were played to Group I subjects through the bone conductivity speakers placed in the gauze wrapped around each subject's head. Each message lasted for approximately fifteen minutes. Following the message, subjects were kept in isolation for another forty-five minutes. On the day after the confinement experience the MMPI and the ICL were given to all groups a second time. The control condition (Group III) was tested at the same time intervals.

A comparison based on all the MMPI and ICL measures between Groups I and II revealed that Group I subjects demonstrated more insight, greater self-understanding, less defensiveness, and a generalized improvement. However, the subjects in Group II (deprivation only, no message) also showed a general improvement though the nature of the changes were different from those in Group I. Group II subjects showed more ego strength and dominance, greater conscious self-acceptance, less depression, and an enhanced sense of personal adequacy. There was, however, for Group II, less of an increase in conscious insight and self-understanding than for Group I. The authors reported that the many contrasts between Groups II and III demonstrated that sensory deprivation alone produced many changes which cannot be attributed merely to the added attention of being tested twice. The authors concluded that presentation of a message during deprivation can greatly facilitate the process of psychotherapy.

Adams (1964) reported on a follow-up of one of the patients from Group I of the above study which demonstrated that exposure to deprivation plus message rendered the patient willing to accept intensive outpatient psychotherapy for the first time. The patient initiated therapy contacts immediately after the experimental session and continued them for the next sixteen months. During the thirteen months prior to the experimental treatment, the subject had been admitted to the hospital as an inpatient three times while in the thirty-month period following the session he required hospitalization only once. It is unfortunate that follow-up data are not provided for the other eleven subjects of Group I.

An interesting study by Robertson (1964) utilized fifty-one psychiatric patients classified as personality disorders and schizophrenics. Each subject (in all groups) was told that his participation was voluntary but that the procedure was a part of the hospital's rehabilitation program. The subjects were first interviewed and their interview behavior rated on each of twenty items of the Symptom Rating Scale. After the interview, the subjects were given the MMPI and the Leary Interpersonal Check List and then assigned to one of the following four groups. Group I (deprivation, message) consisted of fifteen subjects who, one week after the testing, were placed in sensory deprivation for three hours under the conditions described above (Gibby, Adams, & Carrera, 1960). Confinement took place every other day for three days; each subject was subjected to three periods of isolation. The subjects were told the approximate length of the treatment period. During each of the three sessions each subject heard a different twenty-minute recorded message individually prepared for each patient based on the data from the interview, tests, and case history. The contents of the messages centered around the patient's understanding of his problems of adjustment and personality, and suggestions for constructive changes in his attitudes and behavior. One week after the third session, the interview and testing were repeated.

The twelve subjects in Group II (message only) received the

three messages at the same intervals as Group I but did not undergo confinement. Group III (deprivation only) consisted of twelve subjects who underwent deprivation for the same periods as Group I. The twelve subjects in Group IV (control) were simply tested and interviewed twice with the same time interval between administrations as in the other three groups.

The results indicated that the combination of sensory deprivation and therapeutic message did not benefit the subjects any more than did deprivation alone, or the presentation of the message by itself. In terms of positive changes, the subjects in Group I did not do as well as the deprivation only group or the message only group. Also, none of the three experimental groups demonstrated any advantage over the control group in terms of self-actualization, self-disclosure, self-perception, self-awareness, or conscious idealization. Only one experimental group (deprivation only) showed a significant improvement over the controls on the criterion of self-acceptance; one of six test criteria examined.

There is one point of difference between this study and those discussed above which did demonstrate beneficial effects of confinement with a therapeutic message (Gibby & Adams, 1961; Adams, Robertson, & Cooper, 1963). The difference relates to the time delay between the treatment session and the administration of the posttests. In the earlier studies this delay was fifteen minutes (Gibby & Adams, 1961) or one day (Adams et al., 1963) while the Robertson study invoked a longer delay of one week. It is suggested that Robertson's study might have produced more beneficial effects had not a week of normal sensory experience intervened before posttesting.

Cleveland, Reitman, and Bentinck (1963) reported on a study designed to investigate the therapeutic effectiveness of sensory restriction. The total sample consisted of sixty hospitalized patients who were asked to volunteer for a new kind of treatment which involved lying on a soft bed in a quiet room. They were not told the length of confinement. Of the sixty subjects, forty were diagnosed as schizophrenics. The remaining twenty subjects were patients from open psychiatric wards who were diagnosed as either character disorder or anxiety reaction with no history of psychotic behavior. Half the schizophrenic group and all twenty of the non-schizophrenic group were subjected to sensory restriction. The remaining half of the schizophrenic group served as a control group and did not experience isolation.

The isolation cubicle was bare except for a bed, a white-noise generator, and a speaker system. Subjects lay on the bed and were instructed to move as little as possible. They wore translucent eye goggles, loose cotton gloves, and arm-length cardboard gauntlets. Two overhead lights and the white-noise generator remained on for the four hours of isolation.

On the day before isolation, all subjects were interviewed by a clinical social worker. The interview behavior was rated on each of twenty items of the Symptom Rating Scale developed by Jenkins, Stauffacher, and Hester (1959). Later that same day the subjects were given the Holtzman Inkblot Technique, Draw-a-Person Test, and the Bender-Gestalt test. The next morning, those subjects undergoing isolation were confined in the cubicle. Immediately after release from confinement, the subjects were given the same tests again. A day later they were interviewed and rated again on the Symptom Rating Scale. The control subjects who did not undergo isolation were interviewed and tested at the same time intervals.

The results revealed no significant changes in behavior or personality structure for the schizophrenics and non-schizophrenics following exposure to sensory restriction. Thus, these results dramatically contradict most of those discussed above which did suggest the existence of positive therapeutic effects following sensory isolation. There is one important difference to be noted, however, between the Cleveland, Reitman, and Bentinck study showing no therapeutic value and the work of Gibby, Adams, and Carrera (1960), Gibby and Adams (1961), Cooper, Adams, and Gibby (1962), Adams, Robertson, and Cooper (1963) which demonstrated beneficial effects. This difference relates to the type of sensory restriction imposed. The Cleveland *et al.* study utilized perceptual deprivation (the reduced patterning of sensory input), while the other studies utilized sensory deprivation (the total reduction of sensory input). It has been demonstrated in the preceding chapters that behavioral impairments are usually more severe under conditions of perceptual deprivation. The way is clear for a well-controlled study comparing the relative therapeutic values of sensory versus perceptual deprivation.

## C. DISCUSSION

In discussing the research presented in this section dealing with normal subjects, those studies which reported various stress reactions as revealed through introspective or retrospective report and observation will be considered first. Because of the qualitative nature of these observations, it becomes difficult to delimit any differential effects as a function of type of sensory restriction. For example, emotional "stress" reactions are reported for sensory deprivation, perceptual deprivation, and body immobilization for periods as long as seven days and as short as only two hours. The qualitative results of these various studies do not allow the determination of whether one condition produced more deleterious effects as compared to another condition.

A review article by Zuckerman (1964) provides some interesting summary information on the quantity and content of verbal responses to sensory restriction. A very interesting finding by Zuckerman is that the quantity of verbalization seemed to decrease as a function of time in isolation both during a single session and in the second of two isolation experiences. He suggested that the lack of social reinforcement for the verbalizations may be the cause of this decline during a period of isolation. It might also be suggested that an adaptation mechanism may be operative, in line with observations in preceding chapters noting a less severe reaction to a second confinement session. The possibility of adaptation to sensory restriction is considered in Chapter IX. Zuckerman also noted that suggestion or set tended to facilitate verbal reports of all kinds.

As to the content of these verbalized reports, Zuckerman reported the following to be typical of sensory restriction effects: (1) difficulties in directed thinking and concentration (as reported in Chapter IV), (2) a drifting of thought with fantasies and daydreams, (3) disorientation in time, (4) body illusions and delusions, (5) complaints of confinement, restlessness, and need for activity, (6) somatic discomforts, e.g., backache, headache, pains in neck, eyes, (7) paranoid-like delusions, (8) hallucinations and images, (9) various emotional reactions such as anxiety and apprehension, (10) attention to residual stimuli, and (11) a variety of other reactions including claustrophobic complaints, loneliness, body-need complaints.

Zuckerman discussed two attempts (Holt & Goldberger, 1961; Zuckerman, Albright, Marks, & Miller, 1962) to correlate ratings of verbal content during isolation to find clusters. Holt and Goldberger reported two clusters, the first of which was an adaptive syndrome which consisted of unimpaired secondary process thinking, accepted and controlled primary process thinking, imagery, exploration, and self-stimulation. Their second cluster was a maladaptive syndrome which consisted of quitting and unpleasant affect.

The one cluster reported by Zuckerman *et al.* (1962) was called stress response and included manifest anxiety, confinement complaints, claustrophobia, body need discomforts, loss of time and place orientation, thought or concentration difficulties, and attention to residual stimulation. Zuckerman *et al.* reported little evidence of an adaptive cluster.

Some of the studies discussed do yield the tentative generalization that the emotional effects of sensory restriction increase in severity as a function of time in isolation. However, even this is not reported consistently. For example, the longest confinement period used—seven days in sensory deprivation (Zubek, Pushkar, Sansom, & Gowing, 1961)—produced feelings of contentment and euphoria in some subjects after the fifth day of confinement. There is also the finding reported in the majority of the studies that not all subjects suffered degrees of emotional impairment. This phenomenon of individual differences has been noted in preceding chapters and is discussed in greater detail in Chapter VII.

One factor of experimental manipulation which did seem to produce a differential effect was whether or not the subjects knew how long they would be confined. In many of the studies the subjects were told the length of the session prior to confinement. These subjects did report, for the most part, various forms of emotional impairment. However, those subjects who did not know the length of confinement seemed to experience more severe emotional reactions. Further, these studies, in which the length of confinement was unknown, utilized shorter periods of confinement: Ruff, Levy, and Thaler (1961) used four hours; Cohen, Silverman, Bressler, and Shmavonian (1961) used only two hours. Thus it appears that confinement periods as short as two hours were capable of producing reactions at least as severe as the longer periods of confinement when the subjects knew how long the experience would last. This factor would seem to be a crucial variable in sensory restriction research.

Turning to studies using more objective measures of emotional impairment, Zuckerman *et al.* (1962) reported evidence of deterioration in subjects undergoing seven hours of confinement in an iron lung under darkness and white noise conditions. An interesting finding was that certain types of verbalizations, notably manifest anxiety and claustrophobia, tended to increase as a function of time in isolation. However, the intrusion of a testing session reversed this trend which Zuckerman *et al.* (1962) suggested, "raises the possibility of experimentally controlling anxiety response in isolation through the use of auditory stimulation" (p. 12). Thus, the introduction of sensory variation tended to minimize emotional deterioration as well as other reported forms of impairment.

It was demonstrated that sensory restriction increased somatic discomfort beyond that produced by confinement alone with no attempt at visual or auditory restriction. Zuckerman *et al.* (1962) offered two explanations for this finding. First, the emotionally aroused state of the individual may serve to compound the normal discomfort produced by immobilization alone. Second, in sensory restriction there is minimal competition between external and internal stimuli in terms of attention. As a result, internal stimuli in the form of somatic tensions may become dominant.

The study of Zuckerman, Levine, and Biase (1964) using physiological measures of stress provides some of the more objective data in this section. Their finding that stress (when measured by GSR indices of activation) is a function of time in isolation rather than an initial response to a strange and highly suggestive situation is of interest. The authors suggested that a subject will adapt to a situation and show a lowered emotional response after a certain period of confinement. The work of Zubek *et al.* (1961) reporting contentment and even euphoria after the fifth day of isolation is pertinent here. Zuckerman, Levine, and Biase (1964) commented that in many of the long-duration studies, data are reported only on those subjects with the greatest stress resistance, the others having terminated. It is interesting to note that most subjects who terminate do so within the first three days as is noted in Chapter VII. Also of interest is that in much, if not most, other research, subjects are not kept awake so they are able to utilize the defense of sleep.

The verbal measures of stress did not differentiate between the total and partial isolation conditions which possibly suggests that verbal stress reactions are a function of social isolation rather than the amount of sensory restriction *per se.* Finally, the correlations between the various stress response variables indicated that the verbal and the GSR indices were independent, suggesting that the verbal report method of measuring emotional stress may not be the most effective approach. It would be interesting to replicate this particular study and not tell the subjects the duration of confinement. The previous discussion of this factor would suggest that the GSR defined stress reaction would be more severe and would appear earlier.

The discussion of the possible therapeutic effects of sensory restriction demonstrated some degree of success when dealing with selected types of hospitalized patients. In discussing this area, Robertson (1961) offered several points of possible explanation. First is the observation that non-hospitalized normal people have in many cases recovered from great stress by withdrawing into themselves for a period of time by seeking an environment limited in sensory and social contact. Second, he noted that sensory isolation may produce a heightened suggestibility (see Chapter IV) and a loosening of the cognitive processes which, "would provide a means of access to the positive and constructive features of the unconscious" (1961, pp. 345–346). Robertson also suggested that sensory restriction may operate to jar the individual out of overused thought patterns resulting in the facilitation of contact and communication with him. This factor, together with the increased suggestibility, may render the patient more responsive and receptive to therapeutic suggestions and advice.

Several formal theoretical explanations have been offered (for example, Azima & Cramer, 1956; Azima & Cramer-Azima, 1957), the presentation of which is beyond the scope of this volume.

The data presently available do not allow for any specific conclusions but do pose a number of interesting questions which further, and more systematic, research will hopefully investigate. For example, how long a confinement period is necessary to possibly render a patient more amenable to psychotherapy? Rather short periods were used in the studies discussed. Would much longer periods result in greater therapeutic benefits? Which form of sensory restriction might produce the more beneficial results— sensory or perceptual? Also, it has been shown that not all patients derive benefits from sensory restriction. For what kinds of patients might "sensory restriction therapy" be appropriate? In line with this last question is an interesting finding reported by Cooper, Adams, and Gibby (1962). They found that those patients who scored relatively low on Rorschach measures of ego strength (which indicated, according to the authors, that they were relatively poor candidates for orthodox verbal psychotherapy) derived the greatest benefit from isolation. Thus, sensory restriction may prove most useful therapeutically to those patients for whom more traditional verbal psychotherapy is relatively unfruitful. Also of possible predictive value is the finding by the same authors that those patients who functioned least effectively prior to isolation derived the greatest benefit from the experience.

The finding of Gibby and Adams (1961) that isolated patients were more receptive and susceptible to verbal messages is of considerable interest. It is suggested that the technique discussed in Chapter IV to change attitudes might be applicable in the therapeutic context. Briefly, it will be recalled that a subject in isolation is offered the opportunity to expose himself to stimulation by voluntarily choosing to listen to propaganda messages. Further exposures to the propaganda and "correct" answers to questions put to the subject, i.e., answers agreeing with the communication, were rewarded by other forms of stimulation or brief periods of release from confinement. It was proposed that in this manner a change in attitude could be induced. Might not the same technique be applied to the therapy situation in inducing the patient to attend to "therapeutic propaganda" and engage in dialogue with the therapist if these are the only forms of stimulation and contact afforded him?

# CHAPTER VII

# Differences in Tolerance for Sensory Restriction

Evidence of a wide range of individual differences in the various effects of sensory restriction has been noted in the preceding chapters. In addition, not all of the volunteers have been able to endure prolonged or even short periods of isolation and confinement. Some were able to endure it for days while others were forced to terminate within a few hours. The topic of concern in this chapter is research which has been aimed at finding satisfactory predictive measures of isolation tolerance.

First to be considered will be certain field studies which have attempted to develop selection techniques for military and civilian personnel assigned to remote and isolated stations such as the Arctic and Antarctic. In this situation, the type of sensory restriction involved is that of social isolation as discussed in Chapter VIII.

## A. FIELD STUDIES

The approach generally taken in these field studies is to correlate psychiatric assessments with ratings of adjustment in the particular assigned station. Smith (1961) found no predictive relationship between psychiatric assessment and performance, or between a test of "personal autonomy" and performance (Smith & Jones, 1962), for groups spending fourteen to sixteen months in Antarctica.

Nardini, Herrmann, and Rasmussen (1962) reported on their program of neuropsychiatric assessment of military and civilian personnel who were scheduled to "winter over" during the International Geophysical Year. The evaluation procedure included an extensive biographical inventory, an unstructured psychiatric interview (after which the psychiatrist rated each individual on his suitability for Antarctic duty), and Rorschach given by a psychologist. The psychiatrist and psychologist then made a final team rating as to each candidate's suitability. The criteria for assessment included motivation, history of past personal effectiveness, present ego strength and adequacy of defense mechanisms, and adequacy of interpersonal relationships. Applicants showing no defects in these areas were considered sufficiently stable to adjust to the Antarctic conditions.

Behavior during the wintering over period was assessed by peer nominations, supervisor performance ratings, medical symptom check lists, and debriefing interviews at the end of the experience. The authors indicated that the assessment program was successful in eliminating those who would have become totally ineffective or required hospitalization for psychiatric disorders during the stress of Antarctic isolation. Ego strength and adequacy of defense mechanisms were the best predictors of adjustment.

In view of these results, the original criteria were revised and greater emphasis placed on the adequacy of the defense mechanisms rather than on the nature of the mechanisms themselves. Thus, clear-cut neurotic mechanisms, even if bordering on the pathological, were not in themselves sufficient to disqualify a candidate. Only extreme rigidity was considered to be clearly disqualifying. These findings, unfortunately, were based on rather scanty and unreliable records and the criteria for adjustment were poorly defined.

Weybrew, Molish, and Youniss (1961) compared personality trait ratings with adjustment ratings which were based on reported symptoms and attitudinal surveys. They found that those best suited to the Antarctic isolation communicated well with others, displayed little overt hostility, and dealt adequately with aggression. These findings substantiated earlier work by Weybrew (1957) dealing with adjustment to the confinement of submarines.

M. W. Wright, Sisler, and Chylinski (1963) reported on a screening procedure used on 170 civilian technicians who had volunteered for a one-year period of isolation duty on the Mid-Canada Line. A battery of tests which included the MMPI and the Edwards Personal Preference Schedule was administered to the applicants. After completion of the one-year tour of duty, each person's adjustment to the isolation condition was rated by his supervisor on each of two parameters: work and social adjustment.

The results indicated that those who adjusted poorly to the situation, *i.e.*, those who received low ratings, were characterized by mood instability, restlessness, overactivity, oversensitivity, seclusiveness, emotional shallowness, and limited resourcefulness and capacity for dealing with stressful situations.

These findings, as well as some others discussed by Nancy Wright (1964), suggest the predictive value of variables related to getting along with members of a small group rather than difficulty in adjusting to the conditions of isolation, *per se*.

## B. LABORATORY STUDIES OF SENSORY RESTRICTION

The various means of attempting to predict tolerance for sensory restriction include sensory tests, personality tests (both paper-and-pencil and projective), and the use of certain characteristics of reaction to an initial confinement session which are used to predict the reaction to a second session under the same or different conditions.

### 1. SENSORY TESTS OF ENDURANCE

Some writers have suggested that pain sensitivity and satiation may serve as predictors of deprivation tolerance. Petrie, Collins, and Solomon (1958) hypothesized that pain tolerance was positively related to satiability while sensory deprivation tolerance was negatively related to satiability. Satiation, as discussed by Köhler and Wallach (1944), is the apparent diminution in size ˉof an object touched by the hand after a period of stimulation of the same hand by a larger object. Thus, perceptual intensity diminishes after prolonged stimulation with a stronger stimulus. Wertheimer (1955) demonstrated the existence of individual differences in susceptibility to satiation.

In the Petrie, Collins, and Solomon study (1958), satiation was measured by an adaptation of the Köhler method of kinesthetic figural aftereffect. The blindfolded subject felt, with the thumb and forefinger, the width of a block of wood 38.1 mm. wide. With the other hand he fingered a long tapered bar of similar wood until he found the point of subjective equality where the width of the two pieces of wood appeared similar. He then rubbed a wider test block of 63.5 mm. width at a constant rate at varying time intervals.

The purpose of the wider block was, of course, to induce satiation. The apparent decrease in size in subsequent rubbings of the two original pieces of wood was, then, a measure of satiation, expressed in millimeters.

Pain tolerance was measured in the same subjects by an adaptation of the Hardy-Wolff-Goodell dolorimeter. Tolerance for sensory deprivation was measured by confinement in a tank-type respirator under sensory conditions similar to those of the original Bexton, Heron, and Scott (1954) study described earlier.

The results indicated that the mean amount of satiation for those most tolerant of pain was significantly greater than for those least tolerant of pain. The amount of satiation for those most tolerant of deprivation was significantly smaller than for those least tolerant of deprivation.

The authors concluded that:

> The results reported bear out the hypotheses that (i) pain tolerance is positively related to satiability; (ii) sensory deprivation tolerance is negatively related to satiability. It is inferred that satiability may prove to be in part the mechanism of tolerance and intolerance, and that pain tolerance is inversely related to sensory deprivation tolerance. . . . Our findings provide some support for the hypothesis that he who tolerates sensory deprivation least is most susceptible to satiation (Petrie, Collins, & Solomon, 1958, pp. 1431–1432).

Later, Petrie, Collins, and Solomon (1960) studied the same relationships but utilized two different subject populations. One group underwent experimental pain and heat radiation administered by the Hardy-Wolff-Goodell dolorimeter while the other group consisted of people who were ill and hospitalized and undergoing pain as a result of various types of chest surgery.

Satiation and pain tolerance were measured in the same manner as in the previous study. The authors called those who exhibited satiation "reducers" and those who resisted satiation "non-reducers."

The results showed that the reducers in both groups had the greatest tolerance for pain, thus supporting the earlier study. This was interpreted in terms of the reducers' tendencies to reduce the effectiveness of stimulation. The results further indicated that the reduction was cumulative and persisted much longer than the stimulus which caused it.

The authors then suggested that:

If we are right in explaining the tolerance of Reducers for pain as being partially due to a reduction in the intensity of stimulation, then this tendency to reduce should be a handicap in a situation where the environment starves the individual of sensory experience instead of bombarding him with it, as is the case for pain (Petrie, Collins, & Solomon, 1960, p. 84).

Thus, reducers should be less tolerant of sensory restriction than non-reducers.

This relationship held. The non-reducers were better able to tolerate the lack of stimulation as measured by the number of hours they were willing to remain in the tank-type respirator (under the same conditions as in the previous study). Thus, those who were least tolerant of deprivation were most susceptible to pain. Perhaps the tendency to reduce caused the limited stimulation available to be perceived as even less than it actually was.

Dealing with ability to endure pain, Peters, Benjamin, Helvey, and Albright (1963) isolated twenty-three subjects for forty hours under conditions of perceptual deprivation in a full scale model of a multi-man space capsule. Two subjects were confined at a time, wearing translucent goggles and earphones admitting white noise. On the basis of pre-isolation tests of pain endurance, subjects were divided into high, medium, and low pain endurance groups. The relationship between pain endurance and deprivation tolerance was not significant although a trend suggesting a direct relationship was apparent. Thus, this study did not support the Petrie, Collins, and Solomon studies reported above which suggested an inverse relationship.

Investigating this discrepancy, Zubek (1963b) studied thirty-six male subjects undergoing seven days of perceptual deprivation in the Manitoba isolation chamber described in preceding chapters. Twelve subjects terminated after eight to seventy hours, and their mean pain thresholds were compared with those of the twenty-four subjects who completed the seven-day period. The differences were not significant and the slight trend that did appear supported the work of Peters et al. (1963), i.e., a direct relationship.

Zubek concluded that, "in the light of these findings, it appears that pain sensitivity may be just as ineffective a predictor of tolerance for conditions of reduced sensory input as have been a variety of paper-and-pencil tests of personality" (1963b, pp. 641–642). With little encouragement from this comment, the discussion turns to personality tests as possible predictors of sensory deprivation tolerance.

## 2. TESTS OF PERSONALITY

For clarity of discussion this section will be divided into two parts: those studies using paper-and-pencil tests, and those using projective techniques.

*a. Paper-and-Pencil Tests.* Wexler, Mendelson, Leiderman, and Solomon (1958) employed the Edwards Personal Preference Schedule (EPPS) and the MMPI, among others, with seventeen male subjects undergoing thirty-six hours of perceptual deprivation in polio respirators. It is noted that the tests were given several weeks after confinement. None of the MMPI scales discriminated between the successful and the unsuccessful subjects, but more encouraging results were reported with the EPPS. A significant negative relationship was found between length of stay and need Exhibitionism, and non-significant positive relationships were found between time and need Affiliation, need Succorance, and need Nurturance. The authors suggested that those better able to tolerate isolation were desirous of more contact and emotional interaction with others and exhibited a greater dependence on others.

A later study (Kubzansky, Leiderman, Mendelson, Solomon, & Wexler, 1958) utilized more severe conditions of isolation and did not confirm the original findings. In this study, a need for autonomy and independence from others correlated positively with length of stay.

Smith and Lewty (1959), in the study discussed in Chapter VI, confined twenty male and twenty female subjects under conditions of partial perceptual deprivation for as long as they could tolerate the experience. All subjects were administered the Maudsley Medical Questionnaire, a measure of neuroticism. Zuckerman (1964) calculated the correlation between time in isolation and the questionnaire responses and obtained a coefficient of —0.84, suggesting that time in isolation was highly related to freedom from neurotic tendencies. Smith and Lewty suggested that the calm and placid person with average or somewhat below average intelligence was best able to tolerate sensory deprivation.

Tranel (1962) selected twenty male introverts and twenty male extraverts, based on the Myer-Briggs Type Indicator, and exposed them to four hours of perceptual deprivation in a sound-treated room. He reported that extraverts seemed better able to tolerate the isolation period, and that they tended to violate instructions and be more active. Introverts, on the other hand, tended to follow instructions more closely but were less successful in enduring the four-hour isolation period, *i.e.*, they terminated earlier. Data provided by administering the MMPI to a control group who did not undergo isolation showed the introverts to have a more feminine interest pattern and to be more passive and dependent than the extraverts. This is in disagreement with Hull and Zubek (1962) who found the successful subjects to have more feminine interests as measured on the MMPI (see below).

The research of Zuckerman, Albright, Marks, and Miller (1962), presented in Chapter VI, is also of relevance in the present context. To briefly reiterate, the experimental group consisted of twenty-five student nurses who were confined in iron lungs for seven hours under total darkness with white noise presented through earphones. A variety of tests and check lists were given to the subjects as noted in Chapter VI. Of interest here are the correlations between anxiety and stress responses to isolation and scores on the MMPI and the EPPS, which revealed no relationship between the personality variables measured and response to isolation.

Arnhoff and Leon (1963) exposed fifteen subjects to forty-eight hours of sensory deprivation in a McGill-type cubicle, four of whom terminated after twelve to twenty-seven hours of confinement. Prior to isolation all subjects were given Cattell's 16 P-F test. The personality profiles of the successful subjects were then compared with those of the four unsuccessful subjects. The results showed that successful subjects were more enthusiastic, talkative, suspicious, and jealous. The small *N* (four unsuccessful subjects) is, however, a cause for cautious interpretation.

Peters, Benjamin, Helvey, and Albright (1963) exposed twenty-three subjects to forty hours of perceptual deprivation under the conditions noted above. They found no significant relationships between MMPI and EPPS results and length of stay.

Hull and Zubek (1962) suggested several inadequacies of the research designed to relate personality characteristics to adjustment to sensory restriction. They note the existence of small samples, different criteria of evaluating adjustment, greatly differing subject populations, and widely variant conditions of isolation. Accordingly,

Hull and Zubek undertook a more systematic study of the problem. One group of sixteen male subjects was exposed to constant darkness and silence in the isolation chamber while another group of thirty male subjects was exposed to constant light and noise in the chamber. The confinement chamber has been described earlier. The maximum period of confinement for both groups was seven days. Of the total forty-six subjects, thirty completed the week of isolation. Of the sixteen who were unsuccessful, all but one requested release within the first three days.

Prior to isolation subjects were given the Thurstone Temperament Schedule (TTS), the MMPI, and the EPPS. In addition, the subjects filled out a biographical questionnaire containing items relating to leisure activities, health, job preferences, socio-economic factors, and parental background.

The most striking finding of the study was that none of the forty variables measured by the three tests made it possible to differentiate the successful from the unsuccessful. This was the case when the data for the two conditions of isolation were pooled for analysis and also when each was analyzed separately.

Taking a lower level of confidence (.10 instead of .05) the authors noted the existence of two trends. The successful subjects tended to have more feminine interests, as evidenced by their higher scores on the MF scale of the MMPI, and they also scored lower on the impulsive scale of the TTS.

Two significant differences did appear on the biographical questionnaire. Successful subjects were non-smokers, although no subjects gave prohibition of smoking as a reason for terminating early. The authors noted that other research (Myers, Murphy, & Smith, 1961) reported that lack of smoking was not a problem. The second difference was that successful subjects watched less television than unsuccessful subjects. The data also suggested that successful subjects read more books.

A later study by Zubek, Aftanas, Kovach, Wilgosh, and Winocur (1963) dealt with body immobilization for a period of twenty-four hours, as discussed in Chapters IV and V. After immobilization, the subjects were divided into two groups of twenty each, one group with a mean duration of 18.2 hours and the other with a mean duration of 7.7 hours. Comparisons of their performance on the MMPI, which had been administered prior to confinement, revealed the existence of no reliable differences on any scale. The only scale approaching significance was the Manic scale on which the less successful subjects tended to score higher. A further analysis was made of the top twelve and bottom twelve subjects with mean durations of 22.0 hours and 6.4 hours, respectively. No reliable differences were obtained.

Myers (1964b) reports on HumRRO research which utilized 170 subjects, 62 of whom requested release before the end of the ninety-six hours of sensory deprivation. Prior to confinement, biographical data were obtained and the MMPI and EPPS were administered. Myers reported that the unsuccessful subjects tended to be younger, higher on the Psychopathic Deviancy and Hypomanic scales of the MMPI, lower on the Deference scale of the EPPS, and more likely to be classed as smokers, than the successful subjects.

Myers suggested that the successful subject is higher in conformity and perhaps "is more attuned to the cultural requirements for mature responsibility, and more desirous of fulfilling his commitments. In contrast, the younger early release S appears to be a less mature person, not so sensitive to implicit duties prescribed by the culture, and less strongly governed by need to comply with his perceived obligations to others" (1964b, p. 53).

In relating their findings to the relevant literature, Hull and Zubek (1962) note that, "it would appear, then, that the *most* that can be said from the research in this area is that there is some indication that a person low in impulsiveness, possessing some feminine interests and a good imagination, who is able to accept a dependency situation, might be the best candidate for sensory isolation. These conclusions are merely suggestive" (pp. 237–238).

*b. Projective Tests of Personality.* Ruff and Levy (1959b) used the Rorschach in a series of studies utilizing candidates for space travel as subjects. One of the studies involved isolation for only three hours in a dark, soundproof room. The authors provided no other information about the conditions of the study. The Rorschach protocols of those who were rated as best-adjusted to isolation were well organized and suggested little imagination and creativity, although they were not overly rigid. Aggressive impulses tended to be expressed in action rather than fantasy. Little information on the criteria for isolation adjustment and no statistical data were provided by the authors.

Later work (Ruff & Levy, 1959a; Levy, Ruff, & Thaler, 1959) included fifty-two experiments involving isolation for four hours to seven days under conditions of sensory deprivation and perceptual deprivation. Description of specific conditions of isolation, criteria, and statistical support are again lacking. The authors concluded that "the best qualification for a space crew member is a sound ego" (Ruff & Levy, 1959a, p. 796). Ruff, Levy, and Thaler (1959) suggested that schizophrenics and schizoid personalities were poor isolation subjects while passive-dependent individuals with strong egos and few emotional problems were better able to tolerate isolation.

Cohen, Silverman, Bressler, and Shmavonian (1961) exposed four subjects to four hours of isolation in a soundproof chamber. Two of the subjects had been diagnosed by the Rorschach and personal interview as schizoid personalities while the other two appeared to be well integrated. The authors suggested that the withdrawn schizoid personalities might be better able to endure isolation. This suggestion conflicts with that of Ruff, Levy, and Thaler as discussed above but is in agreement with the results of Grunebaum, Freedman, and Greenblatt (1960) whose personality evaluations were based on extensive interviewing. This latter study utilized an eight-hour period of isolation.

A study by Cohen, Rosenbaum, Dobie, and Gottlieb (1959) exposed ten subjects (including normal, neurotic, schizophrenic, and sociopathic individuals) to only one hour of isolation. The subject sat in a chair, wearing earplugs and earphones through which a masking sound was presented. Elbow-length mittens were worn and some subjects wore blacked-out goggles while others wore frosted goggles. The authors reported that the normal and neurotic subjects exhibited an increased sensitivity to residual stimuli in the chamber while the schizophrenic subjects showed a generally positive reaction to the situation.

In a series of studies, Goldberger and Holt (1961a, 1961b) studied the relationship between Rorschach responses and reaction to eight hours of isolation under constant diffuse light and noise. Two subject groups were utilized: fourteen male college students and sixteen unemployed male actors. The nature of the adaptive and maladaptive reactions was determined by objective analysis of the verbalizations made by subjects during isolation. Maladaptive reaction was defined by quitting or verbal preoccupation with doing so. The adaptive college student subjects were characterized by acceptance of their passive, feminine side, emotional lability, and easily displayed affect. This was not confirmed with the actor group.

The authors suggested that the typical mode of defense of an individual was not as important as the effectiveness of the particular defenses. They found that with the Rorschach, those who handled primary process material maturely and effectively adapted better to isolation. Those who reacted negatively to isolation, on the other hand, had handled primary process material with poor control or had avoided it. Conditions of isolation, then, were thought by the authors to be particularly threatening to those unable to defend themselves effectively against the emergence of primary process material. The authors suggested that this material emerged as a function of interference with reality.

Working in the Manitoba laboratory, Nancy Wright and Abbey (1965) investigated the utility of the Rorschach in predicting tolerance for perceptual deprivation. A group of twenty-one male students who had previously served as subjects in perceptual deprivation experiments were used. The conditions of deprivation with unpatterned light and white noise have been described in Chapter I. Fourteen of these subjects had successfully endured a week of confinement while seven had terminated within the first three days. The authors noted that the 2:1 ratio of successful to unsuccessful subjects was characteristic of all the perceptual deprivation work at Manitoba.

Several months after their isolation experience, the subjects were administered the Buhler-Lefever Standardization of the Rorschach (C. Buhler, K. Buhler, & Lefever, 1954). Scoring of the verbatim records by the Holt-Havel system (1960) resulted in two quantitative summary scores: Defense Demand (a measure of amount of primary process material), and Effectiveness of Defense (a measure of control of primary process material).

The results indicated that when the Defense Demand scores were plotted as a function of Effectiveness of Defense, the effectiveness of a subject's control and defense mechanisms was confounded by the amount of drive-dominated material that had emerged. Defense Demand was therefore controlled statistically in order to analyze Effectiveness of Defense. The subjects were rank-ordered according to this Index of Control with the top seven subjects becoming the High Control Group, the next seven the Mid Control

Group, and the bottom seven the Low Control Group. The number of successful and unsuccessful subjects in each of these groups is indicated in Table 7–1.

Statistical analysis revealed no significant difference between observed frequencies and hypothesized frequencies (the 2:1 ratio mentioned above) for the High and Mid Control Groups. However, these values were significant for the Low Control Group. The authors suggested that the Index of Control may be a reliable measure "for predicting whether or not the defense mechanisms of an individual will be effective in controlling the drive-dominated

TABLE 7–1

DIVISION OF SUCCESSFUL AND UNSUCCESSFUL ISOLATION SUBJECTS ON THE BASIS OF CONTROL OF DRIVE-DOMINATED RESPONSES[a]

|  | Index of control | | |
| --- | --- | --- | --- |
| Subjects | High | Middle | Low |
| Successful | 7 | 5 | 2 |
| Unsuccessful | 0 | 2 | 5 |
| | — | — | — |
| Total | 7 | 7 | 7 |

[a] Reprinted by permission from N. Wright and D. S. Abbey, *Percept. mot. Skills*, 1965, **20**, 35–38.

responses that might emerge during his period of reduced sensory stimulation" (Wright & Abbey, 1965, p. 37). These findings lend support to the suggestion discussed earlier that the important discriminatory variable is the adequacy of defense mechanisms rather than the specific nature of the mechanisms themselves. As the authors suggested, the results are subject to one limitation: the Rorschach was administered several months after confinement. The individual's realization that he failed or succeeded in the experience may have confounded his Rorschach results. Work currently in progress at Manitoba involves the administering of the Rorschach prior to confinement (Zubek, 1964).*

### 3. THE BODY-FIELD PERCEPTUAL MODE

A paper by Shmavonian (1964, in conjunction with Cohen) is of interest to this chapter. Their work with the body-field perceptual

* Personal communication.

mode in sensory deprivation, while not done in the context of attempting to predict tolerance for sensory restriction, provides some relevant results nonetheless. The reader is referred to "Personality Through Perception" (Witkin *et al.*, 1954) for a detailed discussion of this personality dimension. Very briefly, it may be said that the "field-dependent" person is rigid and leans heavily upon the external and concrete qualities of stimuli in crystallizing their interpretations, while the "field-independent" person is more flexible and uses internal and abstract stimuli as well as external stimuli in their perceptions. The complexity of personality attributes is appraised by a battery of procedures developed by Witkin including clinical interviews and projective tests.

A subject group of thirty-five males, without any overt evidence of psychopathological or psychophysiological disorders, was separated into three subgroups: twelve body-oriented, twelve field-oriented, and eleven designated as falling midway between the other two groups. Prior to isolation, urine specimens were taken. Subjects were then placed in an 80 db. attenuated dark chamber for a two-hour period of sensory deprivation. Immediately after confinement, tests of sensory discrimination were administered and pain thresholds for electric shock were established. During the two hours of confinement, EEG, GSR, peripheral plethysmography, respiration, and cardiac recordings were obtained. At the end of the two hours, perceptual threshold testing was repeated, second urine specimens collected, and subjects interviewed for degree of discomfort.

A number of differences were reported between the body-oriented and field-oriented subjects. The field-oriented group had the highest overall mean number of nonspecific GSR fluctuations as well as the smallest decrease in number of fluctuations from beginning to end of confinement. Analysis of EEG records revealed that CNS activation (decrease in alpha activity with no increase in theta) appeared to be greater for the field-oriented subjects while the middle group showed the lowest level of activation. When the change in alpha activity over the two-hour period was analyzed, the field-oriented subjects showed a decrease and the body-oriented and middle group showed a slight increase. A review of the beta activity also suggested that field-oriented subjects were the most aroused. Taken together, the results of EEG and GSR "suggested that the field-oriented subjects' central nervous system activities are increased by isolation in the low sensory environment whereas the body-oriented subjects and those whose perceptual mode does not fall in either extreme are decreased" (Shmavonian, 1964, p. 7).

The tests of somatosensory discrimination suggested that field-oriented subjects required greater separation of calipers to identify two points and showed less precision and more overlap than the other groups. The field-oriented group was also less accurate in the identification of letters.

In general, the psychological findings paralleled the psycho-physiological results. More field-oriented subjects asked to be released from confinement and showed the greatest discomfort and emotional inappropriateness. They also gave more evidence of illusory thinking, visual and auditory images, and disorganization of thought.

It seems not unreasonable to suggest that had the period of isolation been extended, a greater number of field-oriented subjects would have terminated the experience earlier than subjects of the other two groups.

### 4. OTHER VARIABLES

Sex differences in endurance ability were studied by Davis et al. (1961) who suggested that women were less able to tolerate isolation in a respirator than men. In two studies (Pollard, Uhr, & Jackson, 1963a, 1963b) involving perceptual deprivation it was found that males stayed significantly more hours than females. Arnhoff and Leon (1963) compared nineteen males and seventeen females who underwent two hours of sensory deprivation and found no significant sex differences on the behavioral measures of Isolation Disturbance, Time Disturbance, and Imagery Disturbance. Smith and Lewty (1959), on the other hand, found females able to endure partial perceptual deprivation (silence with unpatterned vision) for a longer period than males. However, the subjects were recruited from nurses and hospital workers and their average age was greater than that of the usual college student subject population.

Suedfeld (1964) reported a high proportion of first-born individuals among volunteers for a sensory deprivation study. He found that 79 per cent of the twenty-nine volunteers were first-borns, a figure significantly higher than the proportion of first-borns in the subject population from which the sample was drawn, and almost twice the proportion of first-borns in the general population. There is, however, no data to indicate any relation between birth order and tolerance for sensory restriction.

Time estimation as a predictor of endurance has been investigated in the HumRRO program by Murphy, Hampton, and Myers (1962). The HumRRO procedure of ninety-six hours under conditions of sensory deprivation has been described in previous chapters. In this study, of forty-eight subjects confined in sensory deprivation, twenty-five requested early release while the other twenty-three remained the entire ninety-six hours.

A time estimation task was given after four, forty-five, eighty-four, and ninety-six hours in isolation and consisted of asking the subject to estimate the day and time of day. The subjects were not told in advance that this would be asked of them. Instructions for the task were presented aurally by tape recording and subjects indicated their responses by pulling a lever of a Lindsley manipulandum.

The primary data of interest are a comparison between the average time estimation error of the early release and of the successful subjects. Some of the unsuccessful subjects left before the second time estimation at forty-five hours, hence only the estimations obtained after four hours of confinement were of value.

The results revealed a significant difference in average time estimation between the two groups. The unsuccessful subjects overestimated the passage of time significantly more than those who were able to tolerate the ninety-six-hour isolation session. For the early release group, the correlation between time estimation error and duration of confinement was —0.43, indicating that those who made the larger errors in time estimation had relatively shorter confinement. The authors concluded that time estimation error after only four hours of confinement appeared to be a good predictor of endurance for the much longer confinement period.

Smith, Myers, and Murphy (1962) reported on another possible predictor of isolation tolerance investigated in the HumRRO program: activity pattern and restlessness during isolation. The data were collected from the same twenty-five early release and twenty-three successful subjects described above (Murphy, Hampton, & Myers, 1962). As in all the HumRRO studies, the confinement period was ninety-six hours of sensory deprivation.

The data were gathered continuously from the isolation cubicles and recorded every ten minutes during the entire session. To determine the subject's restlessness, two sensing devices were used. One was an arrangement of switches mounted beneath the bed which indicated when the subject was on or off the bed. The other device was a rate of change of movement detector which indicated the amount of gross restlessness occurring on the bed.

The two groups (stayers and quitters) did not differ for the first day time period. The authors noted that the subjects slept a great deal during this period. The data for day two, however, revealed a significantly higher restlessness for the unsuccessful subjects as compared to those who remained for the entire ninety-six hours. Also reported was a negative correlation ($-0.62$) between amount of restlessness and length of endurance indicating that the more restless the subject, the earlier he requested release.

Thus, a predictor of isolation endurance might be the degree of restlessness manifested in the early stages of confinement. One would suspect that had the subjects been kept awake for the initial hours of isolation, the difference in restlessness between stayers and quitters would have been demonstrated during the first day of confinement.

## C. TOLERANCE AS A FUNCTION OF NEED FOR STIMULATION

Zuckerman and Haber (1965) hypothesized that the individual differences in stress reactions may be a function of differences in need for stimulation. Because of its congruence with the sensoristatic model, this approach to tolerance of isolation will be discussed at some length.

Zuckerman and Haber noted earlier work by Vernon and McGill (1960) who attempted to determine if an individual under conditions of sensory deprivation would seek a form of stimulation which ordinarily would hold no interest for him. Fifteen subjects were confined in the Princeton "floating room" and were given the opportunity to push a button illuminating a viewing box containing a simple line drawing of a small and a large circle with a slanting line between them. The authors posited that if a subject spent time looking at the viewer, he was expressing a need for stimulation.

The results indicated that all subjects used the viewing box. More important for the present discussion, however, is the finding that the utilization of the viewer clearly separated successful from unsuccessful subjects. The results are indicated in Table 7–2. Group I were those subjects demanding an early release with an average confinement time of 37.6 hours. The nine subjects in Group II successfully completed their seventy-two-hour confinement period. The time at the viewer during the first day was significantly greater

TABLE 7–2[a]

MEAN VIEWING TIMES OF EARLY RELEASE AND SUCCESSFUL SUBJECTS

| Number of subjects | Mean viewing time (sec.) during first day of S.D.[b] | Mean viewing time (sec.) during total S.D. | Mean time (hr.) in S.D. |
|---|---|---|---|
| Group I 6 | 183.2 | 212.5 | 37.6 |
| Group II 9 | 13.3 | 165.5 | 72 |

[a] Reprinted by permission from J. Vernon, *Inside the black room.* New York: Potter, 1963.
[b] S.D. = Sensory deprivation.

for Group I than for Group II. The authors suggested that this indicated that the need for stimulation was generated early for those who did not adjust well to sensory deprivation. The need for stimulation seemed to increase gradually in both groups suggesting that the need state became more intense as a function of time in deprivation.

Zuckerman, Levine, and Biase (1964) confined thirty-six female subjects in three groups under the following conditions: (1) sensory deprivation, no light or sound; (2) auditory deprivation, light but no sound; and (3) visual deprivation, sound but no light. The conditions were described in Chapter III. On the basis of basal skin conductance increase during the last one and one-half hours of the three-hour confinement period, subjects in the total isolation group were divided into six high and six low GSR responders. These two groups were compared on ratings obtained from post-confinement interviews. Significant differences were found between the groups on need for activity and complaints about isolation. The high GSR responders were rated higher in both cases.

Six weeks after this study, Zuckerman and Haber (1965) obtained twenty-four of the original subjects to participate in a second isolation experience. Twelve of these were high GSR responders and twelve were low GSR responders determined on the basis of the magnitude of their conductance increase during the last one and one-half hours of the original experiment. All subjects were confined under conditions of sensory deprivation in a dark, sound-proof room for three hours. A button was provided to bring stimulation to the subject who was instructed that its use was entirely up to her. By means of a switch the subjects could expose themselves to visual stimulation (strips of colors painted across a blank film strip) or auditory stimulation (tape recorded tones played on a vibraphone). The middle position of the switch activated neither form of stimulation. The stimulation was provided for a period of fifteen seconds. The button had to be pressed ten times for the stimulation to appear.

The response means for high and low GSR responders are noted in Table 7–3. The differences were highly significant with the

TABLE 7–3

RESPONSE MEANS OF HIGH AND LOW GSR REACTORS FOR VISUAL AND AUDITORY REINFORCEMENT[a]

| Type of reinforcement | Reaction to prior isolation | | |
| --- | --- | --- | --- |
| | High GSR | Low GSR | All subjects |
| Auditory | 938 | 239 | 588 |
| Visual | 2114 | 594 | 1354 |
| Both | 3052 | 833 | 1942 |

[a] Reprinted by permission from M. Zuckerman and M. Haber, *J. abnorm. Psychol.*, 1965, in press.

high GSR responders making almost four times as many responses as the low GSR responders. All groups made significantly more responses for the visual than the auditory reinforcement and none of the subjects responded with the switch in the neutral position.

The difference between high and low GSR groups was more marked with the visual reinforcement. Zuckerman and Haber (1965) related this to the previous study (Zuckerman, Levine, & Biase, 1964) in which the group deprived of visual stimulation alone showed more nonspecific GSR reactions than the group deprived of auditory stimulation.

## D. DISCUSSION

The various attempts to develop techniques to predict tolerance for sensory restriction based on personality tests, have produced little in the way of consistent or useful results. However, some interesting new data are available from Zubek's Manitoba laboratory in an unpublished M.A. thesis (1964) by Nancy Wright. Using a very large sample of ninety subjects who had previously been tested under perceptual deprivation, Wright reanalyzed the data using first $t$ test and then the multiple discriminant function to determine if a particular pattern of variables might successfully distinguish successful from unsuccessful subjects. Of the total ninety subjects, thirty had failed to endure a week of confinement, all but one having terminated in the first three days.

Several days before confinement, all subjects took the MMPI, the EPPS, and the Thurstone Temperament Schedule (TTS). The $t$ test analysis of the thirty-eight variables involved revealed that only Deference on the EPPS reached significance in discriminating between the two groups. The twenty-five most potent measures from the three tests were then run on the multiple discriminant function. These measures were rank-ordered according to their contribution to the discriminating power of the function. The top seven measures were: Validity Scale F (MMPI), Dominant (TTS), Neuroticism Index (MMPI), Succorance (EPPS), Exhibition (EPPS), Hypochondriasis (MMPI), and Sociable (TTS). The successful group rated higher than the unsuccessful group on all variables except Dominant. The mean scores for both groups were within the average range on all measures except Sociable on which both groups scored in the low average category.

The characteristic which contributed most to the difference between successful and unsuccessful subjects was the former's attitude toward taking the test. Wright noted that the successful subjects' responses were generally less rational and less pertinent. The results of the other tests suggested that the successful subject tended to be more neurotic, somewhat hypochondriacal and immature, had less capacity for taking initiative and responsibility, had a greater need to be understood by others and to receive help and affection, made friends more easily, and was more sympathetic, cooperative, and agreeable, than the unsuccessful subject.

Wright indicated that forty-five of the sixty successful subjects were correctly predicted as were twenty-three of the thirty unsuccessful subjects. Thus, performance in isolation of sixty-eight of the ninety subjects (75.5 per cent) was correctly predicted by the classification matrix of the multiple discriminant function.

Wright then applied the multiple discriminant function to Rorschach data which was obtained from twenty-one subjects several months after their isolation experience. Fourteen of these subjects had endured the week of isolation while seven had terminated prematurely. Impressive results were reported from the analysis of the Rorschach data. All seven unsuccessful subjects and twelve of the fourteen successful subjects were correctly classified by only three Rorschach variables: average reaction time, number of popular responses, and content scores. A pattern composed of twenty-five groups of variables provided a perfect classification of subjects. Wright noted that because the Rorschach was given after isolation, the results must be considered only suggestive.

The author concluded that a combination of variables may be a more valid predictor of isolation tolerance than individual variables and that the Rorschach may be a better predictor than a combination of even the most discriminating measures from paper-and-pencil tests of personality. Commenting on the contradictory findings reported in this area, Wright noted:

> It would appear that in addition to the small samples, brief periods of isolation and differences attributable to alterations in the conditions of isolation, a major flaw has been the lack of sophistication of the statistical techniques employed. When a more complex method of analysis is used, it is clear that personality characteristics do indeed play an important role in determining an individual's response to sensory isolation (Wright, 1964, p. 37).

Zubek (1965)[*] reports on a cross-validation of the multiple discriminant function data reported above. In this study, thirty-one new subjects were given the same paper-and-pencil tests and exposed to one week of isolation. Of the total sample, eighteen endured the week's confinement while thirteen terminated early. Applying the previously determined weights to the three personality

[*] Personal communication.

tests, Zubek reported that 71 per cent of the subjects were correctly predicted.

Hull and Zubek (1962) suggested the importance of considering the nature of the isolation condition. Predictive value might hold for one type of restriction but not for another. Evidence is available (Hull & Zubek, 1962; Cohen, Silverman, Bressler, & Shmavonian, 1961; Ruff, Levy, & Thaler, 1959) which indicates that slight environmental changes can have important effects on the subject's reaction to confinement. If this is true, differences in conditions of isolation may also affect the type of personality best able to adapt.

Another factor worthy of consideration is that all the research on sensory restriction utilizes volunteer populations. Not all people volunteer for this experience. As Kubzansky noted, "there is no such data available on possible differential reactions of volunteers and nonvolunteers. Similarly, one must leave open the possibility that solitude and perceptual deprivation sought at the individual's own need or whim may have different effects than when imposed by an experimenter who creates a highly artificial situation so that he may systematically observe the subject" (1961, p. 85).

Hull and Zubek (1962) suggested several more reasons for the negative findings resulting from earlier studies using tests of personality. The studies have utilized small samples. Trends are sometimes reported, but for the most part the findings have not reached statistical significance (although some might reach significance with a larger sample). Also, the tests themselves have certain inadequacies and limitations, and the proposition that the traits measured may not be relevant to tolerance of isolation must be considered. Hull and Zubek further suggested that perhaps motivational factors, rather than personality characteristics, were of crucial importance.

The work of Zuckerman lends credence to this suggestion. This approach, using the subjects' actual behavior in a previous isolation situation, has yielded predictability at a level not achieved by using general trait tests (except for Wright's approach). Zuckerman discussed his results in terms of man's "need" for stimulation. His hypothesis was that sensory deprivation is the source of arousal (as measured by GSR) and that subjects who show more arousal in an initial period of isolation have a greater "need" for stimulation than subjects less aroused in the initial experience. This suggests individual differences in this stimulation "need." It would follow, then, that those individuals with the greater "need" would be less tolerant of sensory restriction. The results, as discussed above, strongly support this hypothesis.

Zuckerman reported some very exciting work on the development of a "Sensation Seeking Scale" (Zuckerman, Kolin, Price, & Zoob, 1964) designed to measure the individual level of stimulus "need." The Scale is in the form of a forced-choice questionnaire with items indicating preferences for extreme intensities of stimulation (heat, cold, noise, tastes, colors, musical sounds) as opposed to minimal or zero intensities. Other items contain preferences for irregularity as opposed to routine, enjoyment of anxiety-provoking reactions as opposed to a safety orientation, and so on.

This work has obvious relevance for the sensoristatic model and the postulation of individual differences in optimal level of sensory variation/cortical arousal. It might be suggested that those individuals with a higher optimal sensoristatic level have a greater "need" (in Zuckerman's terms) for varied stimulation while those with a lower sensoristatic level have less of a stimulus "need" and indeed function most adaptively with a minimal/moderate sensory variation input. The latter, then, would be most tolerant of sensory restriction.

The work on satiation reported earlier may also be relevant. It might be suggested that the reducers (those who exhibited satiation) have a higher stimulus "need" and a higher sensoristatic level. (The reducers were less tolerant of sensory restriction than non-reducers.) If the reducers do have a higher stimulus "need" one might reasonably ask why they reduce the intensity of available stimulation. One possible reason might be due to the simple level of stimulation used in satiation (rubbing pieces of wood). The stimulation is highly repetitive and involves minimal sensory variation; hence sensory habituation may occur more readily with reducers than with non-reducers. Thus, those high in stimulus "need," who have a higher sensoristatic level, strive for varied sensory input to a high degree and therefore habituate to repetitive simple stimuli quickly. It would be interesting to compare the relative performances of reducers versus non-reducers on Zuckerman's "Sensation Seeking Scale."

This chapter has provided evidence to support three of the predictions made in Chapter II. Evidence has been presented indicating differences in tolerance for isolation (Prediction 6), and there has been additional evidence on the role of the reinforcing effects of stimulation under conditions of confinement (Prediction 5). The work of Vernon and McGill (1960) provided evidence suggesting that the need for stimulation becomes more intense as a function of time in isolation (Prediction 2). No conclusions have been reached in the search for valid predictors of isolation tolerance, but the provocative work of Zuckerman seems to offer the most fruitful approach.

# CHAPTER VIII

# *Effects of Social Isolation*

In the research discussed in the preceding chapters, subjects were isolated individually and exposed to conditions of sensory or perceptual deprivation. This chapter deals with a different form of isolation in which the chief restriction imposed is that of limited or no social contact with other people. Here the concern is with the effects of confinement to a very specific and monotonous sensory environment on an individual alone or with a small group of people. The subjects are not placed in darkness or under non-patterned stimulation, but are forced to function in a sensory environment which offers little change or sensory variation. Even in situations where a small group of people are confined together, the social stimulation provided by the other people may offer little sensory variation because of the length of confinement. The individual in this situation interacts with the same people day after day in an environment which is fairly "normal" but which nonetheless is constant and unchanging.

Recent technological developments, particularly in the military, have focused attention on the problems of human adaptation to such a restricted and unusual environment. The reference is to the advent of space craft, nuclear submarines, isolated radar and missile stations, and remote scientific outposts, where small groups are forced to operate in isolation for extended periods of time. In these situations, the principal task is often that of routine, monotonous monitoring of automated equipment. The important problem of efficient performance in such an environment is of more than academic or theoretical interest alone. In the not too distant future one can look forward to satellite space stations, lunar colonies, and the like, occupied by small teams of technicians and scientists, being added to the list of extreme environments to which man must adapt. Even more severe problems of adjustment may be expected in long-term confinement to community or small group fallout shelters in the event of nuclear war. In all of these examples neither

147

the physical or social stimulation available is capable of providing much in the way of sensory variation.

Most of this chapter will deal with small group confinement studies, however, some reports of individual isolation with no contact with other people will be discussed first.

## A. INDIVIDUAL SOCIAL ISOLATION

The concern here is the individual functioning without contact with any other person in a somewhat normal sensory environment. Much of the available literature in this area is autobiographical in nature and consists of reports of explorers, sailors, castaways, and prisoners. There are some important differences to be considered between this form of isolation and the sensory and perceptual deprivation research. First, there is no attempt (except possibly in solitary confinement) to reduce the level and/or patterning of sensory stimulation. However, both sensory restriction and social isolation may offer little sensory variation. Second, in laboratory studies of sensory restriction, the subject's life is not endangered, he is not subject to torture and starvation, and he is free to leave whenever he wishes. Third, selective factors are operative in that autobiographical accounts of social isolation can be written only by those who survive the experience. In addition, not all of those who survive such isolation choose to write about it. Finally, the experience of someone who chose solitary isolation, as did Admiral Byrd, may not be the same as that of someone who is isolated against his will.

With these important limitations in mind, the discussion now turns to some of these subjective reports.* Lilly (1956) noted that isolation *per se* functions as a powerful stress on most people and often produces a variety of psychotic-like behaviors including hallucinations, savior types of delusions, superstitiousness, intense love of any living things, conversations with inanimate objects, and a feeling that when one is once again among people he must be careful of what he says lest he be judged insane.

A variety of techniques for counteracting the effects of isolation are reported. Miller (1962) reported that the most frequently described method is some form of mental exercise ranging from

---

* For those interested in reading these fascinating biographical accounts, references can be found in Lilly (1956) and Miller (1962).

counting pebbles to complex intellectual exercises. Edith Bone (1957), for example, during her seven years of solitary confinement, mentally catalogued 27,369 English words. Keeping a log or diary is another frequently used technique, as is some form of work. Many of these isolated people engaged in scientific observations, housecleaning, or, in several cases, just killing flies in an effort to protect themselves from the pressures of isolation.

Lilly (1956) noted that in all cases of survivors of isolation, it was the first exposure that provoked the greatest fear. Apparently some previous experience was of great help despite the symptoms. Another factor found common to all survivors was the conviction that they would inevitably survive.

Because of the anecdotal nature of these reports and their limitations as discussed above, it becomes difficult to draw useful generalizations beyond the obvious comment that such social isolation serves as a source of stress. Lilly (1956) offers the following comments:

> (1) Published autobiographies are of necessity incomplete. Social taboos, discretion to one's self, suppression and repression of painful or uncomfortable material, secondary elaboration, and rationalization severely limit the scope of the material available. (Interviews with two men, each of whom lived alone in the polar night, confirm this impression.)
> (2) Despite these limitations, we find that persons in isolation experience many, if not all, of the symptoms of the mentally ill.
> (3) In those who survive, the symptoms can be reversible. How easily reversible, we do not know. Most survivors report, after several weeks exposure to isolation, a new inner security and a new integration of themselves on a deep and basic level.
> (4) The underlying mechanisms are obscure. It is obvious that inner factors in the mind tend to be projected outward, that some of the mind's activity which is usually reality-bound now becomes free to turn to phantasy and ultimately to hallucination and delusion. It is as if the laws of thought are projected into the realm of the laws of inanimate matter and of the universe (pp. 4–5).

Three empirical studies of individual social isolation are available. Ormiston (1958) confined ten Air Force officer volunteers in an aircraft cockpit capsule for forty-eight hours. The subjects were required to work intermittently on perceptual, intellectual, and compensatory tracking tasks. A group of ten control subjects were confined in the capsule only while performing the above tasks.

Subjects were able to see outside the capsule but the view was considerably restricted. The subjects were allowed to smoke and there were no restrictions on communicating with the monitor. A sleep period of eight and one-half hours was allowed the confined subjects each night.

The following intellectual tasks were used: arithmetic, digit memory, confusing sentences, verbal analogies, nonsense syllables, same-opposite word meanings, and logical reasoning. Perceptual tasks included warning-light monitoring, finding embedded figures, form discrimination, and aerial reconnaissance. No impairments were reported on any of the intellectual tasks and only one perceptual task, aerial reconnaissance, reflected the possibility of impairment.

Observation of the confined subjects revealed a tendency to become increasingly irritable and to exhibit undesirable behavior normally kept under control.

A study by Walters and Henning (1962) involved social isolation of high school male subjects under a number of conditions, only two of which are pertinent in the present context. The main concern of the study was with verbal productivity as a function of isolation versus no isolation, and ego-oriented versus task-oriented instructions. Subjects were isolated in a basement room, provided with food and chemical toilet, and asked not to leave the room under any circumstances. Subjects had been told only that the experiment was designed to study speaking ability and time judgments, not that the effects of isolation were being examined.

Subjects were confined for three-hour or six-hour periods and were instructed to press a buzzer each time they thought thirty minutes had elapsed. The authors reported that the purpose of this was two-fold: it prevented a subject from going to sleep and it disguised the true purpose of the experiment.

The relevant results dealing with isolation revealed that the procedure was a boring and distasteful task for most of the subjects but the procedure did not appear to have made the subjects emotionally disturbed, upset, or anxious. For social isolation, however, six hours is not a very long period of time.

Walters, Callagan, and Newman (1963) investigated the effects of a ninety-six-hour period of social isolation using twenty volunteer long-term prisoners as subjects. Another group of twenty volunteers served as controls. The 6 ft. by 12 ft. isolation cells contained only a bed, toilet, and handbasin. During the day, light was provided by a small window high up on the wall and by an electric light. A dim light was kept on at night. Subjects were allowed to smoke and were provided a regular diet but were not allowed to have reading matter. No indication was given that their behavior or feelings might be influenced by their participation in the experience.

Confined and control subjects were given a number of tests immediately before and immediately after isolation (four days apart for control subjects). Three tests of susceptibility to social influence, a body sway test, autokinetic test, and a conditioning of meaning test were given, as were a manual dexterity test, the Shipley-Hartford Abstraction Test, and a brief test of verbal productivity. In addition, the subjects reactions to the situation were assessed by the following: (1) self-ratings to indicate how anxious they felt about participating in the study, (2) a posttest rating of five concepts—punishment, solitary, prison, authority, society, (3) the Maudsley Personality Inventory to obtain scores for neuroticism and introversion, (4) a brief aggression scale.

The results indicated that significantly more confined subjects reported an increase in anxiety from pre to posttest periods. After isolation, however, the confined subjects rated the concept "solitary" more positively and "society" more negatively than did the control subjects. The confined subjects were somewhat less verbally productive than controls.

Thus, the results of this study suggest that social isolation for ninety-six hours does not result in increased susceptibility to social influence or in mental or psychomotor deterioration. However, it is important to note that the nature of the subject population was such that they might have been more adjusted to a monotonous, little-changing sensory environment than the general population.

## B. SMALL GROUP SOCIAL ISOLATION

As with individual social isolation, there exist a number of anecdotal reports describing the experiences of small groups of people in isolation, in a lifeboat for example, for an extended period of time. These reports are subject to the same criticisms noted above in reference to individual social isolation. Fortunately, some laboratory and field research has been conducted on small groups in isolation and the discussion will be restricted to these studies. The isolation of subjects in pairs will be considered first, then isolation of groups with more than two members.

Research dealing with two men in isolation has been performed at the Naval Medical Research Institute by Haythorn, Altman, and Myers (1965). The purpose of this study was to attempt to match the personalities of the isolated pair in order to facilitate their adaptation to the situation.

The personality dimensions of achievement, affiliation, and dominance needs as measured by the Edwards Personal Preference Schedule and dogmatism as measured by the Rokeach Dogmatism Scale were used in the selection of subjects. The volunteer seamen subjects chosen were in the upper or lower tertiles of the four scales. Each pair was selected to have one of three values—homogeneously high, heterogeneous, or homogeneously low—on each of the four personality variables.

Subjects were confined in pairs for ten days in a small room in which they ate, slept, and worked. The only intrusions from the outside world were loudspeaker announcements of reveille, chow time, taps, and task instruction. About seven hours of each day were devoted to a Combat Information Center Task, and vigilance and decoding tasks. The rest of the time was used for cleaning the room and free interaction. The control condition involved performance of the same tasks in the same room, which the subjects left at the end of the work period.

On the tenth day of the study, the subjects took the Subjective Stress Scale discussed in Chapter VI and the Subjective Symptomatology Questionnaire developed by Myers, Murphy, Smith, and Windle (1962). Subjects were also interviewed at this time.

The results of the Subjective Stress Scale indicated that confinement was more stressful than the control condition. The control subjects demonstrated a quick recovery to normal emotional feeling state while the confined subjects showed a persisting emotional decrement.

That confinement was more stressful than the control condition was also suggested by the fact that two of the nine confined dyads terminated before the end of the ten-day period. Also, two of the remaining dyads displayed serious overt hostility toward each other. None of the control dyads terminated early or gave evidence of hostile relations between the members.

The authors stated that the composition of the isolated pairs was a significant determinant of subjective response to the stress of confinement. This seemed most true of the variables of need dominance and need achievement.

Dealing with a larger group of individuals in isolation, Taylor (1961) reported on his observations and research on male prisoners in New Zealand. In his role as prison psychologist, he had identified six cases of deterioration among the prisoners.

> These men were withdrawn, displaying a minimal response to their environment. They lacked spontaneity, had fixed expressions, and spoke without feeling. While they operated physically as persons, they seemed to have ceased to function as individuals. In some ways their symptoms resembled those of reactive depression, but they showed no suicidal tendencies and maintained a moderate level of physical activity. Two of the men displayed compulsive symptoms, one going through a ritual before entering or leaving his cell, and the other ending every reply with the phrase, " . . . and a dog biscuit." The men were serving sentences ranging from two years to life imprisonment, and the symptoms arose at a different time in each case, varying from six months to nine years after the beginning of the sentence. None of the men was under solitary confinement (Taylor, 1961, p. 374).

A program of psychotherapy and some relaxation of rules led in all cases to a restoration of the previous level of functioning.

These observations led to an experiment to test if deterioration is an effect of imprisonment and whether it is characterized by a loss of cognitive efficiency and a lowering of motivation. Three groups were utilized. Group A consisted of prisoners who were serving their first sentences. Group B was a matched group of individuals on probation. The final group (C) consisted of longer term prisoners who had served previous sentences. Taylor (1961) predicted that this latter group would show more deterioration than the "first-termers" making up Group A. Tests were selected which measured word fluency, problem solving, speed and efficiency, and perception of social incongruity. Subjects were tested twice, with a six-month interval between the testing sessions.

Taylor reported that the hypothesis that deterioration is an effect of imprisonment was not supported. The only two tests reflecting any significant deterioration were Koh's Block Design Test and the McGill Delta Block Test. The author suggested that perhaps deterioration begins with cognitive functions and then spreads to a change of attitude, outlook, motivation, and emotional orientation.

Research has been conducted on social isolation by Ruff, Levy, and Thaler (1959) at the Aerospace Medical Laboratory at Wright-Patterson Air Force Base. Groups of five men were confined for a five-day period in a compartment 17 ft. long, 7 ft. wide, and 6 ft. high under simulated operational conditions. Behavioral measures were taken from the groups as a whole and from the individual members and included observation, objective and projective tests, and physiological and biochemical measures. Detailed results were not provided but the authors noted that crew members began their confinement periods with a positive attitude toward each other which was maintained throughout the five-day period.

Analysis of projective tests administered during confinement revealed a trend toward regressive behavior. Also noted were occasional transient signs of ego impairment which were most common during periods of maximum fatigue. On the other hand, subjects frequently appeared capable of more mature and flexible handling of certain conflict areas after confinement than before. The authors suggested that this may have represented a therapeutic effect of group support during a stressful experience.

In general, most subjects were able to handle conflicts with their characteristic methods of adaptation. The most common problem was the development of hostility toward other group members which was usually dealt with by the mechanisms of suppression, denial, and undoing.* Anger was seldom expressed directly though it often appeared in indirect form. Physiological and biochemical measures revealed individual variations from day to day but these did not follow any overall pattern. The authors concluded that on the whole, the experience was no more than moderately stressful.

Research conducted by the Navy Medical Neuropsychiatric Research Unit (Gunderson, 1963; Gunderson & Nelson, 1963) was aimed at measuring emotional reactions of scientists and naval personnel who experienced prolonged social isolation at stations in Antarctica. Each station operated under extreme conditions of climate. The groups were completely isolated and confined to small

* This would seem to contradict the previous statement that the subjects maintained a positive attitude toward one another.

quarters for many months, where they faced danger, hardship, restricted activity, and periods of inevitable monotony.

Questionnaires indicating the presence and intensity of a variety of somatic and emotional symptoms were given to a number of Antarctic groups on three occasions for each of two years. The first testing occurred at the end of the summer near the close of a period of great activity. The second testing occurred after three to four months of absolute isolation and relative inactivity. The final testing was administered at the end of a long winter at the beginning of limited outdoor activities. It was predicted that the second testing period would yield the most pronounced effects of the isolation experience.

The influence of the number of persons in a group was investigated by grouping subjects in terms of the number of men assigned to the stations. Thus members of three small stations (15–20 men), two medium-sized stations (30–40 men), and one large station (80–100 men) were grouped and compared for each of two expeditions.

Table 8–1 indicates the variations in incidence of symptoms as a function of size of station and year. Inspection of Table 8–1 reveals that the size of the group does not seem to be a factor in incidence of emotional and somatic complaints. The earlier of the two expeditions reported more emotional and physical difficulties. The most frequently reported symptoms in both expeditions were sleep disturbances and depression. Also frequently reported for both years were headaches, feeling easily annoyed or irritated, and soreness of muscles.

Table 8–2 shows the incidence of symptoms reported over the three time periods for all subjects. It is noted that items which consistently showed a low incidence, little variation over time, or no apparent relation to the clusters were not included in this table.

These data reveal a general trend toward an increased incidence of symptoms over time. Almost all the symptoms were reported by a higher percentage of subjects at midwinter than at prewinter in both years.

The symptoms showing significant shifts toward greater severity from pre- to midwinter testing in the first expedition included difficulty in falling asleep or staying asleep, waking up at night, bad dreams, feeling blue, feeling lonely, easily annoyed or irritated, feeling critical of others, headaches, feeling tired during the day, and pains in the lower back. Those showing significant shifts in

TABLE 8-1

INCIDENCE OF COMMON PHYSICAL AND EMOTIONAL SYMPTOMS IN ANTARCTIC GROUPS OF VARYING SIZE AT MIDWINTER[a]

(PERCENTAGES)

|  | Expedition I | | | | Expedition II | | | |
|---|---|---|---|---|---|---|---|---|
|  | Small | Medium | Large | Total | Small | Medium | Large | Total |
| Headaches | 51[b] | 35 | 41 | 41 | 33 | 34 | 27 | 31 |
| Pains in heart or chest | 18 | 11 | 25[b] | 19 | 17 | 18 | 10 | 15 |
| Heart pounding or racing | 18 | 11 | 31[b] | 22 | 17 | 18 | 23 | 19 |
| Nausea or upset stomach | 26 | 25 | 21 | 23 | 40[b] | 34 | 25 | 32 |
| Frequent urination | 36 | 25 | 45[b] | 36[c] | 12 | 26 | 25 | 22 |
| Soreness of muscles | 49[b] | 44 | 46 | 45[c] | 36 | 35 | 30 | 33 |
| Nervousness & shakiness | 21 | 11 | 20 | 18 | 17 | 14 | 27[b] | 19 |
| Difficulty sleeping | 64 | 76[b] | 71 | 72[c] | 67 | 52 | 40 | 51 |
| Feeling blue | 46 | 60[b] | 59 | 56[c] | 38 | 35 | 33 | 35 |
| Need to do things slowly | 26[b] | 15 | 18 | 19 | 24 | 12 | 23 | 19 |
| Objectionable thoughts | 31[b] | 24 | 21 | 24[c] | 14 | 17 | 13 | 14 |
| Feeling that people watching | 8 | 9 | 15 | 11 | 19 | 26[b] | 22 | 20 |
| Feeling lonely | 28 | 33 | 42 | 37 | 48[b] | 37 | 43 | 42 |
| Need to ask others what to do | 5 | 7 | 16 | 11 | 19 | 20 | 25[b] | 21 |
| Feel easily annoyed | 56[b] | 44 | 48 | 48[c] | 48 | 26 | 23 | 27 |
| Took alcohol or medicine | 13 | 13 | 26[b] | 19[c] | 7 | 8 | 5 | 7 |
| Tired during day | 41 | 46 | 40 | 42 | 48 | 65[b] | 53 | 54[c] |
| Waking up at night | 46 | 60[b] | 60[b] | 58[c] | 57 | 42 | 32 | 42 |
| N | 39 | 55 | 80 | 174 | 42 | 65 | 60 | 167 |

[a] Reprinted by permission from E. K. Gunderson, Arch. gen. Psychiat., 1963, 9, 362–368.

[b] Indicates subgroup with highest incidence of symptom; the percentage for that sample differs significantly from percentages for one or more of the other samples (p is less than .05, two-tailed test).

[c] Indicates that percentage is significantly greater (p is less than .05, two-tailed test) than that for total sample of other Expedition.

TABLE 8–2

INCIDENCE OF COMMON SYMPTOMS IN ANTARCTIC GROUPS AT
THREE TIME PERIODS[a]
(PERCENTAGES)

| | Expedition I | | | Expedition II | | |
|---|---|---|---|---|---|---|
| Item | 1st | 2nd | 3rd | 1st | 2nd | 3rd |
| Sleep disturbances: | | | | | | |
| Difficulty falling asleep or staying asleep | 34[b] | 72 | 54 | 31[b] | 51 | 49 |
| Waking up at night | 31[b] | 58 | 49 | 22[b] | 42 | 38 |
| Depression: | | | | | | |
| Feeling blue | 34[b] | 56 | 42 | 18[b] | 35 | 34 |
| Feeling lonely | 28[c] | 37 | 35 | 24[b] | 39 | 37 |
| Feeling people were watching or talking about you | 8 | 11 | 11 | 4[b] | 20 | 12 |
| Preferring to be alone[d] | 21[c] | 28 | 21 | | | |
| Being quiet and sad at parties | | | | 16[c] | 21 | 24 |
| Aggression: | | | | | | |
| Feeling easily annoyed or irritated | 35[c] | 49 | 46 | 19[b] | 27 | 34 |
| Feeling critical of others | 35[c] | 49 | 49 | | | |
| Finding others short-tempered or unkind | 14[b] | 30 | 39 | | | |
| Burning up with anger | | | | 4[b] | 14 | 17 |
| Anxiety: | | | | | | |
| Sudden fright for no apparent reason | 4 | 7 | 8 | 2[b] | 10 | 14 |
| Bad dreams | 6[c] | 18 | 20 | 8 | 11 | 9 |
| Nervousness and shakiness under pressure | 14 | 18 | 22 | 15 | 19 | 27 |
| Feeling uneasy without knowing why | 14 | 22 | 17 | 8 | 17 | 20 |
| Sudden noises making you jump | | | | 16[c] | 32 | 30 |
| Difficulty in making up your mind | | | | 8 | 19 | 19 |
| Somatic complaints: | | | | | | |
| Headaches | 24[c] | 41 | 43 | 31 | 31 | 31 |
| Pains in the heart or chest | 16 | 19 | 20 | 9[c] | 15 | 18 |
| Pains in lower part of back | 26[c] | 31 | 32 | 20 | 21 | 28 |
| Nausea or upset stomach | 19 | 23 | 19 | 26[b] | 32 | 38 |
| Itching | 12 | 15 | 13 | 17[c] | 27 | 27 |
| Unable to use eyes because of pain | | | | 8[c] | 11 | 11 |
| N | 112 | 177 | 130 | 98 | 168 | 90 |

[a] Reprinted by permission from E. Gunderson, *Arch. gen. Psychiat.*, 1963, **9**, 362–368.

[b] Significant change at the .01 level.

[c] Significant change from 1st to 2nd administrations at the .05 level by the binomial sign test.

[d] Administered in only one of the two expeditions.

the second expedition were the same and the severity tended to be of a larger magnitude. There was a rather wide range of individual differences with many of the men reporting slight, if any, deterioration.

Another study reported by Gunderson and Nelson (1963) using Antarctic groups discussed the development of a set of attitude measures dealing with individual reactions to and satisfaction with Antarctic life and the group's affective and work relationships. These measures revealed a general decline in work satisfaction, social relationships, and group accomplishments as a function of prolonged isolation. A point of great interest was that a few of the groups studied showed very little decline in these variables. Unfortunately, no information was provided on the nature of these non-deteriorating groups.

Mullin (1960) reported a study based on interviews of some eighty-five scientific and naval personnel, conducted at American Antarctic stations. The interviewing was conducted by two psychiatrists and two psychologists and occurred at the end of the wintering-over period at several small isolated stations (twelve to forty men). The men were questioned during two visits on successive years.

It appears that the physical danger, hardship, or extreme cold did not represent important stresses to the men. Indeed, the absence of hardship and danger was seen as a considerable disappointment to many of the younger members. The major stresses appeared to center around (1) individual adjustment to the group, (2) the "sameness" of the environment, and (3) the absence of many usual sources of gratification.

Any stress that was produced by the isolation was not manifested in overtly expressed hostility. Fights and angry arguments were very rare. To explain the probable repressed hostility, Mullin noted that, "group and individual tensions and irritations are ever present, but the most important lesson a wintering-over man learns is that he cannot afford to alienate the group; that in this tight little society he is dependent in large measure upon the goodwill of the next man and of the group as a whole for his vital feelings of security, worth and acceptance" (1960, pp. 323–324).

One way in which the stress and apparently repressed aggression were manifested was in the extraordinary frequency of headaches which could not be ascribed to any physical cause. Of particular interest was the finding that the officers and civilians had more headaches than the enlisted men. Mullin noted that the enlisted men had a variety of socially acceptable techniques for expressing their hostility and tensions, e.g., vigorous horseplay, loud complaining, and swearing. The more sophisticated officer-scientist members were more limited in their techniques of expression and were possibly under a greater self-imposed necessity for controlling their aggression.

A widespread phenomenon of the dark indoor winter season was insomnia. This difficulty in sleeping was attributed to the accumulation of tensions, reduced physical activity, group suggestibility, and an intense need for stimulation.

Another result of the isolation of the winter months was a widespread lack of intellectual energy. Most of the men had planned intellectual activities during their isolation, such as learning a language, correspondence courses, writing. Although there was a great deal of time available, few of the men even made a start on their projects. Related to this intellectual lethargy was the finding of impaired memory, alertness, and concentration among many of the men. Mullin reported that "it is probable that the intellectual anergia and impaired alertness . . . bear some relationship to the factor of prolonged exposure to 'sameness'—the same few faces and personalities, the same limited physical milieu, the same relatively simple routine of life—plus a long period of limited physical activity and mobility; or, in short, the effect of the reduction in the amount and variety of meaningful sensory stimulation over a prolonged period of time" (1960, pp. 324–325).

The majority of the men felt that they had accrued some positive benefits from the experience in terms of more self-discipline, greater adaptability and tolerance, more patience, and a better understanding of themselves and others. However, none of them expressed any overwhelming desire to repeat the experience.

Finally, relevant information is available from a review by Rohrer (1960) on submarine habitability and adjustment to polar isolation. Two major dimensions, size of group and length of stay, were considered to affect adjustment to polar isolation. The large station, numbering about 100 men, seemed to require less of an adjustment than small stations. Rohrer identified several distinct phases of adjustment to the polar social isolation. Phase I occurs on arrival at the station and may last for as long as six weeks. The chief characteristic during this period is a greatly heightened anxiety which results in increased aggression for some. Phase II occurs during the winter months of darkness, where the work load is lessened, with a corresponding increase in depression. Phase III occurs when the sun returns. Work activities increase with a corresponding decrease in depression.

Literature on submarine habitability also revealed an increased initial anxiety during the first exposure to isolation, which lasted, in some cases, as long as sixty hours. Rohrer noted the crew's preoccupation with food and suggested that this is the most important single factor in maintaining morale. A similar finding is reported in the study by Rasmussen (1963) below. One suggested way to reduce the anxiety of the initial hours in isolation is to engage the people in activities which are functionally oriented and meaningful to them.

Thus far, the discussion of small group social isolation has dealt primarily with studies conducted under naturalistic or field conditions using highly realistic confinement situations such as prison or Antarctic station. The remainder of this chapter will deal with research investigating psychological aspects of confinement in a fallout shelter. In the event of a nuclear attack, what will be the reactions of survivors facing a prolonged period of confinement in the limited space and probably overcrowded conditions of an underground shelter?

One such study was carried out by the American Institute for Research (Altman, Smith, Meyers, McKenna, & Bryson, 1960). Four groups of thirty subjects each were confined to a room 20 ft. long, 12 ft. wide, and 7 ft. high under four different conditions. The major experimental variables were temperature ranging from "comfortable" (74°F) to "hot" (85°F) and the presence or absence of a trained leader. Three groups were confined for one week while the fourth group remained for two weeks. Subjects were paid volunteers of both sexes and ranged in age from seven to seventy-two years.

The results of the study were quite optimistic with the authors reporting no apparent serious psychological or social stress in most of the subjects. The presence of trained leaders seemed to have a beneficial effect in that they increased the overall adjustment to the experience and also enhanced attitudes toward shelters and Civil Defense. Emotional agitation and tension were reported to be greatest immediately after entrance into the shelter and again just prior to release. Most subjects manifested a steadily increasing desire to leave but this seemed not to become overwhelming during the two-week maximum confinement period. The authors noted that adjustment to the confinement experience seemed to be a fairly direct reflection of the subjects' pre-shelter patterns of adjustment. There was little direct inter-personal conflict in all groups which was further minimized in the two groups functioning under a designated leader. There was also a rapid development of strong individual loyalties and a general high degree of group cohesion. Almost every subject from all groups commented, after confinement, that they could not have been confined with a better group.

The authors concluded that the results support the generally optimistic conclusions from shelter habitation studies undertaken in Sweden, Germany, and the United States, both with family and group shelters. The investigators encountered fewer and less severe problems than they had anticipated and noted that, "shelter confinement *per se* will not be overwhelmingly stressful if reasonable management, space, ventilation, temperature, sanitation, light, and sustenance are provided" (Altman *et al.*, 1960, pp. 96–97).

Rasmussen (1963) reported on two habitability studies sponsored by the Navy Bureau of Yards and Docks and conducted by the Naval Medical Research Institute. The first study was undertaken under winter conditions and the second under hot summer conditions, with both studies lasting two weeks. The subjects were volunteer seamen who had just completed basic training and who were subjected to very rigid medical and psychiatric screening. The author noted that 50 per cent of the volunteers were rejected for the summer test and 33 per cent for the winter test. Approximately 100 highly selected subjects served in each study. Two other conditions in reference to the subjects were introduced. First, they were not told how long they were going to be confined, and second, no reward of any kind was offered. These two conditions did allow for a more faithful simulation of actual shelter conditions in spite of the rigid selection standards.

The shelter is shown in Figure 8–1. The structure, five feet underground, was 48 ft. long and 25 ft. wide and was designed for a capacity of 100 people. It is interesting to note that the space provided was about one-tenth the roominess found on nuclear submarines.

To study psychological discomfort, subjects ranked twenty-one discomfort indices. The results of the ranking are shown in Table 8–3. The first column refers to discomfort which approached the limits of individual tolerance. The second column refers to discomfort which was present and noticeable over prolonged periods

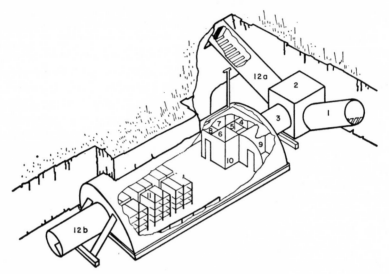

FIG. 8–1. Cutaway diagram of shelter.

KEY: 1—entrance; 2—Diesel generator room; 3—entry passage-blast door between 2 and 3 not shown; 4—trash room; 5—undressing room; 6—shower room; 7—filter room; 8—drying room; 9—chemical toilets (6); 10—washtub occupies this space; 11—bunks (changed during construction; now 5 double rows 5 bunks high, total of 50 bunks); 12a and 12b—emergency exits.

[Reprinted by permission from J. Rasmussen, *J. Amer. Dietetic Ass.*, 1963, **42**, 109–116.]

but which did not approach the limits of human tolerance. It can be seen that the leading source of discomfort for both winter and summer tests was the lack of water for washing. Food ranked second in the winter test but was lower in the summer test.

In the winter tests, debriefing interviews revealed lengthy and emotional complaints about the food. The high temperatures of the summer test produced a number of signs of heat stress including loss of appetite, apathy, and irritability. The debriefing interviews revealed a focus on the discomforts produced by heat, humidity, and dirt, and the existence of a greatly increased irritability with

## TABLE 8–3

### Subjective Importance of Discomfort Sources by Ranking Scale, Day 7, Winter and Summer Tests[a]

| Discomfort source | Acuteness of discomfort | Generality of discomfort |
|---|---|---|
| *Winter test* | | |
| Lack of water for washing | 1 | 1 |
| Food | 2 | 2 |
| Crowding of shelter | 3 | 3 |
| Dirt | 4 | 4 |
| Behavior of others | 5 | 5 |
| Boredom | 6 | 6 |
| Noise | 7 | 7 |
| Temperature and humidity | 8 | 9 |
| Toilet facilities | 9 | 12 |
| Lack of exercise | 10 | 11 |
| Odors | 11 | 8 |
| Bunks | 12 | 10 |
| Lack of privacy | 13 | 13 |
| Physical symptoms | 14 | 14 |
| Lights while sleeping | 15 | 15 |
| Lack of organization | 16 | 18 |
| Inability to concentrate | 17 | 16 |
| Concern about outside | 18 | 17 |
| Sleeping difficulty | 19 | 20 |
| Inadequate leadership | 20 | 19 |
| Lights while awake | 21 | 21 |
| *Summer test[b]* | | |
| Lack of water for washing | 1 | 1 |
| Food | 4 | 5 |
| Crowding of shelter | 5 | 3 |
| Dirt | 3 | 4 |
| Behavior of others | 8 | 8 |
| Boredom | 9 | 10 |
| Noise | 7 | 7 |
| Temperature and humidity | 2 | 2 |
| Toilet facilities | 15 | 14 |
| Lack of exercise | 12 | 12 |
| Odors | 6 | 6 |
| Bunks | 10 | 9 |
| Lack of privacy | 16 | 13 |
| Physical symptoms | 11 | 11 |
| Lights while sleeping | 14 | 16 |
| Lack of organization | 20 | 19 |
| Inability to concentrate | 17 | 17 |
| Concern about outside | 18 | 18 |
| Sleeping difficulty | 13 | 15 |
| Inadequate leadership | 21 | 21 |
| Lights while awake | 19 | 20 |

[a] Reprinted by permission from J. E. Rasmussen, *J. Amer. Dietetic Ass.*, 1963, **42**, 109–116.

[b] Listed in order of importance during winter test.

others. This, however, did not lead to overt aggressive behavior which was probably a function of the constant presence of several officer-observers. It is interesting to speculate on the results had the observers not out-ranked the subjects. In summary, Rasmussen noted that, "shelter equipment and/or factors in the physical environment ranked ahead of other people *per se* as sources of psychologic discomfort" (1963, p. 115).

## C. DISCUSSION

In Chapter I, social isolation was discussed as another method of restricting variable sensory input. Though less severe than sensory and perceptual deprivation techniques, social isolation nonetheless involves prolonged exposure to monotonous unchanging stimulation. True, the presence of other people in the small group isolation situation may provide meaningful and varied stimulation *for a time*, but prolonged confinement can minimize even this source of varied sensory input. The other people in the situation are, after all, almost as constant and unchanging (after repeated exposure to them) as the physical stimulation available. Thus, the sensoristatic model would predict many of the same types of behavioral and emotional impairments demonstrated under conditions of sensory and perceptual deprivation; albeit less severe impairments. Such impairments would also be expected to increase directly with time in isolation and inversely with the number of people in the confinement situation. In other words, longer confinement with only a few other people (or none at all) would be expected to produce greater impairments than shorter or longer confinements with a larger group.

Unfortunately, social deprivation has not been the subject of as much systematic research as has sensory and perceptual deprivation. Furthermore, much of what research is available has been handicapped by the lack of operationally defined concepts, appropriate objective measurement techniques, replication attempts, and general criteria of scientific rigor. With these serious limitations in mind, an overview of the work discussed in this area is offered.

Dealing with individual social isolation first, it was found that the most serious consequences occurred when the individual was alone. This situation most closely parallels the sensory and perceptual deprivation conditions. The anecdotal "data" discussed suggests an emotional deterioration similar in nature to that produced by sensory and perceptual deprivation as discussed in Chapter VI. One suspects that had tests of intelligence and perception been administered to these individuals undergoing years of confinement, they would have reflected deterioration more severe than that noted in the short-term sensory and perceptual deprivation studies.

Dealing with two subjects confined together (Haythorn, Altman, & Myers, 1965), a high degree of hostility engendered in the dyad in the relatively short ten-day confinement period was noted. It must also be remembered that in addition to the relatively short confinement period, the subjects were volunteers and had tasks to occupy seven hours of each day. It would be interesting to study comparable dyads confined for ten days with no work tasks to perform.

Dealing with a somewhat larger subject group (five), Ruff, Levy, and Thaler (1959) noted the existence of some emotional impairment though the experience as a whole was seen as only moderately stressful. Limiting factors of this study include the short five-day period of isolation and the fact that the subjects had work to perform.

The previously discussed investigations on the men in Antarctic confinement provide some data on the effects of long-term isolation. The subjects showed general emotional impairment which increased in severity as a function of time in confinement. Of particular interest is the finding that the size of the group seemed to have no relation to the incidence of emotional and somatic complaints in the reports of Gunderson (1963) and Gunderson and Nelson (1963). The small groups observed consisted of fifteen to twenty men while the largest consisted of eighty to one hundred men. The comment above that the larger the group, the fewer the disturbances is obviously not borne out by the above studies, but is in agreement with the review by Rohrer (1960). Perhaps it might be hypothesized that behavioral and emotional impairments can be minimized by the addition of group members only up to a certain number. Once this number is reached, adding new members might not add appreciably to the available sensory variation, perhaps due to the formation of cliques and subgroups in the very large groups. Thus, each individual would interact with and receive sensory variation from only the members of his particular subgroup, regardless of the size of the total group. This points to the need for a systematic research program involving carefully observed effects on individuals in dyads, triads, and so on, to determine the point of diminishing returns.

Also of great interest is the finding that not all individuals or groups showed adverse effects of social isolation. This points again to individual differences in tolerance for conditions of isolation and to the practical, as well as theoretical, importance of developing valid predictive techniques. Also needed is research to identify predictive factors for group tolerance of isolation. The influence of such factors as group composition, leadership behaviors, and other group characteristics is presently unknown. Equally open to research efforts is the problem of introducing effective levels of sensory variation into the monotonous little-changing world of social isolation. A number of techniques have been suggested, *e.g.*, games, exercises, presence of women, but little if any research has been performed. In short, the area of social deprivation may be in the same position that sensory and perceptual deprivation found itself eight to ten years ago—systematic research is sorely needed.

Research of Zubek and his associates previously reported is of relevance. Some of these studies utilized two different control groups: ambulatory and recumbent. The ambulatory groups simply came to the laboratory at appointed times for testing. The recumbent control condition, however, resembles the small group social isolation situation. In Zubek, Aftanas, Hasek, Sansom, Schludermann, Wilgosh, and Winocur (1962), the recumbent control subjects were confined for one week in groups of five or six in a windowless room 24 ft. long and 12 ft. wide. Subjects were required to lie quietly on mattresses except when eating or using the washroom. Except for these restrictions on gross body movements, the environment was quite normal with the subjects being able to talk, read, listen to the radio, and watch television. They were not allowed to see the outside world, however. Tests of intelligence and perception as described in Chapters IV and V were administered.

On the tests of numerical reasoning, space relations, and verbal fluency, the recumbent controls performed at a lower level than the ambulatory control subjects. Only on numerical reasoning, however, were these differences significant. The other nine tests of intelligence produced no difference between the ambulatory and recumbent positions. There were no differences reported on the perceptual tests. Upon release from confinement, many of the recumbent controls reported the subjective experiences of increased brightness of objects, vividness of colors, and feelings of detachment. These experiences were noted by almost the same number of recumbent controls as those who underwent a week of perceptual deprivation in complete isolation (see Chapters IV and V).

Thus, there is some indication that certain intellectual functions may be impaired under social isolation. It is noted that the subjects were exposed to a relatively rich and varying sensory environment provided particularly by radio and television. It would be interesting to replicate this approach with a reduced level of sensory stimulation, i.e., without television and radio. A greater level of impairment would be predicted under these conditions.

Finally, brief mention is made of the effects of social isolation as experienced in the fallout shelter habitability studies. Both studies were quite optimistic about life among the subterranean survivors and noted the existence of no apparent serious psychological or social stress. Indeed, it might almost be looked upon as a pleasant holiday—away from the cares of the world! One would hope, of course, to be confined with an equally highly selected group of compatriots and a firm, but friendly, group leader who is respected by all—as long as he has the shotgun!

Editorializing aside, there are two important differences between these studies and the Antarctic observations which produced more serious effects. The most obvious difference is the shorter confinement period utilized in the fallout shelter studies. Second, these subjects were able to leave if the situation became intolerable, a benefit not allowed in the polar stations.

# CHAPTER IX

# Summary and Discussion

## A. SUMMARY

The time is at hand for summation and reflection. First, a brief review of the findings in the preceding chapters would seem to be in order, along with a check on the predictions set forth earlier. The seven predictions of the sensoristatic model are noted again.

(1) Conditions of reduced sensory input will result in measurable changes in activation level.

(2) The sensoristatic drive state is induced by conditions of restricted sensory variation input and becomes increasingly intense as a function of time and amount of deprivation or restriction.

(3) When conditions of sensory restriction disturb the sensoristatic balance, the organism will exhibit gross disturbances of functioning, e.g., perception, cognition, learning.

(4) When stimulus variation is restricted, central regulation of threshold sensitivities will function to lower sensory thresholds. Thus, the organism becomes increasingly sensitized to stimulation in an attempt to restore the balance.

(5) Organisms will exhibit evidence of learning in situations where the only apparent reinforcement is a change in sensory variation. Thus, under conditions of sensory restriction, increases in stimulus variability will have reinforcing properties.

(6) There exist individual differences in the need for sensory variation. These individual differences may be partially due to the early postnatal levels of stimulation as discussed in Chapter II.

(7) Reduction of the patterning of stimulus input will result in greater behavioral effects than simply reduction of the level of stimulation. Deprivation of variation in stimulation rather than level of stimulation per se, induces a more intense sensoristatic drive state. Hence, behavioral disturbances should be greater under perceptual deprivation conditions than under sensory deprivation conditions, as these were defined in Chapter I.

Chapter III noted a variety of physiological effects as a consequence of sensory restriction. A progressive slowing of the frequencies of brain waves in the alpha band was demonstrated which seemed to persist for some time after release from isolation. This disturbance of electrical activity of the brain was greater under perceptual deprivation than sensory deprivation. Also suggested was the possibility of fluctuation in brain wave activity as a function of the stimulus variation provided by talking and reported hallucinations. Similarly, the performance of physical exercise, with its attendant kinesthetic and proprioceptive stimulation, was shown to offset to some degree the effects of sensory restriction.

A somewhat consistent decrease in the electrical resistance of the skin as measured by GSR was demonstrated. Rather consistent increases appeared in cutaneous and pain sensitivities with some suggestion of an increase in visual and auditory sensitivities. This supports the contention of Vernon, McGill, Gulick, and Candland (1961) that the sensorily deprived individual becomes more attuned to any and all stimulation. Thus, Chapter III is seen as providing evidence in support of Predictions 1, 4, 6, and 7.

Dealing with cognitive functions, evidence introduced in Chapter IV revealed that most subjects in sensory and perceptual deprivation conditions reported difficulties in directed thinking, concentration, etc., to a rather high degree. Objective tests of intellectual functioning, however, did not reveal as severe an impairment. Some functions, such as verbal reasoning, arithmetic problems, and digit span, showed no impairment under any form of sensory restriction while other functions showed impairment under one type of restriction but not under another.

The evidence indicates a somewhat greater impairment under perceptual as opposed to sensory deprivation. What functions are impaired under sensory restriction seem to be restored to their pre-confinement levels once a normal level of sensory input is reinstated. There is also an indication (Zubek, Aftanas, Hasek, Sansom, Schludermann, Wilgosh, & Winocur, 1962) that the intellectual impairments that do occur do not get any worse with time in isolation. It was even suggested that, at least in some cases, the degree of impairment might decrease toward the end of confinement. Body immobilization for seven days produced some impairments though not as severe as sensory or perceptual deprivation. Finally, the role of exercise in eliminating many impairments was noted.

Of great interest for further research was the suggestion that some cognitive abilities might show an improvement under sensory restriction. The evidence was, however, contradictory. The proposition that a subject may be rendered more persuasible under sensory restriction received some degree of support and the implications of this for a brainwashing technique were noted. Chapter IV, then, provides evidence to support Predictions 3, 6, and 7.

The data reviewed in Chapter V dealing with perceptual effects again reveal a discrepancy between self-reports and objective test results. Most subjects undergoing sensory restriction reported a rather wide range of perceptual disturbances during isolation which persisted, in some cases, for as much as one day after isolation. Objective tests of perceptual functioning, however, have not revealed such a wide range of perceptual deterioration. There is some indication that the effects that do occur are generally greater under perceptual deprivation, though there were exceptions. The objectively reported impairments showed very little persistence beyond the period of confinement. Body immobilization produced some impairments, though the range of effects was not as great as under sensory or perceptual deprivation. Finally, the effect of exercise was again shown to counteract the effects of isolation to a great degree. Some evidence is thus provided to support Predictions 3, 6, and 7.

Chapter VI revealed evidence indicating varying degrees of emotional impairment in subjects undergoing sensory restriction, which effects often, but not always, increased in severity as a function of time in isolation. However, some subjects reported no negative changes whatsoever in affective feeling states. Perhaps a self-selection factor is operative in that people who consider themselves to be low in stress resistance fail to volunteer for this kind of research. Data were also presented which suggest a possible therapeutic value of sensory restriction when dealing with selected types of hospitalized patients. Patients may be rendered more susceptible to therapeutic suggestions after a period of isolation but there was no evidence to indicate that sensory restriction, *per se,* can effect lasting personality changes. Some evidence, then, is available to support Predictions 3 and 7.

Chapter VII dealt with a variety of techniques attempting to predict a person's tolerance for sensory restriction. In general, most of the attempts at prediction, using paper-and-pencil and projective tests, provided very discouraging and inconsistent results. However, the very important work of Wright (1964) using a larger sample and the multiple discriminant function of analysis, did indicate a very high predictive value of a combination of variables from paper-and-pencil tests. Wright's work further suggested that the Rorschach may be a more valid predictor than even a combination of the most discriminating measures from more objective tests. The other approach discussed which is highly promising involves the subject's actual behavior in a previous confinement situation. Zuckerman's work, showing that those subjects demonstrating a higher arousal in an initial period of isolation were less tolerant of a later period of isolation, has important implications for the sensoristatic position. Support for Predictions 5 and 6 is noted in this chapter.

A less severe form of sensory restriction, social isolation, was the topic of discussion in Chapter VIII. This area has not been the subject of as intensive or systematic research as has sensory and perceptual deprivation. Thus the findings are more speculative or suggestive than those discussed in previous chapters. The findings on the effects of social isolation are also limited by the general lack of physiological or other objective test measures. In general, it seems that individual social isolation produced the most severe effects as compared to isolation with a small group. However, even confinement with a group of other people seemed to produce emotional and cognitive impairments when the period of confinement was as long as several months. Some support is suggested by these findings for Predictions 3, 6, and 7.

## B. EXPERIMENTAL TECHNIQUES TO DEMONSTRATE A DRIVE FOR STIMULATION

The major question of interest in this section is how to submit the sensoristatic drive for stimulus variation to experimental test within the framework of research on sensory restriction. In a paper presented to the 1964 annual meeting of the American Psychological Association, Jones discussed five different research strategies or techniques for the demonstration of drive associated with sensory restriction. Three of these approaches provide direct tests for the drive concept; the other two provide indirect tests.

The first of the direct tests involves allowing the subject to execute an instrumental escape response. In virtually every study reported in the preceding chapters, subjects were able to terminate the isolation experience whenever they felt they could no longer continue. A number of studies discussed in Chapter VII reported data on "quitters," but none have utilized the escape procedure as a direct test of the drive hypothesis. Jones suggests that such a procedure would be relatively simple. The independent variable could be either different lengths of confinement and/or different degrees of severity of sensory restriction. "Dependent variables would be latency or amplitude of the escape response, or, for Ss having received pre-training, resistance to extinction. Should latencies be found shorter and amplitudes greater over increasing lengths of deprivation, support for the drive hypothesis would be inferred" (Jones, 1964, p. 3). It is suggested that support for Prediction 2 would also be inferred.

The second direct test suggested by Jones would involve an avoidance response in which the subject is permitted some response which would prevent or delay confinement. Nothing of this sort has appeared in the literature but a variation of this procedure has been reported in a number of studies by Rossi and Solomon (1964a, 1964b, 1964c, 1964d). In their research, subjects undergoing perceptual deprivation were permitted a button-pressing response which resulted in "time-off" (in the form of a shortened duration of isolation) but did not provide immediate escape or avoidance.

The first two studies (Rossi & Solomon, 1964a) investigated (1) whether the activity involved in button-pressing would be rewarding in itself, independent of a time-off reward; and (2) the existence of any relation between amount of button-pressing for a time-off reward and descriptions of feeling states while in isolation. In both studies, the subject sat in a lounge chair in a sound-attenuated, air-conditioned cubicle with translucent halved ping-pong balls covering eyes and white noise presented through earphones. Subjects were not told how long they would be confined but were told that the period would not exceed five hours. A button was strapped to the subject's preferred hand and he was told that his time in isolation would be reduced by two minutes for every 100 button-presses. Thus, 3000 button-presses would reduce the time by one hour, and so on. Actually, the time was not reduced at all, regardless of the number of button presses. All subjects spent three hours in isolation no matter how many times they pressed the button.

In Study I, ten subjects were placed in isolation exactly one week apart. On one occasion they were told button-pressing would result in time off (as above). On the other occasion they were told button-pressing could be engaged in to relieve any felt need for activity. The results indicated that button-pressing for time off was significantly greater than for activity reward. Four of the subjects in the "time-off" condition pressed the button over 14,000 times. Of great interest is that four subjects did not press the button *at all* under either condition.

In Study II, nine different subjects were isolated under the "time-off" reward instructions. After isolation they completed an adjective check list which described pleasant states, unpleasant states, or neutral states. The results indicated that the percentage of pleasant adjectives varied inversely with amount of button-pressing while the percentage of unpleasant adjectives varied directly with amount of button-pressing.

In another study by Rossi and Solomon (1964d), ten subjects were confined in two isolation sessions one week apart, with one session being more uncomfortable than the other. The conditions of isolation were the same as reported above with several exceptions. In the "comfortable" session, rubber goggles with paper-covered lens were used instead of the ping-pong balls, and white noise was presented by a loudspeaker rather than through earphones. In the "uncomfortable" session, halved ping-pong ball eyecups were attached firmly, earphones were used for the white noise, and the cubicle temperature was kept between 85°F and 90°F. Before and after each session, the subject rated his state of well-being on a semantic differential-type scale. The results indicated that significantly more button-pressings occurred in the uncomfortable session than in the comfortable one. The ratings of well-being were lower in the uncomfortable session as compared to the comfortable session.

Another report by Rossi and Solomon (1964b) investigated the effects of three different amounts of time-off rewards: one minute, two minutes, and three minutes off for every 200 button-presses. The conditions of isolation were the same as those described above

(Rossi & Solomon, 1964a). The results indicated a significant positive relationship between amount of button-pressing and amount of time-off reward. There were no significant differences in the mean responses for the three one-hour segments. Subjects responded equally during the first, second, and third hours of confinement.

Jones (1964) suggests that this technique used by Rossi and Solomon could be used, with slight variation, to provide a more direct test of the drive hypothesis by a design similar to that discussed under the escape procedure. He suggests that subjects be kept in isolation for varying periods of time before being allowed to button-press for time off. If the response rate is found to increase directly with length of prior deprivation, then support for the drive concept and for Prediction 2 could be inferred.

The escape and avoidance paradigms as discussed thus far ignore one major question: what aspects of the restricted stimulus environment motivate escape and avoidance responses? What characteristics of sensory input serve as reinforcers of the escape or avoidance responses? The reference here is to the specific properties or characteristics of stimuli sequences as discussed in Chapter II (e.g., Berlyne's "collative" properties; Jones' statistical properties of information, complexity, and fluctuation). Two approaches were suggested to clarify this aspect of the drive process. First, the sensory environment to which a subject could "escape" might be varied. Thus, environments differing in complexity, incongruity, surprisingness, information, etc., to which the subject can expose himself might be provided. Thus, as Jones suggests,

> If Ss regularly make escape responses which propel them into an environment rich in information but do not make escape responses which propel them into an environment rich in complex but predictable stimuli (which contain no information), then the drive process would be demonstrated as contingent upon the lack of information in the deprived environment rather than upon the undifferentiated clutter of dimensions simultaneously manipulated in most experiments (Jones, 1964, p. 5).

An alternative approach would be to selectively eliminate the various properties of stimuli in the isolation session and note which characteristic(s) resulted in the strongest escape or avoidance responses.

A similar procedure is provided by Jones' third suggested direct test of the drive hypothesis which he calls the "consummatory" procedure. In this approach, subjects are exposed to sensory restriction for varying periods of time before being allowed to make instrumental responses which introduce stimuli possessing specific properties. Jones reported on several studies which found initial response rates to be a direct linear function of prior deprivation. These results were obtained using the stimulus property of information as an incentive condition. He interprets these results as supportive of a drive interpretation of information deprivation. No support was found for drive processes associated with Jones' two other statistical properties of stimuli: complexity or fluctuation. In the work of Zuckerman and Haber (1965) discussed in Chapter VII, subjects in isolation were permitted a response which exposed them to a random tone series or a random array of colored strips. There was a significant increase in response rate over the three-hour session which suggested the operation of a cumulative motivational process. This suggests support for Prediction 2.

An indirect strategy suggested by Jones involves the use of physiological measures of arousal, such as the EEG and GSR. The study by Zuckerman, Levine, and Biase (1964) discussed in Chapters II and VII illustrates this approach. Subjects were isolated for three hours under one of three conditions: visual deprivation, auditory deprivation, or visual and auditory deprivation. Nonspecific GSR measures were significantly higher when both visual and auditory modalities were deprived than when only one was restricted. Zuckerman and Haber (1965) took from this previous experiment twelve high GSR responder subjects and twelve low responders. In a three-hour session of visual and auditory restriction, the high GSR responders made significantly more responses for the random visual or auditory stimulation described above than did the low responders. Thus, the two groups might be considered as differing in the drive level with which they entered isolation.

The second indirect approach suggested by Jones involves the use of verbal report. A serious limitation, as has been noted in the preceding chapters, is the oft-reported discrepancy between verbal report and other indices. Jones suggests that a possible reason for this discrepancy may be due to the demand characteristics of the experiment as discussed below (Orne, 1962).

The discussion now turns to a consideration of variables other than reduction of sensory input which might serve to confound some of the results reported in sensory restriction research.

## C. THE ROLE OF SET OR SUGGESTION

Several writers have suggested that perhaps some of the behavioral effects of sensory restriction may be due, in part, to preconfinement anticipations or expectations on the part of the subjects. The reference here is to the demand characteristics of Orne (1962) and Orne and Scheibe (1964), and to suggestion or set.

Orne uses the term "demand characteristics" to refer to certain implicit and explicit cues that indicate to the subject what is expected of him in the experimental situation, and so bias his response. Thus, Orne is concerned with the subject's perception of the experiment as a social situation. The results of an experiment are seen as including two distinct components: (1) the true experimental effect entirely contingent upon the antecedence of the independent variable, and (2) the effect induced by the social cues that attend the experimental situation. This latter effect is unrelated to the independent variable.

Orne and Scheibe (1964) contend that some of the rather dramatic effects produced in many of the sensory restriction studies may result from the demand characteristics of the situation. They note the existence of a number of subtle cues in sensory restriction experiments which may serve to bias the subject's behavior, independent of the restriction of sensory input. They suggest, for example, that the use of a panic button may function in the manner of "instructions," serving to increase the subject's expectation that he may be in for an unpleasant experience. Psychiatric and physical examinations administered in some studies may similarly affect the subject's expectations. The mere presence of observation windows and microphones may serve as "instructions" for as one of Orne and Scheibe's subjects remarked, "If you didn't expect to see or hear something unusual, why were you looking and listening?" (1964, p. 4).

Orne and Scheibe performed an experiment to determine if the effects usually produced under sensory restriction could be produced in a situation where there was no sensory restriction, but which did contain the cues usually found in sensory restriction research. The experimental group of male subjects were exposed to pre-isolation conditions designed to imply that certain effects were expected to emerge. The same conditions were structured for the control group in such a way as to lead them to expect nothing to happen.

The isolation chamber in which the experimental subjects were individually confined was a small room furnished with a desk and two chairs, and was amply illuminated. Sounds from other parts of the building and from outside were clearly audible and there were no restrictions on movement. Food and water were provided in the room. A simple arithmetic task was provided but it was made clear that the subject could do as little or as much as he wished, or none at all. Subjects were not told how long they were to be confined and all were released after four hours. It can be seen that the isolation experience was definitely not of the sensory or perceptual deprivation variety. It more closely parallels the social isolation procedure as discussed in Chapter VIII.

Prior to and after isolation, a battery of ten tests of cognitive and perceptual abilities was administered. The tests chosen were some of those on which previous investigators had reported significant impairments as a result of sensory restriction: mirror tracing, spatial orientation, word recognition, reversible figures, digit-symbol, test of mechanical ability, simple form perception, size constancy, spiral aftereffect, and logical deductions. In addition, a post-isolation interview was held with each subject.

The results indicated that the two groups differed significantly on a number of tests. Also, data based on subjective reports of the subjects and on the experimenters' clinical impressions indicated that the experimental subjects exhibited a significantly greater number of sensory and perceptual deprivation "symptoms" than did the control subjects. The authors concluded that a subject's behavior can be differentially manipulated by altering the implicit and explicit cues in the experimental situation. Orne and Scheibe (1964) did not suggest that sensory or perceptual deprivation does not produce effects on behavior, but they do point out that the demand characteristics of the experimental situation may be an important confounding variable. Further research was suggested to determine the actual extent to which the reported behavioral effects of sensory restriction are related to the reduction of sensory input. One approach suggested was to use conditions of maximal sensory restriction while varying the demand characteristics. In this manner, the situation could be structured in various ways so that different groups perceive the sensory restriction as a means to a variety of experimental purposes. "It is not possible to eliminate demand characteristics, but they can be varied with relative ease. Cues provided by the deprivation manipulations themselves must remain fairly constant, but the other cues can be systematically varied, thereby creating a variety of totally distinct sets of demand characteristics for different groups. Such studies would go far toward clarifying the actual effects of reduced sensory input" (Orne & Scheibe, 1964, pp. 11–12).

Jackson and Kelly (1962) investigated the role of suggestion and prior knowledge in sensory restriction research. The fourteen male subjects were confined for only one hour under perceptual deprivation. Prior to confinement, subjects were given information regarding the anticipated results, *i.e.,* they were told of unusual images, ideas, feelings, and so on, reported by previous subjects. The subjects were also given an "hallucinogenic drug" (actually a placebo), told that unusual experiences were quite normal under these circumstances, and instructed to report on their thoughts, images, *etc.,* during confinement.

Most of the subjects reported experiences similar to and as extreme as those reported in longer confinement sensory restriction studies. For instance, twelve of the subjects reported visual experiences and all fourteen reported auditory experiences. All subjects complained of cognitive difficulties and twelve reported some degree of emotional impairment.

Jackson and Pollard (1962, 1963) discussed three non-deprivation variables which they suggest are capable of biasing the results of sensory restriction research, particularly in studies of eight hours or less duration. These confounding variables include: (1) the subject's set or expectations about what is "supposed" to happen, (2) the subject's motivation to perform in accordance with or contrary to these expectations, and (3) the effects of using "free associative-like" experimental instructions.

In the article by Jackson and Pollard (1962), emphasis is placed on the realization that more and more subjects have varying degrees of knowledge about expected results of sensory restriction research due to its increasing popularity. They also note that even if subjects are naive at the time of the experiment, the demand characteristics (in Orne's terms) of the situation are highly provocative and suggestive. Also, they note that the pre-isolation instructions often provide a great deal of information about what is expected to occur. For example, Pollard, Uhr, and Jackson (1962) exposed twenty-four subjects who received no information about expected effects to eight hours of sensory deprivation. Another group of twelve subjects were provided information about previous studies and were confined for only three hours. The results indicated that the average number of reported experiences for the "suggestion" group was significantly greater than for the non-suggestion group, even though the latter were in isolation five hours longer.

Jackson and Pollard (1963) reported on a most interesting study designed to investigate the effects of the confounding variables listed above in affecting the reported results of sensory restriction research. A group of forty-eight college students were given several questionnaires. One set of questions related to general experimental sophistication and included biographical information, previous experience as a subject, sources of knowledge about sensory deprivation, and knowledge about sensory deprivation. The subjects' expectations were determined by asking for their predictions about sensory deprivation effects based on their own previous knowledge and a brief description given them of a deprivation situation. Additional questionnaires related to naturally occurring unusual experiences.

None of the subjects reported that they had ever participated in sensory restriction research, though half of them had participated in one or more psychological experiments. Three-fourths of the subjects checked one or more sources of information about sensory restriction, with textbooks and courses being the most prevalent. Subjects described a wide variety of expected effects of sensory restriction: becoming neurotic or psychotic, subjects can't stand it, hallucinations, increased anxiety, abnormal effects, quick fatigue.

Next, subjects were asked if they would volunteer for a deprivation experiment and twenty-eight of the forty-eight said that they would. For half of these, curiosity was the major motivation for volunteering.

Subjects were then provided with a description of a deprivation experiment and asked to predict various effects during isolation. Forty-five of the subjects predicted effects in one or more of the following categories: fears, anxieties, disorganized thoughts, delusions, hallucinations, body seeming to be of abnormal size. The authors suggested that, "a simple description of the experimental conditions is sufficient to permit people to make very specific statements about what 'will' happen. Exposure to the experiment itself is probably sufficient to stimulate many very particular expectations" (Jackson & Pollard, 1963, pp. 5–6).

Subjects were also asked to predict post-deprivation performance on tests of cognitive, motor, and perceptual abilities relative to pre-deprivation performance. Approximately 75 per cent of the subjects predicted that post-deprivation performance would indicate impairments on the functions tested.

Of particular interest and significance were the data on naturally occurring unusual experiences. Over 75 per cent of the subjects reported one or more unusual experiences (occurring in their natural environments) with the largest number reported in the thinking category. Reported feeling states consisted of irrational fears, depression, anxiety, and mood swings. Visual hallucinatory-type experiences were reported as well as some auditory experiences. In brief, then, a large number of these subjects reported experiences similar to those reported by subjects in sensory restriction research. It is emphasized that these reported experiences were not produced by isolation techniques, but seemed to occur in the normal everyday lives of the subjects. It is interesting to speculate, of course, on the possible role of demand characteristics, suggestion, etc., on the subjects in responding to this questionnaire. It seems that the subjects were specifically asked to report unusual experiences with categories specified for them, i.e., visual, auditory, taste, etc. It might reasonably be asked if this research designed to investigate the role of such confounding variables on sensory restriction research might not itself be influenced by the same variables.

Jackson and Pollard's study (1963) does suggest, however, that a group of subjects similar to groups typically chosen for deprivation experiments are quite sophisticated and do seem to enter the situation with numerous expectations of what "should" happen to them and what is expected of them. The reporting of the unusual experiences is in accord with Jackson and Pollard's suggestion that these ordinarily repressed sensations and thoughts may be elicited during deprivation because of different expectations, a permissive free-associative atmosphere, and suggestion.

As noted above with Orne and Scheibe, Jackson and Pollard do not suggest that all the reported effects of sensory and perceptual deprivation are due to extra-deprivation variables. They do suggest, however, that these non-deprivation factors must be considered when interpreting past research and designing future research.

Not all research designed to investigate the possible confounding role of set, suggestion, and the like, have reported such affirmative results. Zuckerman and Cohen (1964b) reported a study which attempted to test the role of expectations and positive suggestion on reported visual sensations during isolation. The subjects were fifty-eight males and were divided into a control group and three suggestion groups. All groups were confined for one hour under perceptual deprivation. Prior to confinement, subjects were interviewed to determine their prior knowledge of the results of sensory restriction research and their expectations as to their own reactions.

The control group (I, $N = 15$) were told that they would be confined for one hour and were asked not to sleep, to move as little as possible, and to make no noise except when reporting their experiences. They were told to report during isolation their thoughts, images, daydreams, *etc.*

Group II (mild suggestion group, $N = 15$) was given the same instructions as the control group. In addition, however, they were told that peculiar thoughts and unusual experiences such as images, were entirely normal under the circumstances.

Group III (mild suggestion and placebo group, $N = 15$) was given the same instructions as Groups I and II. They were also given a pill to take and told the following: "Because of the short time you will spend under these conditions of sensory deprivation you are being given a drug which will facilitate these unusual experiences including hallucinations and odd feelings" (p. 656).

Group IV (extended suggestion and placebo group, $N = 13$) was given two pills and even stronger suggestions as to the occurrence of images and other unusual experiences under the conditions.

The results indicated no relationship between reports of visual sensations and either the subjects' previous knowledge of the effects of sensory restriction or their expectations as these were determined in the pre-confinement interviews. The results of the four conditions revealed that only the least structured and meaningful type of reported visual sensation increased with suggestion. The authors noted as questionable whether such reports could be considered "hallucinations."

In an effort to determine if other kinds of responses could have been influenced by suggestion, the authors rated post-isolation interviews on the following variables: manifest anxiety, need for activity, claustrophobic response, disorientation for time and place, somatic discomforts, paranoid-like feelings, and a number of other frequently reported responses to sensory isolation. Analysis of the four groups revealed that none of the variables yielded frequency distributions which differed significantly from chance.

The authors noted that the lack of significant differences was accounted for by the high percentages of reported visual sensations in the control and mild suggestion groups. Thus, the results point to the need for control groups in research on the role of suggestion.

Another study which did not find positive effects of set was reported by Myers, Murphy, and Terry (1962) as part of the HumRRO program. The 120 enlisted Army personnel serving as subjects were asked to predict the experimental outcomes of four days of sensory deprivation without actually undergoing four days of confinement. Subjects were confined for only thirty minutes in the experimental cubicles and then given a description of the four-day condition. Following this they were given an objective questionnaire of 242 items which included a variety of feelings and reactions grouped into twenty-three categories or factors. Some of these factors included reported visual sensations, speech difficulties, dreams, loss of touch with reality, lonesomeness, temporal orientation, anger, worry and fright. The subjects were asked to judge whether the items would apply with greater than normal frequency, normal frequency, or less than normal frequency to an imagined four-day period of confinement.

These predicted frequencies were then compared with actually obtained frequencies from previous research using 115 cubicle and 116 control subjects. The cubicle subjects had completed the questionnaire on termination of ninety-six hours of isolation while the control subjects completed them after four days of normal

Army life. Cubicle subjects had reported greater frequency on nineteen of the twenty-three factors. A rather wide discrepancy between predicted and obtained frequencies was reported. The predicted frequencies were correct on only four factors and incorrect on the remaining nineteen factors. Furthermore, the errors in prediction were not all slight displacements. For example, nine of the nineteen incorrect predictions represented actual contradictions.

The authors concluded that the expected or desired results by the experimenters were apparently not so transparent to the subjects even when they were given a description of the experiment and exposed to a brief confinement session. It might be suggested that the Army personnel subjects in this study differ in terms of pre-experiment knowledge of sensory deprivation and in general research sophistication from the college student subjects used in other studies investigating set or suggestion. In departments of psychology which are very active in research, the college sophomore (or even freshman) has usually been exposed as a subject to a variety of research studies. The college student may be more highly motivated to help (or hinder) the experimenter. Many basic texts in psychology now include information about sensory and perceptual deprivation research providing knowledge of the effects of such research which might not be available to the Army subject.

At any rate, enough data is available which demonstrates the possible confounding effect of pre-confinement set or suggestion to indicate its importance in the design of future research.

## D. THE VOLUNTEER SUBJECT

One serious limitation of the vast research discussed in the earlier chapters is the restriction of the subject population to volunteers. This problem, of course, is not unique to sensory restriction research—most psychological research involving human subjects must deal with this limitation. Since, however, personality variables may be relevant, as discussed in Chapter VII, it is possible that volunteers may represent a unique personality constellation which may influence the results of sensory restriction research. Furthermore, the rather restricted range of educational and other background factors found in a college population may serve to impose additional limitations on the generality of the data.

Myers (1964b) supplies the following data on the nature of volunteer and non-volunteer populations. He noted that of the 551 enlisted Army personnel in the HumRRO program to whom the research was described, approximately 73 per cent volunteered to undergo the ninety-six hours of sensory deprivation. It is noted that, in contrast to the majority of the research using college students, the HumRRO Army subjects received no monetary rewards for volunteering. Myers reported that the two most frequently given reasons for volunteering were (1) wanting to contribute to a scientific effort, and (2) wanting to see how they would react to the stressful situation. Others said they volunteered because they wanted to use the time to think about personal problems, to plan for the future, or to catch up on their sleep.

Of those who did not volunteer, a large number said they were afraid they would not be able to last the full time and would thus fail themselves and the experimenters. Other reasons given for not volunteering included dislike of being in the dark for a long period of time, being too restless to do nothing for four days, and concern about the palatability of the liquid diet.

Biographical and personality test data were secured from all subjects, both volunteers and non-volunteers. Background data obtained included age, education, marital status, basis of Army duty (volunteer or draftee), integrity of home, size of family, order of birth, and smoking habits. The following tests were administered: MMPI, EPPS, achievement scale of the Iowa Picture Inventory Test; and from the Army battery, the General Technical aptitude (a general intelligence measure), and the Combat Information sub-test (predictive of potential performance under the stresses of combat).

The results indicated that the volunteers for confinement tended to be younger than non-volunteers, and generally had volunteered for the Army instead of being draftees. The volunteers were higher in aptitude for stressful combat duty and were lower in Depression and Psychopathic Deviancy (MMPI) than the non-volunteers. Also, there were nonsignificant trends toward lower scores in Hysteria and Psychasthenia (MMPI) among the volunteers. Myers concluded that these differences seemed to indicate that the volunteer subject is a sounder and more stable personality than the non-volunteer.

A replication of this approach attempting to distinguish volunteer from non-volunteer would certainly seem to be in order using the traditional college student subject group. Should such results verify Myers' findings, the generality of the sensory restriction data is indeed subject to cautious interpretation.

## E. BODY IMMOBILIZATION

Zubek (1963a) suggested that the degree of motor activity permitted during isolation may be one of the most important variables operating in sensory and perceptual deprivation experiments. He further suggested that some of the apparently contradictory results reported in the literature may be related to differences in motor activity. In some of the studies reviewed in the previous chapters, subjects were not restricted in terms of body movement, in other studies subjects were allowed to get out of bed only for toilet activities, while in others, cardboard cuffs on arms and legs, and instructions, restricted movement a great deal. In the tank-type respirator studies and the body immobilization studies of Zubek and his associates, motor activity was severely restricted. Thus, a somewhat wide range of motor activity is evident in past research.

The degree of motor activity permitted during isolation may influence confinement endurance. Zuckerman (1964) commented that isolation endurance is lowest in the water-immersion studies, intermediate in the tank-type respirator confinement studies, and highest in bed-confinement studies. He also noted, however, that restrictions on movement did not reduce endurance unless the restrictions were so severe that they produced painful somatic discomforts. The study of Zubek, Aftanas, Kovach, Wilgosh, and Winocur (1963) involving twenty-four hours of uninterrupted body immobilization in a coffin-like box demonstrated that severe immobilization could be as stressful as almost any pain-producing situation. Zuckerman (1964) commented that the more severe the immobilization confinement, the stronger the stress effects.

In the Zubek and Wilgosh study (1963), subjects were immobilized in the coffin-like box for seven days but were unstrapped periodically to minimize pain and cramps. The study revealed, as discussed earlier, that body immobilization alone with no visual or auditory deprivation produced intellectual and perceptual impairments similar to those produced by visual and auditory deprivation research, though a smaller range of performance tasks was affected.

Similarly, body immobilization alone produced a decrease in occipital lobe frequencies though the decrease was less than that produced by a similar period of darkness and silence. Zubek and Wilgosh accounted for their results in terms of disturbance of the ARAS as a result of a decrease in the level and variability of stimulation from tactile-kinesthetic senses.

Highly relevant to this discussion is the demonstration by Zubek (1963a) of the facilitating effects of exercise during isolation in counteracting the impairments produced by sensory restriction. Zubek suggested that the performance of exercises may provide sufficient variability of kinesthetic and proprioceptive stimulation to counteract most of the effects of unvarying stimulation from the visual and auditory sense modalities. This explanation is supported by French (1960) who commented on the role of somatic sensory excitation in producing a powerful excitatory influence upon the reticular formation.

These findings on the influence of body immobilization and the counteracting effects of exercise have obvious and important implications for sensory restriction research in which the subject is instructed to lie quietly for long periods of time. They raise the distinct possibility that the behavioral impairments reported may be as much a function of restricted motility as reduced visual and auditory input.

## F. ADAPTATION TO ISOLATION

In Chapter IV, the study by Zubek, Aftanas, Hasek, Sansom, Schludermann, Wilgosh, and Winocur (1962) provided some evidence to suggest the possibility that subjects might be able to adapt to a condition of sensory restriction. To reiterate briefly, four of the subjects had undergone two exposures to one week of sensory restriction with a year interval in between. Three of these four subjects reported that the second period was much easier to endure. Zubek et al. (1962) also discussed other reports which seemed to suggest the possibility of adaptation. Ruff, Levy, and Thaler (1961) discussed eight subjects who participated in two or three confinement studies. Most of these subjects reported that each period seemed easier than the preceding one. Studies using the water-immersion technique (Lilly, 1956; Lilly & Shurley, 1961) provided subjective reports indicating that repeated exposures were less fear-provoking and easier to endure. These studies, unfortunately, did not provide any supportive data using objective performance measures.

More objective measures were employed in a study reported by Pollard, Uhr, and Jackson (1963a) comparing two confinement sessions. A sample of twelve male and twelve female subjects were confined for two eight-hour periods of perceptual deprivation one week apart. The subject lay on a mattress which was covered by a white translucent semi-cylinder providing diffuse illumination. Hands were lightly bound into cotton mitts, and feet were separated and bound so they could not touch each other. White noise was presented through earphones.

Subjects were told they were going to participate in an experiment measuring the effects of various psychoactive drugs. Prior to isolation subjects were screened, tested, and given a capsule which they were told might or might not contain an active drug. Subjects were not told how long they would be confined and were asked to report their experiences during confinement. After confinement, subjects were again tested. A control group underwent the same testing procedures at the same time intervals.

The results supported the subjectively reported apparent adaptation noted above. The subjects reported only about one-third as many effects during the second session as compared to the first. This significant decrement during the second confinement was also apparent when the comparison was made between the first three hours of each session. Furthermore, fewer effects were reported during the latter part of each session when compared to the earlier part.

It would be of interest to investigate the effects of repeated exposure to confinement alone without the possible confounding influence of taking the drug. One might suspect that the subjects were more anxious during the first confinement due to their concern over possible effects of the "drug." Experiencing no adverse effects of the "drug" during the first confinement perhaps induced less anxiety during the second exposure. Also, the authors suggested that the subjects were more familiar with the environment the second time and were also aware that confinement would end either when requested by them or after eight hours. Of great interest is the finding that not all subjects endured the total eight hours of confinement: only fourteen of the twenty-four completed the first session, while thirteen completed the second session. The authors noted that in general those who remained the total time in the first session also remained the entire time in the second session, and those who tended to quit early the first time also did so the second time. Thus, it is suggested that much of the in-confinement data came from those subjects most resistant to the stresses of isolation. Those who were least resistant quit early both times. Of course, this is an apparent problem with all the long-term confinement studies. If the data are restricted to only those subjects completing the session then the results are taken only from those most tolerant of this stressful situation. Zubek *et al.* (1962) commented that the degree of intellectual impairment did not get any worse with time and even, in some cases, seemed to decrease toward the end of the isolation period—again suggestive of adaptation. In this particular study, twenty-nine of the original forty-two subjects stayed in isolation for the prescribed week. The mean duration of the "quitter" group was 47.4 hours. Interestingly enough, these early release subjects showed the same degree of impairment as did the successful subjects during the first three days for each group.

The problem of possible adaptation to sensory restriction poses one other question. The reference here is to the physiological effects reported in Chapter III. For example, EEG records revealed a progressive slowing of brain wave frequencies over extended periods of isolation. Zubek *et al.* (1963; Zubek, 1964a), dealing with two weeks of perceptual deprivation, found progressive decreases in mean occipital lobe frequencies over time. The mean decrease during the second week was twice as great as during the first week. Such data reveal no indication of a decreased cortical change as time in isolation increased. These data, too, are taken only from those subjects able to endure the long-term confinement.

Thus, there is some evidence to tentatively suggest an adaptation effect to isolation at the "psychological" level but no such speculation can proceed from physiological measurements of effects. Zubek *et al.* (1962) suggest, "It appears that as a result of prior experience the situation becomes less novel and stressful and that S has learned various techniques and devices to help him cope with the environment" (p. 186). This remains a tantalizing problem for future research grant applications.

## G. WHAT IS THE NORMAL SENSORY ENVIRONMENT?

What is normal stimulation? What is the necessary baseline amount and type of stimulation from which sensory restriction subjects are being deprived? The previous chapters noted the existence of a number of reports of unusual experiences, feeling states, *etc.*, under conditions of reduced sensory input. The question of concern in this section relates to the number of people who may experience similar phenomena in a normal sensory environment. In the study of Myers, Murphy, Smith, and Windle (1962), and Jackson and Pollard (1963) discussed earlier, the authors noted that some people reported having experiences in a normal environment similar to those reported by isolated subjects.

Myers (1964a) noted that the HumRRO studies have revealed that the incidence of sensory restriction symptomatology varies among control groups in a normal environment as a function of the nature of intervening activity. He also noted that on some behavioral tests it made a difference if the control group was tested in a lighted or a dark test room. Zubek *et al.* (1962) found that a control group asked to lie quietly in a room and provided with normal sensory input frequently reported visual and auditory experiences of varying degrees of complexity. Thus, it would seem that "normal life" is somewhat inconstant in its stresses and apparently cannot be assumed to be devoid of unusual or bizarre experience. It is obvious that the manner in which baselines are defined can have a profound effect on experimental outcomes.

## H. TESTING: DURING OR AFTER CONFINEMENT

The sensoristatic model would predict that a testing intrusion during confinement would serve to increase the level of sensory variation increasing, in turn, the level of activation with its consequent focusing of attention (cognitive change) and arousal of interest (motivational change) (Schultz, 1964b). Differences in tested behavioral effects with testing occurring during or after isolation have been noted. These differences may be due, at least in part, to this introduction of stimulation which may seriously mitigate the conditions of minimal sensory input.

In Chapter III the suggestion of fluctuation in brain wave activity as a function of behavioral activity was noted. It was seen that self-generated stimulation in the form of reported hallucinations (Heron, 1961) and verbal activity (Mendelson, Kubzansky, Leiderman, Wexler, & Solomon, 1961) did serve to increase level of activation. It seems reasonable to suggest that if self-initiated stimulation can increase the activation level then the external stimulation provided by a testing intrusion can certainly serve the same purpose. Thus, the very act of testing may serve to produce a more alert subject. However, it would seem that the complete return to a normal sensory environment provided by termination of isolation would result in an even higher level of activation. Thus, it may be suggested that, as Zubek (1964c) has noted, behavioral impairments would be more severe when testing occurs during isolation, even though the testing intrusion may produce a more alert subject.

The discussion now turns to a brief overview of theoretical attempts to account for the effects of sensory restriction, other than the proposed concept of sensoristasis.

## I. OTHER THEORETICAL APPROACHES TO SENSORY RESTRICTION

Zubek (1964c) notes the existence of three types of theoretical approaches which attempt to account for the effects of reduced environmental stimulation. These theoretical efforts include: (1) psychoanalytic interpretations which suggest changes in the relationship between id and ego functioning (Rapaport, 1958) or a weakening of the ego for reality testing (Goldberger & Holt, 1958, 1961a); (2) psychological interpretations which posit a disruption of the evaluative processes by which techniques used in dealing with the environment are monitored and corrected (Bruner, 1961) or which discuss man's continual search for order and meaning in an unorganized perceptual environment (Freedman & Greenblatt, 1959); and (3) neurophysiological models emphasizing the role of the RAS and cortical activation. The main points of the psychoanalytic and psychological theoretical attempts will be briefly discussed here, a neurophysiological approach having been offered in Chapter II.

### 1. PSYCHOANALYTIC APPROACHES

Rapaport (1958) contends that, in a situation of reduced external stimulation, the ego is less able to maintain its autonomy from the id. As a result, the effectiveness of the ego's control over id impulses becomes impaired. The primary process material is then capable of emerging from the id into consciousness. It is this emergence of id impulses which is considered to be the causal factor in the reported delusions, hallucinations, difficulties in thinking, *etc.* Thus, proper functioning of the ego is closely associated with appropriate levels of external stimulation. In a situation of stimulus deprivation, environmental or perceptual supports used by the ego to test reality are removed and ties with reality are weakened. Following this, there is a decrease in ego functioning.

Working somewhat within the general theoretical framework of Rapaport, Goldberger and Holt (1958, 1961a) maintain that proper functioning of the secondary process depends on constant contact with reality. A loss of reality contact, as in sensory restriction, facilitates a regression to the primary processes. Thus, in sensory restriction, rational and purposive thinking give way to unrealistic modes of thought or thought containing inappropriate drive intrusions.

Individual differences in reaction to sensory restriction are accounted for by Goldberger and Holt by the assumption that, "people differ significantly not only in the extent of their dependence on reality contact for maintaining efficient secondary process thought, but also in their resistance to regression and in their general modes of handling the primary process once it begins to become evident in the conscious stream of thought" (1961a, p. 131). There are two extreme modes by which the normal person deals with the primary process. First, there is the mature person with a well-developed ego who is not to be overwhelmed by instinctual impulses. With this person, primary process manifestations are controlled, modulated, and anxiety-free. Hence, he would be expected to show little disturbance in a situation of curtailed sensory inputs. In sensory or perceptual deprivation he may temporarily abandon secondary thought processes, but he can easily and quickly return to efficient and goal-oriented thought.

At the other extreme, Goldberger and Holt speak of the person with an immature ego in whom the intrusion of primary process into conscious thought provokes anxiety or guilt. Primary process manifestations become highly disruptive to this person and will, in sensory isolation, lead to a number of forms of unpleasant affect and perhaps to termination.

Several studies performed by Goldberger and Holt were discussed in Chapter VII. The authors interpreted the results as strongly supporting the psychoanalytic proposition. To reiterate briefly, the results (with the college student population only) demonstrated that those who handled primary process manifestations effectively reacted in an adaptive way to isolation, while those who evidenced poor control of the primary process reacted negatively to isolation.

"Man is to a large extent dependent on continual commerce with his usual environment to maintain his highest level of thought functioning. Many of the effects of isolation may be understood as the emergence into awareness of a kind of thinking usually found in dreams, psychosis, and artistic creation" (Goldberger & Holt, 1961a, p. 141).

## 2. PSYCHOLOGICAL APPROACHES

Grunebaum, Freedman, and Greenblatt (1960; Freedman, Grunebaum, & Greenblatt, 1961) invoke the notion of perceptual degradation to account for the disturbing effects of sensory isolation. They suggested that a properly functioning organism constantly seeks to impose structure on his environment according to a learned set of relationships which have proved useful in the past. The perceptual processes of the organism are constantly engaged in reality testing and in structuring the environment into the previously existing schemata. The authors postulated that it is this process of attempting to incorporate non-order into previously existing schemata which accounts for the perceptual changes and distortions reported in sensory restriction research.

In sensory isolation, the subject is exposed to a lack of stimulus patterning as to expectations, i.e., he doesn't know what will happen next or what to do about it. Grunebaum et al. (1960) suggested that the subject's handling of this unstructured situation is dependent on his defensive and adaptive resources. They reported that those who could not tolerate an eight-hour period of sensory deprivation appeared to be those in whom, "reality testing was impaired and where acting-out of impulses was a central defense, i.e., borderline states and psychopathic personalities. Schizoid subjects seem particularly well able to tolerate isolation through the use of withdrawal because it is a situation harmonizing with this defense" (Grunebaum et al., 1960, p. 881).

A somewhat similar approach has been suggested by Bruner (1961) who views perception as instrumental behavior that permits an organism to carry on its necessary transactions with the environment. Perceptual and cognitive activity, to Bruner, depend on a dynamically stable equilibrium which, in turn, depends on contact with heterogeneously patterned stimulation. To support this contention he notes the work of Ditchburn (1957) which indicated that if a visual pattern is stabilized completely on the retina, and is not even displaced by the natural tremor of the eye, it will disappear from view. The cessation of visual experience in a Ganzfeld, discussed in Chapter V, may also be supportive evidence.

The organism must develop a model of the environment if it is to operate effectively. If sensory restriction is imposed early in life, the organism is prevented from developing such a model so that later adult transactions with the environment are impaired, as was discussed in Chapter II. "Without such prior learning, the centrifugal control functions of the nervous system are without a program, without a basis for predicting that certain events are more likely than others or preclude others, and have no basis for selectivity toward stimuli" (Bruner, 1961, p. 201).

Hence, contact with a rich sensory environment is necessary in childhood to develop an adequate internal model of the external world. For the adult, effective functioning depends on the continued maintenance of contact with an appropriately rich sensory environment (relative to that in which early learning took place). Stimulus deprivation in adult life, then, would interfere with this maintenance need of the organism and would disrupt the evaluation process by which the models and strategies used in dealing with the environment are monitored and corrected. Thus, "One may suggest that one of the prime sources of anxiety is a state in which one's conception or perception of the environment with which one must deal does not 'fit' or predict that environment in a manner that makes action possible" (Bruner, 1961, p. 206).

This overview of some of the theoretical positions posited to account for the effects of sensory restriction has purposefully not been exhaustive. The reader is referred to the original sources for more thorough coverage. The relative utility of these various positions and of the sensoristatic model must await the test of future research. The author's bias should by this point be evident. "The neurophysiological theories seem to be the most promising" (Zubek, 1964c, p. 42).

# Bibliography

Adams, H. B. Therapeutic potentialities of sensory deprivation procedures. *Int. ment. Hlth. Res. Newsltr.*, 1964, **6**, 7–9.

Adams, H. B., Robertson, M. H., & Cooper, G. D. Facilitating therapeutic personality changes in psychiatric patients by sensory deprivation methods. Paper presented to *XVII Int. Congr. Psychol.*, 1963.

Aftanas, M. & Zubek, J. Effects of prolonged isolation of the skin on cutaneous sensitivity. *Percept. mot. Skills*, 1963, **16**, 565–571. (a)

Aftanas, M. & Zubek, J. Long-term after-effects following isolation of a circumscribed area of the skin. *Percept. mot. Skills*, 1963, **17**, 867–870. (b)

Aftanas, M. & Zubek, J. Interlimb transfer of changes in tactual acuity following occlusion of a circumscribed area of the skin. *Percept. mot. Skills*, 1964, **18**, 437–442.

Altman, J. W., Smith, R. W., Meyers, R. L., McKenna, F. S., & Bryson, S. *Psychological and social adjustment in a simulated shelter.* Pittsburgh: American Institute for Research, 1960.

Arnhoff, F. N. & Leon, H. V. Personality factors related to success and failure in sensory deprivation subjects. *Percept. mot. Skills*, 1963, **16**, 46.

Arnhoff, F. N., Leon, H. V., & Brownfield, C. A. Sensory deprivation: effects on human learning. *Science*, 1962, **138**, 899–900.

Azima, H. & Cramer, F. J. Effects of partial perceptual isolation in mentally disturbed individuals. *Dis. nerv. Syst.*, 1956, **17**, 117–122.

Azima, H. & Cramer-Azima, F. J. Studies on perceptual isolation. *Dis. nerv. Syst.*, 1957, **18**, 80–85.

Barnes, G. W. & Kish, G. B. Reinforcing properties of the termination of intense auditory stimulation. *J. comp. physiol. Psychol.*, 1957, **50**, 40–43.

Barnes, G. W. & Kish, G. B. Reinforcing properties of the onset of auditory stimulation. *J. exp. Psychol.*, 1961, **62**, 164–170.

Barnes, G. W., Kish, G. B., & Wood, W. O. The effect of light intensity when onset or termination of illumination is used as reinforcing stimulus. *Psychol. Rec.*, 1959, **9**, 53–60.

Beach, F. A. & Jaynes, J. Effects of early experience upon the behavior of animals. *Psychol. Bull.*, 1954, **51**, 239–263.

Bennett, A. M. H. Sensory deprivation in aviation. In P. Solomon *et al.* (Eds.), *Sensory deprivation.* Cambridge, Mass.: Harvard Univer. Pr., 1961. Pp. 161–173.

Bennett, E. L., Diamond, M. C., Krech, D., & Rosenzweig, M. R. Chemical and anatomical plasticity of brain. *Science*, 1964, **146**, 610–619.

Berlyne, D. E. Novelty and curiosity as determinants of exploratory behavior. *Brit. J. Psychol.*, 1950, **41**, 68–80.

Berlyne, D. E. An experimental study of human curiosity. *Brit. J. Psychol.*, 1954, **45**, 256–265.

195

Berlyne, D. E. *Conflict, arousal, and curiosity.* New York: McGraw-Hill, 1960.

Berlyne, D. E. Conflict and the orientation reaction. *J. exp. Psychol.,* 1961, 62, 476–483.

Berlyne, D. E. Novelty. *New Soc.,* May 28, 1964.

Berlyne, D. E. & Koenig, I. D. V. Some possible parameters of photic reinforcement. Unpublished manuscript, 1964.

Berlyne, D. E. & McDonnell, P. Effects of stimulus complexity and incongruity on duration of EEG desynchronization. *EEG clin. Neurophysiol.,* 1965, in press.

Berlyne, D. E., Craw, M. A., Salapatek, P. H., & Lewis, J. L. Novelty, complexity, incongruity, extrinsic motivation and the GSR. *J. exp. Psychol.,* 1963, 66, 560–567.

Bernhaut, H. *et al. J. Neurophysiol.,* 1953, 16, 21.

Bexton, W. H. Some effects of perceptual isolation on human subjects. Unpublished doctoral dissertation, McGill Univer., 1953.

Bexton, W. H., Heron, W., & Scott, T. H. Effects of decreased variation in the sensory environment. *Canad. J. Psychol.,* 1954, 8, 70–76.

Bindra, D. *Motivation: a systematic reinterpretation.* New York: Ronald Press, 1959.

Bone, E. *Seven years' solitary.* London: Hamish Hamilton, 1957.

Brownfain, J. J. Stability of the self-concept as a dimension of personality. *J. abnorm. soc. Psychol.,* 1952, 47, 597–606.

Bruner, J. S. Neural mechanisms in perception. *Psychol. Rev.,* 1957, 64, 340–358.

Bruner, J. S. The cognitive consequences of early sensory deprivation. In P. Solomon *et al.* (Eds.), *Sensory deprivation.* Cambridge, Mass.: Harvard Univer. Pr., 1961. Pp. 195–207.

Buhler, C., Buhler, K., & Lefever, D. W. *Rorschach standardization studies.* Los Angeles: Western Psychological Services, 1954.

Burney, C. *Solitary confinement.* New York: Clerke & Cockeran, 1952.

Butler, R. A. Discrimination learning by rhesus monkeys to visual-exploration motivation. *J. comp. physiol. Psychol.,* 1953, 46, 95–98.

Butler, R. A. The effect of deprivation of visual incentives on visual exploration in monkeys. *J. comp. physiol. Psychol.,* 1957, 50, 177–179.

Butler, R. A. & Alexander, H. M. Daily patterns of visual exploratory behavior in the monkey. *J. comp. physiol. Psychol.,* 1955, 48, 247–249.

Cannon, W. B. *Bodily changes in pain, hunger, fear, and rage.* New York: Appleton-Century, 1929. (2nd ed.)

Cannon, W. B. *The wisdom of the body.* New York: Norton, 1932.

Clark, B. & Graybiel, A. The break-off phenomenon; a feeling of separation from the earth experienced by pilots at high altitudes. *J. aviat. Med.,* 1957, 28, 121.

Cleveland, S. E., Reitman, E. E., & Bentinck, C. Therapeutic effectiveness of sensory deprivation. *Arch. gen. Psychiat.,* 1963, 8, 51–56.

Cofer, C. N. & Appley, M. H. *Motivation: theory and research.* New York: Wiley, 1964.

Cohen, B., Rosenbaum, G., Dobie, S., & Gottlieb, J. Sensory isolation: hallucinagenic effects of a brief procedure. *J. nerv. ment. Dis.,* 1959, **129,** 486–491.

Cohen, S. I., Silverman, A. J., & Shmavonian, B. M. Psychophysiological studies in altered sensory environments. *J. Psychosom. Res.,* 1962, **6,** 259–281.

Cohen, S. I., Silverman, A. J., Bressler, B., & Shmavonian, B. M. Problems in isolation studies. In P. Solomon *et al.* (Eds.), *Sensory deprivation.* Cambridge, Mass.: Harvard Univer. Pr., 1961. Pp. 114–129.

Cohen, W. Spatial and textural characteristics of the Ganzfeld. *Amer. J. Psychol.,* 1957, **70,** 403–410.

Cohen, W. Color perception in the chromatic Ganzfeld. *Amer. J. Psychol.,* 1958, **71,** 390–394. (a)

Cohen, W. Some perceptual and physiological aspects of uniform visual stimulation. Washington, D. C.: Res. & Dev. Div., Office of the Surgeon-General, Dept. of the Army, Progress Report #1, 1958. (b)

Cooper, G. D., Adams, H. B., & Gibby, R. G. Ego strength changes following perceptual deprivation. *Arch. gen. Psychiat.,* 1962, **7,** 75–79.

Cooper, R. M. & Zubek, J. P. Effects of enriched and restricted early environment on the learning ability of bright and dull rats. *Canad. J. Psychol.,* 1958, **12,** 159–164.

Davis, J. M. *et al.* Sensory deprivation: role of social isolation. *Arch. gen. Psychiat.,* 1961, **5,** 84–90.

Davis, J. M., McCourt, W. F., & Solomon, P. Sensory deprivation: (1) effects of social contact; (2) effect of random visual stimulation. Paper presented to American Psychiatric Association, 1958.

Davis, J. M., McCourt, W. F., & Solomon, P. Effect of visual stimulation on hallucinations and other mental experience during sensory deprivation. *Amer. J. Psychiat.,* 1960, **116,** 889–892.

Davis, R. Somatic activity under reduced stimulation. *J. comp. physiol. Psychol.,* 1959, **52,** 309–314.

Dember, W. N. *Psychology of perception.* New York: Holt, Rinehart, & Winston, 1960.

Ditchburn, R. W. Report to the experimental psychology group, Univer. of Reading, Reading, England, 1957. In P. Solomon *et al.* (Eds.), *Sensory deprivation.* Cambridge, Mass.: Harvard Univer. Pr., 1961, p. 200.

Doane, B., Mahatoo, W., Heron, W., & Scott, T. Changes in perceptual function after isolation. *Canad. J. Psychol.,* 1959, **13,** 210–219.

Duffy, E. The conceptual categories of psychology: a suggestion for revision. *Psychol. Rev.,* 1941, **48,** 177–203.

Duffy, E. The concept of energy mobilization. *Psychol. Rev.,* 1951, **58,** 30–40.

Duffy, E. *Activation and behavior.* New York: Wiley, 1962.

Fiske, D. W. Effects of monotonous and restricted stimulation. In D. W. Fiske & S. R. Maddi (Eds.), *Functions of varied experience.* Homewood, Ill.: Dorsey Press, 1961, Pp. 106–144.

Fiske, D. W. & Maddi, S. R. *Functions of varied experience.* Homewood, Ill.: Dorsey Press, 1961.

Fox, S. Self-maintained sensory input and sensory deprivation in monkeys:

a behavioral and neuropharmacological study. *J. comp. physiol. Psychol.*, 1962, **55**, 438–444.

Freedman, S. J. & Greenblatt, M. *Studies in human isolation.* Wright-Patterson AFB, Ohio: WADC Technical Report 59-266, 1959.

Freedman, S. J., Grunebaum, H. U., & Greenblatt, M. Perceptual and cognitive changes in sensory deprivation. In P. Solomon *et al.* (Eds.), *Sensory deprivation.* Cambridge, Mass.: Harvard Univer. Pr., 1961. Pp. 58–71.

Freedman, S. J. & Held, R. Sensory deprivation and perceptual lag. *Percept. mot. Skills,* 1960, **11**, 277–280.

Freeman, G. L. The relationship between performance level and bodily activity level. *J. exp. Psychol.,* 1940, **26**, 602–608.

Freeman, G. L. *The energetics of human behavior.* Ithaca, N. Y.: Cornell Univer. Pr., 1948.

French, J. D. Neurophysiology. (Section 1, Vol. 2). In J. Field (Ed.), *Handbook of physiology.* Baltimore: Williams & Wilkins, 1960.

French, J. D., Hernandez-Peon, R., & Livingston, R. B. Projections from cortex to cephalic brain stem (reticular formation) in monkeys. *J. Neurophysiol.,* 1955, **18**, 44–55.

Gellhorn, E. Motion and emotion: the role of proprioception in the physiology and pathology of the emotions. *Psychol. Rev.,* 1964, **71**, 457–472.

Gibby, R. G. & Adams, H. B. Receptiveness of psychiatric patients to verbal communication. *Arch. gen. Psychiat.,* 1961, **5**, 366–370.

Gibby, R. G., Adams, H. B., & Carrera, R. N. Therapeutic changes in psychiatric patients following partial sensory deprivation. *Arch. gen. Psychiat.,* 1960, **3**, 57–64.

Girdner, J. B. An experimental analysis of the behavioral effects of a perceptual consequence unrelated to organic drive states. *Amer. Psychologist,* 1953, **8**, 354–355. (Abstract)

Goldberger, L. & Holt, R. R. Experimental interference with reality contact (perceptual isolation): I. Method and group results. *J. nerv. ment. Dis.,* 1958, **127**, 99–112.

Goldberger, L. & Holt, R. R. Experimental interference with reality contact: individual differences. In P. Solomon *et al.* (Eds.), *Sensory deprivation.* Cambridge, Mass.: Harvard Univer. Pr., 1961. Pp. 130–142. (a)

Goldberger, L. & Holt, R. R. *A comparison of isolation effects and their personality correlates in 2 divergent samples.* Wright-Patterson AFB, Ohio: Aeronautical Systems Div., ASD, TR 61-417, 1961. (b)

Goldfarb, W. Emotional and intellectual consequences of psychologic deprivation in infancy: a reevaluation. In P. Hock & J. Zubin (Eds.), *Psychopathology of childhood.* New York: Grune & Stratton, 1955. Pp. 105–119.

Grissom, R. J., Suedfeld, P., & Vernon, J. Memory for verbal material: effects of sensory deprivation. *Science,* 1962, **138**, 429–430.

Grunebaum, H. U., Freedman, S. J., & Greenblatt, M. Sensory deprivation and personality. *Amer. J. Psychiat.,* 1960, **116**, 878–882.

Gunderson, E. K. Emotional symptoms in extremely isolated groups. *Arch. gen. Psychiat.,* 1963, **9**, 362–368.

Gunderson, E. K. & Nelson, P. D. Adaptation of small groups to extreme environments. *Aerospace Med.,* 1963, **34**, 1111–1115.

Haber, W. B. Effects of loss of limb on sensory functions. *J. Psychol.*, 1955, **40**, 115–123.

Harlow, H. F. Motivation as a factor in the acquisition of new responses. In M. Jones (Ed.), *Nebraska symposium on motivation.* Lincoln, Neb.: Univer. Nebraska Pr., 1953. Pp. 24–49.

Harris, A. Sensory deprivation and schizophrenia. *J. Ment. Sci.*, 1959, **105**, 235–237.

Harvey, O. J., Hunt, D. E., & Schroder, H. M. *Conceptual systems and personality organization.* New York: Wiley, 1961.

Haythorn, W. W., Altman, I., & Myers, T. I. *Emotional symptomatology and stress in isolated groups.* Bethesda, Md.: Naval Medical Research Institute, Research Task MR 005.12-2005.01, Subtask 1, 1965.

Hebb, D. O. *The organization of behavior.* New York: Wiley, 1949.

Hebb, D. O. Drives and the CNS (conceptual nervous system). *Psychol. Rev.*, 1955, **62**, 243–254.

Held, R. & White, B. Sensory deprivation and visual speed: an analysis. *Science*, 1959, **130**, 860–861.

Hernandez-Peon, R., Scherrer, H., & Jouvet, M. Modification of electrical activity in cochlear nucleus during "attention" in unanaesthetized cats. *Science*, 1956, **123**, 331–332.

Heron, W. The pathology of boredom. *Scientific Amer.*, 1957, **196**, 52–56.

Heron, W. Cognitive and physiological effects of perceptual isolation. In P. Solomon *et al.* (Eds.), *Sensory deprivation.* Cambridge, Mass.: Harvard Univer. Pr., 1961. Pp. 6–33.

Heron, W., Doane, B., & Scott, T. Visual disturbance after prolonged perceptual isolation. *Canad. J. Psychol.*, 1956, **10**, 13–18.

Hochberg, J., Triebel, W., & Seaman, G. Color adaptation under conditions of homogenous visual stimulation (Ganzfeld). *J. exp. Psychol.*, 1951, **41**, 153–159.

Hodes, R. Electrocortical synchronization resulting from reduced proprioceptive drive caused by neuromuscular blocking agents. *EEG clin. Neurophysiol.*, 1962, **14**, 220–232.

Holland, J. G. Human vigilance. *Science*, 1958, **128**, 61–67.

Holt, R. R. & Goldberger, L. Assessment of individual resistance to sensory alteration. In B. E. Flaherty (Ed.), *Psychophysiological aspects of space flight.* New York: Columbia Univer. Pr., 1961. Pp. 248–262.

Holt, R. R. & Havel, J. A method for assessing primary and secondary process in the Rorschach. In M. A. Rickers-Ovsiankina (Ed.), *Rorschach psychology.* New York: Wiley, 1960.

Hull, J. & Zubek, J. Personality characteristics of successful and unsuccessful sensory isolation subjects. *Percept. mot. Skills*, 1962, **14**, 231–240.

Jackson, C. W. Toward the establishment of baselines in sensory deprivation research. Paper presented to the American Psychological Association, 1964.

Jackson, C. W. & Kelly, E. L. Influence of suggestion and subjects' prior knowledge in research on sensory deprivation. *Science*, 1962, **132**, 211–212.

Jackson, C. W. & Pollard, J. C. Sensory deprivation and suggestion: a theoretical approach. *Behav. Sci.*, 1962, **7**, 332–342.

Jackson, C. W. & Pollard, J. C. Some non-deprivation variables which influence the "effects" of experimental sensory deprivation. Paper presented to the Midwestern Psychological Association, 1963.

Jenkins, R. L., Stauffacher, J., & Hester, R. A symptom rating scale for use with psychotic patients. *Arch. gen. Psychiat.*, 1959, **1**, 197–204.

Jones, A. Supplementary report: information deprivation and irrelevant drive as determiners of an instrumental response. *J. exp. Psychol.*, 1961, **62**, 310–311.

Jones, A. How to feed the stimulus hunger—problems in the definition of an incentive. Paper presented to the American Psychological Association, 1964.

Jones, A., Wilkinson, H., & Braden, I. Information deprivation as a motivational variable. *J. exp. Psychol.*, 1961, **62**, 126–137.

Karsten, A. Psychische sättigung. *Psychol. Forsch.*, 1928, **10**, 142–254.

Katz, D. Psychologische versuche mit amputierten. *Z. Psychol. Physiol.*, 1920, **85**, 83–117.

Kerle, R. H. & Bialek, H. The construction, validation and application of a subjective stress scale. Presidio of Monterey, Calif.: U. S. Army Leadership Human Research Unit, 1958.

King, J. A. Parameters relevant to determining the effect of early experience on the adult behavior of animals. *Psychol. Bull.*, 1958, **55**, 46–59.

Kish, G. B. Learning when the onset of illumination is used as reinforcing stimulus. *J. comp. physiol. Psychol.*, 1955, **48**, 261–264.

Köhler, W. & Wallach, H. Figural after-effects: an investigation of visual processes. *Proc. Amer. Phil. Soc.*, 1944, **88**, 269–357.

Kubzansky, P. E. The effects of reduced environmental stimulation on human behavior: a review. In A. D. Biderman & H. Zimmer (Eds.), *The manipulation of human behavior*. New York: Wiley, 1961. Pp. 51–95.

Kubzansky, P. E. & Leiderman, P. H. Sensory deprivation: an overview. In P. Solomon *et al.* (Eds.), *Sensory deprivation*. Cambridge, Mass.: Harvard Univer. Pr., 1961. Pp. 221–238.

Kubzansky, P. E., Leiderman, P. H., Mendelson, J., Solomon, P., & Wexler, D. A comparison of two conditions of sensory deprivation. Paper presented to the American Psychological Association, 1958.

Lana, R. E. Manipulation-exploration drives and the drive reduction hypothesis. *J. gen. Psychol.*, 1960, **63**, 3–27.

Leiderman, P. H. *Imagery and sensory deprivation: an experimental study.* USAF MRL tech. docum. Rep., No. 62-28, 1962.

Leiderman, P. H., Mendelson, J. H., Wexler, D., & Solomon, P. Sensory deprivation: clinical aspects. *Arch. Internal Med.*, 1958, **101**, 389–396.

Leuba, C. Toward some integration of learning theories: the concept of optimal stimulation. *Psychol. Rep.*, 1955, **1**, 27–33.

Levy, E., Ruff, G., & Thaler, V. Studies in human isolation. *AMA J.*, 1959, **169**, 236–239.

Lilly, J. Mental effects of reduction of ordinary levels of physical stimuli on intact healthy persons. *Psychiat. Res. Rep.*, 1956, **5**, 1–9.

Lilly, J. & Shurley, J. T. Experiments in solitude, in maximum achievable physical isolation with water suspension, of intact healthy persons. In B. E. Flaherty (Ed.), *Psychophysiological aspects of space flight.* New York: Columbia Univer. Pr., 1961. Pp. 238–247.

Lindsley, D. B. Common factors in sensory deprivation, sensory distortion, and sensory overload. In P. Solomon *et al.* (Eds.), *Sensory deprivation.* Cambridge, Mass.: Harvard Univer. Pr., 1961. Pp. 174–194.

McReynolds, P. A restricted conceptualization of human anxiety and motivation. *Psychol. Rep.,* 1956, **2**, 293–312.

Maddi, S. R. & Fiske, D. W. An appraisal of the proposed conceptual framework. In D. W. Fiske & S. R. Maddi (Eds.), *Functions of varied experience.* Homewood, Ill.: Dorsey Press, 1961. Pp. 431–448.

Marx, M. H., Henderson, R. L., & Roberts, C. L. Positive reinforcement of the bar-pressing response by a light stimulus following dark operant pretests with no after-effect. *J. comp. physiol. Psychol.,* 1955, **48**, 73–76.

Mendelson, J., Kubzansky, P., Leiderman, P., Wexler, D., DuToit, C., & Solomon, P. Catechol amine excretion and behavior during sensory deprivation. *Arch. gen. Psychiat.,* 1960, **2**, 147–155.

Mendelson, J. H., Kubzansky, P. E., Leiderman, P. H., Wexler, D., & Solomon, P. Physiological and psychological aspects of sensory deprivation—a case analysis. In P. Solomon *et al.* (Eds.), *Sensory deprivation.* Cambridge, Mass.: Harvard Univer. Pr., 1961. Pp. 91–113.

Miller, S. Ego-autonomy in sensory deprivation, isolation, and stress. *Int. J. Psycho-Anal.,* 1962, **43**, 1–20.

Montgomery, K. C. A test of two explanations of spontaneous alternation. *J. comp. physiol. Psychol.,* 1952, **45**, 287–293.

Moruzzi, G. & Magoun, H. W. Brain stem reticular formation and activation of the EEG. *EEG clin. Neurophysiol.,* 1949, **1**, 455–473.

Mullin, C. S. Some psychological aspects of isolated Antarctic living. *Amer. J. Psychiat.,* 1960, **117**, 323–325.

Murphy, C. W. *et al.* Absence of increased corticoid excretion with stress of perceptual deprivation. *Canad. J. Biochem. Physiol.,* 1955, **33**, 1062–1063.

Murphy, D. B., Hampton, G. L., & Myers, T. I. Time estimation error as a predictor of endurance in sustained sensory deprivation. Paper presented to the American Psychological Association, 1962.

Murphy, D. B., Myers, T. I., & Smith, S. Reported visual sensations as a function of sustained sensory deprivation and social isolation. Presidio of Monterey, Calif.: US Army Leadership HRU Draft res. Rep., Pioneer VI, 1962.

Murphy, J. P. & Gellhorn, E. The influence of hypothalamic stimulation on cortically induced movements and on action potentials of the cortex. *J. Neurophysiol.,* 1945, **8**, 341–364.

Myers, T. I. Some further data from the Subjective Stress Scale (SSS). Paper presented to the Eastern Psychological Association, 1964. (a)

Myers, T. I. The isolation experience. Unpublished manuscript, 1964. (b)

Myers, T. I., Murphy, D. B., & Smith, S. Progress report on studies of sensory deprivation. Presidio of Monterey, Calif.: US Army Leadership Human Research Unit res. memo., March, 1961.

Myers, T. I., Murphy, D. B., & Smith, S. The effect of sensory deprivation and social isolation on self-exposure to propaganda and attitude change. Paper presented to the American Psychological Association, 1963.

Myers, T. I., Murphy, D. B., Smith, S., & Windle, C. Experimental assessment of a limited sensory and social environment: summary results of the HumRRO program. Presidio of Monterey, Calif.: US Army Leadership Human Research Unit res. memo., February, 1962.

Myers, T. I., Murphy, D. B., & Terry, D. F. The role of expectancy in subjects' responses to sustained sensory deprivation. Paper presented to the American Psychological Association, 1962.

Nardini, J. E., Herrmann, R. S., & Rasmussen, J. E. Navy psychiatric assessment program in the Antarctic. *Amer. J. Psychiat.*, 1962, **119**, 97–105.

Nissen, H. W. The nature of the drive as innate determinant of behavioral organization. In M. Jones (Ed.), *Nebraska symposium on motivation*. Lincoln, Neb.: Univer. Nebraska Pr., 1954. Pp. 281–321.

Olds, J. Physiological mechanisms of reward. In M. Jones (Ed.), *Nebraska symposium on motivation*. Lincoln, Neb.: Univer. Nebraska Pr., 1955. Pp. 73–139.

Ormiston, D. W. The effects of sensory deprivation and sensory bombardment on apparent movement thresholds. *Amer. Psychologist*, 1958, **13**, 389. (Abstract)

Orne, M. T. On the social psychology of the psychological experiment: with particular reference to demand characteristics and their implications. *Amer. Psychologist*, 1962, **17**, 776–783.

Orne, M. T. & Scheibe, K. E. The contribution of nondeprivation factors in the production of sensory deprivation effects: the psychology of the "panic button." *J. abnorm. soc. Psychol.*, 1964, **68**, 3–12.

Peters, J., Benjamin, F., Helvey, W., & Albright, G. Study of sensory deprivation, pain, and personality relationships for space travel. *Aerospace Med.*, 1963, **34**, 830–837.

Petrie, A., Collins, W., & Solomon, P. Pain sensitivity, sensory deprivation, and susceptibility to satiation. *Science*, 1958, **128**, 1431–1433.

Petrie, A., Collins, W., & Solomon, P. The tolerance for pain and for sensory deprivation. *Amer. J. Psychol.*, 1960, **73**, 80–90.

Pollard, J. C., Uhr, L., & Jackson, C. W. A comparison of relatively neutral versus relatively suggestive instructions on sensory deprivation behavior. Paper presented to the Midwestern Psychological Association, 1962.

Pollard, J. C., Uhr, L., & Jackson, C. W. Studies in sensory deprivation. *Arch. gen. Psychiat.*, 1963, **8**, 435–454. (a)

Pollard, J. C., Uhr, L., & Jackson, C. W. Some unexpected findings in experimental sensory deprivation: psychopharmacological interaction of placebo-potentiated suggestion. Paper presented to the American Psychiatric Association, 1963. (b)

Porter, R. W. Hypothalamic involvement in the pituitary-adrenocortical response to stress stimuli. *Amer. J. Physiol.*, 1953, **172**, 515–519.

Rapaport, D. The theory of ego autonomy: a generalization. *Bull. Menn. Clinic*, 1958, **22**, 13–35.

Rasmussen, J. E. Psychologic discomforts in 1962 Navy protective shelter tests. *J. Amer. Dietetic Ass.*, 1963, **42**, 109–116.

Riesen, A. H. Excessive arousal effects of stimulation after early sensory deprivation. In P. Solomon *et al.* (Eds.), *Sensory deprivation.* Cambridge, Mass.: Harvard Univer. Pr., 1961. Pp. 34–40.

Robertson, M. H. Sensory deprivation and some therapeutic considerations. *Psychol. Rec.,* 1961, **11,** 343–347.

Robertson, M. H. Facilitating therapeutic changes in psychiatric patients by sensory deprivation methods. Research Foundation of the Nat. Ass. for Mental Health, final progress report, November 30, 1964.

Rohrer, J. H. Implications for fallout shelter living from studies of submarine habitability and adjustment to polar isolation. In G. W. Baker & J. H. Rohrer (Eds.), *Human problems in the utilization of fallout shelters.* Washington, D. C.: NAS-NRC, 1960. Pp. 21–30.

Rosenbaum, G., Dobie, S. I., & Cohen, B. D. Visual recognition thresholds following sensory deprivation. *Amer. J. Psychol.,* 1959, **72,** 429–433.

Rossi, A. M. & Solomon, P. Button-pressing for a time-off reward during sensory deprivation: I. relation to activity reward; II. relation to descriptions of experience. *Percept. mot. Skills,* 1964, **18,** 211–216. (a)

Rossi, A. M. & Solomon, P. Button-pressing for a time-off reward during sensory deprivation: III. effects of varied time-off rewards. *Percept. mot. Skills,* 1964, **18,** 794–796. (b)

Rossi, A. M. & Solomon, P. Button-pressing for a time-off reward during sensory deprivation: IV. relation to change in ratings of well-being. *Percept. mot. Skills,* 1964, **19,** 520–522. (c)

Rossi, A. M. & Solomon, P. Button-pressing for a time-off reward during sensory deprivation: V. effects of relatively comfortable and uncomfortable sessions. *Percept. mot. Skills,* 1964, **19,** 803–807. (d)

Ruff, G. E. & Levy, E. Z. Psychiatric research in space medicine. *Amer. J. Psychiat.,* 1959, **115,** 793–797. (a)

Ruff, G. E. & Levy, E. Z. Psychiatric evaluation of candidates for space flight. *Amer. J. Psychiat.,* 1959, **116,** 385–391. (b)

Ruff, G. E., Levy, E. Z., & Thaler, V. H. Studies of isolation and confinement. *Aerospace Med.,* 1959, **30,** 599–604.

Ruff, G. E., Levy, E. Z., & Thaler, V. H. Factors influencing the reaction to reduced sensory input. In P. Solomon *et al.* (Eds.), *Sensory deprivation.* Cambridge, Mass.: Harvard Univer. Pr., 1961. Pp. 72–90.

Schlosberg, H. Three dimensions of emotion. *Psychol. Rev.,* 1954, **61,** 81–88. (a)

Schlosberg, H. Fatigue, effort and work output. Presidential address, Eastern Psychological Association, 1954. (b)

Schultz, D. P. Primacy-recency within a sensory variation framework. *Psychol. Rec.,* 1963, **13,** 129–139.

Schultz, D. P. *Panic behavior.* New York: Random House, 1964. (a)

Schultz, D. P. Spontaneous alternation behavior in humans: implications for psychological research. *Psychol. Bull.,* 1964, **62,** 394–400. (b)

Scott, T. Literature review of the intellectual effects of perceptual isolation. Defense Res. Bd., Dept. of Nat. Defense, Canada, Report HR66, July, 1957.

Scott, T., Bexton, W. H., Heron, W., & Doane, B. K. Cognitive effects of perceptual isolation. *Canad. J. Psychol.,* 1959, **13,** 200–209.

Shewchuck, L. & Zubek, J. A technique of intermittent stimulation for measurement of tactual sensitivity: apparatus and preliminary results. *Canad. J. Psychol.*, 1960, **14**, 29–37.

Shmavonian, B. M. Toward increased application of psychophysiological methods in sensory deprivation research. Paper presented to the American Psychological Association, 1964.

Shurley, J. T. The hydro-hypodynamic environment. *Proceedings of the Third World Congr. of Psychiat.*, Vol. 3. Toronto, Canada: Univer. Toronto Pr., 1963. Pp. 232–237.

Smith, S. & Lewty, W. Perceptual isolation using a silent room. *Lancet*, 1959, 342–345.

Smith, S., Murphy, D. B., & Myers, T. I. The effect of sensory deprivation and social isolation on conformity to a group norm. Paper presented to the American Psychological Association, 1963.

Smith, S., Myers, T. I., & Murphy, D. B. Activity pattern and restlessness during sustained sensory deprivation. Paper presented to the American Psychological Association, 1962.

Smith, W. M. Scientific personnel in Antarctica: their recruitment, selection and performance. *Psychol. Rep.*, 1961, **9**, 163–182.

Smith, W. M. & Jones, M. B. Astronauts, Antarctic scientists and personal autonomy. *Aerospace Med.*, 1962, **33**, 162–166.

Solomon, P., Kubzansky, P. E., Leiderman, P. H., Mendelson, J. H., Trumbull, R., & Wexler, D. (Eds.). *Sensory deprivation.* Cambridge, Mass.: Harvard Univer. Pr., 1961.

Stellar, E. The physiology of motivation. *Psychol. Rev.*, 1954, **61**, 5–22.

Suedfeld, P. Birth order of volunteers for sensory deprivation. *J. abnorm. soc. Psychol.*, 1964, **68**, 195.

Suedfeld, P., Grissom, R. J., & Vernon, J. The effects of sensory deprivation and social isolation on the performance of an unstructured cognitive task. *Amer. J. Psychol.*, 1964, **77**, 111–115.

Suedfeld, P., Vernon, J., Stubbs, J., & Karlins, M. The effects of repeated confinement on cognitive performance. *Amer. J. Psychol.*, 1964, in press.

Taylor, A. Social isolation and imprisonment. *Psychiatry*, 1961, **24**, 373–376.

Teuber, H., Krieger, H. P., & Bender, M. B. Reorganization of sensory function in amputation stumps: two-point discrimination. *Fed. Proc.*, 1949, **8**, 156.

Thompson, W. R. Early environment—its importance for later behavior. In P. Hock & J. Zubin (Eds.), *Psychopathology of childhood.* New York: Grune & Stratton, 1955. Pp. 120–139.

Thompson, W. R. Motivational factors in development. *Australian J. Psychol.*, 1958, **10**, 127–143.

Thompson, W. R. Early environmental influences on behavioral development. *Amer. J. Orthopsychiat.*, 1960, **30**, 306–314.

Thompson, W. R. & Schaefer, T. Early environmental stimulation. In D. W. Fiske & S. R. Maddi (Eds.), *Functions of varied experience.* Homewood, Ill.: Dorsey Press, 1961. Pp. 81–106.

Tranel, N. Effects of perceptual isolation on introverts and extraverts. *J. Psychiat. Res.*, 1962, **1**, 185–192.

Vernon, J. *Inside the black room.* New York: Potter, 1963.

Vernon, J. & Hoffman, J. Effects of sensory deprivation on learning rate in human beings. *Science,* 1956, **123,** 1074–1075.

Vernon, J. & McGill, T. The effects of sensory deprivation upon rote learning. *Amer. J. Psychol.,* 1957, **70,** 637–639.

Vernon, J. & McGill, T. Utilization of visual stimulation during sensory deprivation. *Percept. mot. Skills,* 1960, **11,** 214.

Vernon, J. & McGill, T. Sensory deprivation and pain thresholds. *Science,* 1961, **133,** 330–331.

Vernon, J., McGill, T., Gulick, W., & Candland, D. Effect of sensory deprivation on some perceptual and motor skills. *Percept. mot. Skills,* 1959, **9,** 91–97.

Vernon, J., McGill, T., Gulick, W., & Candland, D. The effect of human isolation upon some perceptual and motor skills. In P. Solomon *et al.* (Eds.), *Sensory deprivation.* Cambridge, Mass.: Harvard Univer. Pr., 1961. Pp. 41–57.

Walters, R. H., Callagan, J. E., & Newman, A. F. Effect of solitary confinement on prisoners. *Amer. J. Psychiat.,* 1963, **119,** 771–773.

Walters, R. H. & Henning, G. B. Social isolation, effect of instructions, and verbal behaviour. *Canad. J. Psychol.,* 1962, **16,** 202–210.

Weinberger, N. & Lindsley, D. Behavioral and EEG arousal to contrasting novel stimulation. *Science,* 1964, **144,** 1355–1357.

Wertheimer, M. Figural aftereffect as a measure of metabolic efficiency. *J. Pers.,* 1955, **24,** 56–73.

Wexler, D., Mendelson, J., Leiderman, P., & Solomon, P. Sensory deprivation: a technique for studying psychiatric aspects of stress. *Arch. neurol. Psychiat.,* 1958, **79,** 225–233.

Weybrew, B. An exploratory study designed to suggest clusters of traits and assessment tests related to submarine adjustment. New London, Conn.: USNMRL, Rep. #279, 1957.

Weybrew, B., Molish, H. B., & Youniss, R. P. Prediction of adjustment to the Antarctic. New London, Conn.: USNMRL Rep. #350, 1961.

White, R. W. Motivation reconsidered: the concept of competence. *Psychol. Rev.,* 1959, **66,** 297–333.

Wilson, J. J., Wilson, B. C., & Swinyard, C. A. Two-point discrimination in congenital amputees. *J. comp. physiol. Psychol.,* 1962, **55,** 482–485.

Witkin, H. A., Lewis, H. B., Hertzman, M., Machover, K., Meissner, P. P., & Wapner, S. *Personality through perception.* New York: Harper, 1954.

Wright, M. W., Sisler, G. C., & Chylinski, J. Personality factors in the selection of civilians for isolated northern stations. *J. appl. Psychol.,* 1963, **47,** 24–29.

Wright, N. Use of the multiple discriminant function in the prediction of success or failure in perceptual deprivation. Unpublished M. A. thesis, Univer. Manitoba, 1964.

Wright, N. & Abbey, D. S. Perceptual deprivation tolerance and adequacy of defenses. *Percept. mot. Skills,* 1965, **20,** 35–38.

Ziskind, E. & Augsburg, T. Hallucinations in sensory deprivation: method or madness? *Science,* 1962, **137,** 992.

Zubek, J. P. Counteracting effects of physical exercises performed during prolonged perceptual deprivation. *Science,* 1963, **142,** 504–506. (a)

Zubek, J. P. Pain sensitivity as a measure of perceptual deprivation tolerance. *Percept. mot. Skills,* 1963, **17,** 641–642. (b)

Zubek, J. P. Behavioral and EEG changes after 14 days of perceptual deprivation. *Psychon. Sci.,* 1964, **1,** 57–58. (a)

Zubek, J. P. Behavioral changes after prolonged perceptual deprivation (no intrusions). *Percept. mot. Skills,* 1964, **18,** 413–420. (b)

Zubek, J. P. Effects of prolonged sensory and perceptual deprivation. *Brit. Med. Bull.,* 1964, **20,** 38–42. (c)

Zubek, J. P., Aftanas, M., Hasek, J., Sansom, W., Schludermann, E., Wilgosh, L., & Winocur, G. Intellectual and perceptual changes during prolonged perceptual deprivation: low illumination and noise level. *Percept. mot. Skills,* 1962, **15,** 171–198.

Zubek, J. P., Aftanas, M., Kovach, K., Wilgosh, L., & Winocur, G. Effect of severe immobilization of the body on intellectual and perceptual processes. *Canad. J. Psychol.,* 1963, **17,** 118–133.

Zubek, J. P., Flye, J., & Aftanas, M. Cutaneous sensitivity after prolonged visual deprivation. *Science,* 1964, **144,** 1591–1593.

Zubek, J. P., Flye, J., & Willows, D. Changes in cutaneous sensitivity after prolonged exposure to unpatterned light. *Psychon. Sci.,* 1964, **1,** 283–284.

Zubek, J. P., Pushkar, D., Sansom, W., & Gowing, J. Perceptual changes after prolonged sensory isolation (darkness and silence). *Canad. J. Psychol.,* 1961, **15,** 83–100.

Zubek, J. P., Sansom, W., & Prysiazniuk, A. Intellectual changes during prolonged perceptual isolation. *Canad. J. Psychol.,* 1960, **14,** 233–243.

Zubek, J. P. & Welch, G. EEG changes after prolonged sensory and perceptual deprivation. *Science,* 1963, **139,** 209–210.

Zubek, J. P., Welch, G., & Saunders, M. EEG changes during and after 14 days of perceptual deprivation. *Science,* 1963, **139,** 490–492.

Zubek, J. P. & Wilgosh, L. Prolonged immobilization of the body: changes in performance and in the electroencephalogram. *Science,* 1963, **140,** 306–308.

Zuckerman, M. The development of an Affect Adjective Check List for the measurement of anxiety. *J. consult. Psychol.,* 1960, **24,** 457–462.

Zuckerman, M. Perceptual isolation as a stress situation. *Arch. gen. Psychiat.,* 1964, **11,** 255–276.

Zuckerman, M., Albright, R. J., Marks, C. S., & Miller, G. L. Stress and hallucinatory effects of perceptual isolation and confinement. *Psychol. Monogr.,* 1962, **76** (30).

Zuckerman, M. & Cohen, N. Sources of reports of visual and auditory sensations in perceptual isolation experiments. *Psychol. Bull.,* 1964, **62,** 1–20. (a)

Zuckerman, M. & Cohen, N. Is suggestion the source of reported visual sensations in perceptual isolation? *J. abnorm. soc. Psychol.,* 1964, **68,** 655–660. (b)

Zuckerman, M. & Haber, M. The need for stimulation as a source of stress response to perceptual isolation. *J. abnorm. Psychol.*, 1965, in press.

Zuckerman, M., Kolin, E. A., Price, L., & Zoob, I. Development of a sensation seeking scale. *J. consult. Psychol.*, 1964, **28**, 477–482.

Zuckerman, M., Levine, S., & Biase, D. V. Stress response in total and partial perceptual isolation. *Psychosom. Med.*, 1964, **26**, 250–260.

# Author Index

Numbers in italics show the pages on which the complete references are listed.

# Subject Index

## A

Activation, *see* Arousal

Activity, 14

Adaptation to sensory restriction, 77, 118, 187–189

Adaptive behavior, 18, 23

Affect Adjective Check List (AACL), 105, 106, 107–108

Affective impairments, 22, 23, 25, 99–122, 151, 152, 155–157, 162, 165, 171, 172, 179

Alertness, 6, 17, 36, 83

Alpha activity, 17, 22, 36, 37–38, 56, 57, 135, 170

Alternation behavior, 27

Amputees, 52

Anger, 99, 104, 154, 158, 183

Anxiety, 99, 100, 101, 102, 103, 104, 106, 107, 111, 118, 119, 120, 151, 160, 180, 181, 183, 194

Anxiety states, 108–109, 116

Arousal, 6, 13, 15–27, 29, 30, 31, 32, 35, 56, 57, 59, 97, 169, 190, 191
individual differences in level of, 25–27

Attention, *see* Alertness

Attitude change, 72–75, 80, 122

Auditory flutter fusion, 55–56

Auditory sensitivity, 170

Auditory stimulation as reinforcement, onset, 28
termination, 29

Autokinetic effect, 85, 97

Autonomic nervous system, 15, 20

## B

Bender-Gestalt Test, 86–87, 117

Beta activity, 135

Biochemical changes, 44–45

Birth order as a predictor of isolation tolerance, *see* Predictors of isolation tolerance

Blood pressure, 19, 20, 21

Body-field perceptual mode, 134–136

Body immobilization, 40–41, 54, 68–69, 77, 92, 95, 97, 104, 118, 130–131, 170, 171, 186–187

Boredom, 1, 3, 4, 15, 72, 99, 101, 150

Brainwashing, 5, 80–81, 171

Break-off phenomenon, 2

## C

Catechol amine, 45, 58

Cattell's 16 P-F test, 129

Circulation, 46

Cochlear nucleus, 18

Cognitive impairments, *see* Intellectual impairments

Complexity, 24

Conformity, 72, 75

Critical flicker frequency, 85

Cue function, 18, 20, 23, 26

Curiosity, 6, 27, 29, 30

Cutaneous sensitivity, 58, 59, 170

## D

Delta waves, 20

Demand characteristics, 176, 177, 179, 180, 181

Depressives, 108–109

Diencephalon, 15

Draw-a-Person test, 117

Dreams, 103, 109, 155, 183

Drive
neurophysiologically-based, 6, 11, 14, 29–34, *see also* Sensoristasis
non-visceral, 14, 29
primary, 13–14, 28, 29, 33
secondary, 14

## E

Edwards Personal Preference Schedule (EPPS), 105, 124–125, 128, 129, 130, 131, 141, 152, 185

Ego, 132, 191–192

Ego strength, 108, 111, 112, 114, 122, 124

Electric shock, 108, 109, 135

Electroencephalogram (EEG), 17, 18, 21, 22, 24, 35–42, 56, 57, 104, 135, 176, 189

Epileptic seizure, 19

Epinephrine, 45, 58

Exploration, 6, 14, 27, 28, 29–30, 32, 33